OXFORD POLITICAL THEORY

Series Editors: Will Kymlicka, David Miller, and Alan Ryan

LEVELLING THE PLAYING FIELD

OXFORD POLITICAL THEORY

Oxford Political Theory presents the best new work in contemporary political theory. It is intended to be broad in scope, including original contributions to political philosophy, and also work in applied political theory. The series contains works of outstanding quality with no restriction as to approach or subject matter.

OTHER TITLES IN THIS SERIES

Multicultural Citizenship
Will Kymlicka

Real Freedom for All
Philippe Van Parijs

Reflective Democracy
Robert E. Goodin

Justice as Impartiality
Brian Barry

Democratic Autonomy
Henry S. Richardson

The Liberal Archipelago
Chandran Kukathas

On Nationality
David Miller

Republicanism
Phillip Pettit

Creating Citizens
Eamonn Callan

The Politics of Presence
Anne Phillips

Deliberative Democracy and Beyond
John S. Dryzek

The Civic Minimum
Stuart White

LEVELLING THE PLAYING FIELD

THE IDEA OF EQUAL OPPORTUNITY AND ITS PLACE IN EGALITARIAN THOUGHT

ANDREW MASON

OXFORD
UNIVERSITY PRESS

Great Clarendon Street, Oxford OX2 6DP

Oxford University Press is a department of the University of Oxford.
It furthers the University's objective of excellence in research, scholarship,
and education by publishing worldwide in

Oxford New York

Auckland Cape Town Dar es Salaam Hong Kong Karachi
Kuala Lumpur Madrid Melbourne Mexico City Nairobi
New Delhi Shanghai Taipei Toronto

With offices in

Argentina Austria Brazil Chile Czech Republic France Greece
Guatemala Hungary Italy Japan South Korea Poland Portugal
Singapore Switzerland Thailand Turkey Ukraine Vietnam

Oxford is a registered trade mark of Oxford University Press
in the UK and in certain other countries

Published in the United States
by Oxford University Press Inc., New York

Reprinted 2011

ISBN 978-0-19-926441-4

Printed in the United Kingdom by
Lightning Source UK Ltd., Milton Keynes

For Matthew and Sam

PREFACE

I have been preoccupied with this book since I moved to Southampton, some eight years ago now. This move coincided with my eldest son starting school. Though my interest in the subject matter grew out of a relatively abstract concern with the idea of equality of opportunity, the book has in various ways been influenced by reflecting upon the fraught experience of parenting in an unequal society.

Many people have helped me to bring the book to fruition, and I would like to thank them for giving their time so generously. David Miller and David Owen read the penultimate draft and made many suggestions that enabled me to improve the final version. Roger Crisp and John Horton read an early version and their detailed comments forced me to rethink many of its central ideas. I presented a paper based on some of these ideas to an ECPR workshop on Equality of Opportunity held at the University of Granada in April 2005, which was organized by Ian Carter and David Miller. I learned much from the other papers and from the responses I received to mine. I presented a revised version of the same paper to a workshop in the Department of Philosophy, University of Copenhagen and to a seminar in the School of Public Policy, University College London. I am grateful to the participants for sharing their thoughts on it, especially Richard Bellamy, Alex Brown, Tony Draper, Ross Harrison, Nils Holtug, Claus Jensen, Sune Laegaard, and Kasper Lippert-Rasmussen.

A number of other people have commented on individual chapters, or on articles which these chapters have drawn upon. I would like to thank Chris Armstrong, Chris Brown, Matthew Clayton, Cécile Fabre, Matt Matravers, Andrew Moore, Hillel Steiner, Peter Vallentyne, Alex Voorhoeve, and Andrew Williams, for doing so.

I could not have completed this book without the receipt of an AHRB Research Leave Scheme Award, or without the distraction of my family, that is, Lynn, Sam, and Matthew.

CONTENTS

INTRODUCTION 1

1. THE SIMPLE VIEW 15

2. THE DESERT OF THE BEST QUALIFIED 39

3. RAWLSIAN FAIR EQUALITY OF OPPORTUNITY 68

4. COUNTERACTING CIRCUMSTANCES 89

5. EQUALITY, PRIORITY, AND SUFFICIENCY 112

6. MITIGATING PRINCIPLES 134

7. A RESPONSIBLE EGALITARIANISM 158

8. INDIVIDUALISM AND PERSONAL RESPONSIBILITY 194

9. CONCLUSION 216

Bibliography 225

Index 233

Introduction

Suppose that the top 10 per cent of earners in a polity receive more than one-quarter of the total income, whilst the wealthiest 10 per cent own half of all the total wealth.[1] What normative premises, or further facts, would be required to determine whether these inequalities are just or unjust? One traditional view is that they are just if and only if there is equal opportunity for all; equality of opportunity can legitimate some inequalities of outcome, for it levels the playing field in the way that justice requires. Can inequalities of outcome such as these be reconciled with equality of opportunity or do they show that it is being systematically violated?

On reflection, it is clear that we cannot address this question satisfactorily without some account of equality of opportunity. Constructing such an account is far from straightforward, however. 'Equal opportunity for all' is a fine piece of political rhetoric but the concept that supposedly lies behind it is slippery to say the least. Like all political ideals, it is radically contested; there is little consensus on what counts as equality of opportunity. But this is not the only problem that is encountered in trying to improve our grasp on it. The ideal seems to self-destruct on close examination. We move from one interpretation of the ideal to another, motivated by the attempt to overcome difficulties, and end up with a position that seems unrecognizable at all as a conception of equal opportunity.[2]

[1] Statements such as these raise many questions but they are one way of representing the distribution of wealth and income in Britain in the early 1990s, according to the data provided by the 1995/6 Family Resources Survey. See K. Rowlinson, C. Whyley, and T. Warren, *Wealth in Britain: A Lifecycle Perspective* (London: Policy Studies Institute, 1999), 2–4.

[2] See B. Barry, 'Equal Opportunity and Moral Arbitrariness', in N. Barry (ed.), *Equal Opportunity* (Boulder, CO: Westview Press, 1988), 29–33; J. Richards,

It is natural to begin with the apparently simple idea that equality of opportunity requires advantaged social positions to be subject to open competition. According to the most plausible way of understanding this common-sense view, equality of opportunity entails that selection procedures for jobs and educational places must be suitably designed to identify the best-qualified candidates. As many have argued, however, even if this is a necessary condition of equal opportunity, it cannot be a sufficient condition of it. For if it were, equality of opportunity would permit differences in people's social circumstances, such as the economic class or the culture into which they were born, to have too deep an impact on their prospects. The ideal would be compatible, for example, with a society in which those born to a lower economic class have radically different prospects from those born to a higher economic class as a result of the way that the different resources at their disposal influence their access to the qualifications required for success. The solution, it might be thought, is to suppose that equality of opportunity not only requires open competition for advantaged social positions, but also fair access to qualifications. Let me call this vision of what it is to level the playing field 'the meritocratic ideal of equality of opportunity', without prejudging the issue of how it might be defended.

This meritocratic ideal may seem highly unstable, however. On the surface, at least, it appears to be motivated by the desire to prevent differences in people's social circumstances from significantly affecting their prospects in life relative to each other. Yet if the reason for doing so is that an individual's social circumstances are beyond his control (they are simply a matter, let us say, of being born into a particular family, class, or culture), then the same can be said of his 'natural circumstances', such as the genetic potential with which he happens to have been born. Consistency would seem to require preventing differences in people's natural circumstances from significantly affecting their relative life prospects not just their social circumstances.[3] Does this reveal an incoherence at the very heart of

'Equality of Opportunity', in A. Mason (ed.), *Ideals of Equality* (Oxford: Blackwell, 1998), 53.

[3] J. Rawls, *A Theory of Justice* (Cambridge, MA: Harvard University Press, 1971), 73–4; P. Singer, *Practical Ethics*, 2nd edn (Cambridge: Cambridge University Press, 1993), 39.

the ideal of equality of opportunity? Does it show that equality of opportunity collapses into equality of outcome?

The short answer to these questions is, 'Not without much more argument'. It might seem that we are confronted by a stark choice between retreating to an unacceptably thin conception of equality of opportunity which holds that it consists in open competition for advantaged social positions and nothing more, and a much more expansive notion which maintains that it requires us to counteract the differential effects of anything that is beyond a person's control. But those who accept the idea that equality of opportunity requires counteracting the effects of differences in people's social circumstances have strategies they can use to try to show that this does not commit them to the idea that it also requires counteracting the effects of differences in people's natural endowments. The most prominent amongst these is the argument that when the effects of different social circumstances have been redressed, people deserve the benefits they receive: in other words, when there is fair access to qualifications, and the best-qualified candidates are appointed to advantaged social positions, they deserve these positions and the rewards attached to them by the market.

Even if the ideal of equality of opportunity, strictly thought out, does require us to counteract the effects of different natural endowments as well as the effects of differences in social circumstances, we would not be led inexorably to the conclusion that this entails equality of outcome. For such an approach is consistent with allowing people's life prospects to be influenced by their values and choices. Indeed, it is consistent with the idea that those who are ambitious and want material success may legitimately end up with a greater share of resources than those who value leisure or spending time with their families. Some have wanted to claim that a deeper conception of equality of opportunity emerges from these reflections, with a more radical vision of what is required to level the playing field. From this standpoint, the underlying motivation of the ideal of equality of opportunity, properly understood, is to counteract the effects of people's different natural and social circumstances whilst permitting inequalities of condition that emerge as a result of their choices. When inequalities arise from differences in choice, they are just; indeed if we do not allow inequalities to arise in this way, we fail to give personal responsibility its due.

Even though this radical vision of what it is to level the playing field has its attractions, we should not simply assume that equality of opportunity requires us to *neutralize* the effects of differences in social circumstances and natural endowments, a conclusion which emerges from this radical conception, when the counteracting of these effects is treated as equivalent to fully cancelling them out, so that no inequalities of access to advantage are generated by them. For we might interpret 'counteract' as 'mitigate' instead, where mitigating the effects of differences in people's circumstances would mean preventing them from having an undue impact on their access to advantage. Of course, this idea needs further development and more defence. (What is it for these differences to have 'an undue impact'? If people's social circumstances and natural endowments are, in some sense, arbitrary from the moral point of view, to borrow a phrase of John Rawls, then does not this require us to prevent differences in them from having any effects on people's prospects?) But one of my aims in this book is to make a mitigation approach of this sort seem plausible by refining it in the face of criticism.

The position I have outlined allows us to reconsider the relationship between equality of opportunity and other egalitarian principles. It becomes clear that we do not have to choose between equality of opportunity, on the one hand, and placing limits on inequalities of wealth and income, on the other. This is not simply because equality of opportunity itself has implications for what kinds of inequalities of wealth and income are permissible. It does have implications for this issue, but my point is that justice may also place independent limits on inequalities of outcome. How would this work in the context of a mitigation approach? An approach of this kind might involve principles for allocating advantaged social positions (such as the principle that these should be allocated to the best-qualified candidates) and principles that determine what is to count as fair access to qualifications (such as the principle that everyone should have available to them an education which enables them to acquire basic skills). Taken together we might think of these principles as spelling out what equality of opportunity requires. They might then be combined with further principles that limit in other ways the degree and kind of inequalities of outcome that are permissible. As John Rawls recognized, equality of opportunity is just one aspect of justice and allows space for other principles to govern inequalities of wealth and income. Indeed, we cannot understand the significance of equality of opportunity unless we view it in relation to these other principles. If we are going to invoke the metaphor of levelling the playing field, we might hold that a level playing field cannot be achieved by equality of opportunity alone, but only by limiting inequalities of outcome in other ways as well.

I. *Analysing 'Equality of Opportunity' and Understanding Its Place in Egalitarian Thought*

This book is concerned with reaching a better understanding of the ideal of equality of opportunity and its place in egalitarian thought rather than, say, with identifying the social, political, and economic obstacles that currently stand in the way of implementing equality of opportunity and reducing inequalities of wealth and income in societies such as Britain. So what is the proper way of approaching these issues?

My project is clearly a philosophical rather than an empirical one, but that does not settle the issue of how we should approach it. We need to provide an analysis of the concept of equality of opportunity and an account of its relationship to other egalitarian principles, but how should we go about this task? Peter Westen maintains that any statement about equality of opportunity involves specifying three elements: the agent or class of agents to whom the opportunities belong, the goal or set of goals towards which the opportunities are directed, and the obstacles which the agent or class of agents is not hindered by in relation to these goals. He, in effect, believes that any statement which attributes equality of opportunity to members of a group can be translated into the following form: members of that group equally enjoy a lack of obstacles of a certain kind to the attainment of a certain goal.[4] Westen's analysis conforms to a widely accepted view that the best way of proceeding is to analyse the separate concepts of 'equality' and 'opportunity', then combine

[4] See P. Westen, 'The Concept of Equal Opportunity', *Ethics* 95 (1985), 838–41; I. Carter, 'Equal Opportunity and Equal Freedom', a paper presented to the workshop on Equality of Opportunity at the ECPR Joint Sessions, Granada, 14–19 April 2005.

the results.[5] Whilst this approach (and Westen's illuminating version of it) can be helpful in understanding many claims that are made about equality of opportunity or its absence, I do not assume that it can make sense of all those claims. My aim is to help us to understand better our ordinary notion of equality of opportunity, and we should leave open the possibility that much of what people mean by 'equality of opportunity' might not be captured particularly well in terms of this abstract analysis.

In this spirit, my approach is to try to recover the meaning of the ideal by starting from an account of the role it plays in our thought and practice. Crudely stated, my view is that the point of the notion of equality of opportunity is to spell out, at least in part, what it is for individuals to face a playing field that is level in appropriate respects. (I say 'at least in part' because I want to leave open the possibility that levelling the playing field in the way that justice requires may involve more than simply providing equality of opportunity.) Admittedly this is a vague idea that is amenable to different interpretations, not least because it does not by itself give us any help in identifying the respects in which a playing field needs to be level in order for equality of opportunity to be achieved. Some ways of spelling it out might involve making claims that can be captured in terms of Westen's analysis, but there may be other ways of doing so that cannot be properly understood in this way. For example, it may be that the best way of unpacking our ordinary notion of equality of opportunity would make little or no reference to equality in the strict sense at all, but would invoke instead some sort of prioritarian commitment to benefiting the worse off, or would appeal to the idea that we should promote the conditions necessary for everyone to be

[5] See Westen, 'The Concept of Equal Opportunity'; A. Goldman, 'The Justification of Equal Opportunity', *Social Philosophy and Policy* 5 (1987), 88–103. Most writers think that any adequate analysis of equality of opportunity must at least provide us with an account of what an opportunity is: Michael Levin claims: 'Before attempting to say what equality of opportunity, or opportunity rights, are, one must say something about what an opportunity is' (Michael Levin, 'Equality of Opportunity', *Philosophical Quarterly* 31 (1981), 110). T. D. Campbell writes: 'One pre-requisite [of a successful formulation and justification of principles of equality of opportunity] is an adequate analysis of the concept of an opportunity' (T. D. Campbell, 'Equality of Opportunity', *Proceedings of the Aristotelian Society* 106 (1974–5), 51). See also J. Nickel, 'Equal Opportunity in a Pluralistic Society', *Social Philosophy and Policy* 5 (1987), 110; D. A. Lloyd Thomas, 'Competitive Equality of Opportunity', *Mind* 86 (1977), esp. 388–91.

in a position to lead a decent life. (Antony Flew may be right that the label equality of opportunity is a rather misleading characterization of the ideal in question, even if he is mistaken in supposing that it is reducible to the idea of open competition for scarce opportunities.[6]) We should also leave open the possibility that equality of opportunity might be a complex ideal that consists of more than one principle, with different principles governing different aspects of people's circumstances or different kinds of good, some of which are committed to strict equality of some sort (or, at least, to limiting inequalities of access to particular kinds of goods, such as education), whilst others merely require providing everyone with access to some of the goods that they need in order to be able to lead a decent life (e.g. basic skills). Indeed, this is what I propose.

My argument begins in Chapter 1 with a consideration of what I call the simple view, the idea that equality of opportunity requires open competition for advantaged social positions. I unpack that idea and argue it is not really so simple. The notion of an open competition, and the idea of a qualification which it presupposes, are more complicated than they seem, and need to be embedded within a broader account of justice in general or equality of opportunity in particular. For the reason given earlier, the simple view must in any case be regarded as incomplete: it is implausible to suppose, for example, that open competition for advantaged social positions is a sufficient condition of equality of opportunity. Reflection upon the simple view suggests that any adequate account of equality of opportunity must include at least two components: the idea that there should be open competition for advantaged social positions and that there should be fair access to the qualifications required for success in these competitions. I stipulate that any account which has this structure is meritocratic in character.

In Chapter 2, I consider the most obvious way of developing a meritocratic account, in terms of the idea of desert. According to this approach, the best-qualified candidates should be appointed to

[6] A. Flew, *The Politics of Procrustes* (London: Temple Smith, 1981), 21, 45. In fact the idea of 'open competition for scarce opportunities' might be adequately captured using Westen's analysis, for it would seem that it can be expressed by saying that everyone should be equally unobstructed by factors such as class, gender, and race, from securing jobs and educational places. Cf. Carter, 'Equal Opportunity and Equal Freedom'.

advantaged social positions because they deserve to be, provided there is fair access to qualifications. David Miller's version of this approach is the most sophisticated available, so I focus on it. He maintains that the best-qualified applicants for jobs deserve them because they are the most likely to come to deserve the rewards attached to them, at least when the market is functioning properly. Against this approach I argue that our ordinary judgements about economic desert are sensitive to effort-making, not just achievement, and the degree of effort that people make corresponds in a highly imperfect way to their qualifications. Appointing people to jobs on the basis of their qualifications, and then allowing the market to reward them for their performance, does not therefore seem to be a promising way of giving them what they deserve. Even if we were to insist that economic desert tracks achievement alone, and that effort matters only to the extent that it results in achievement of the relevant sort, there is good reason to deny that the market can be designed to reward economic desert in the way Miller proposes.

In the face of these difficulties, we should entertain the possibility that our intuitions about desert can be better preserved by an account which defends the idea that there is a principled reason for appointing the best-qualified candidates for advantaged social positions but makes no claim that they deserve these positions, and which rejects a 'pre-justicial' notion of desert, defining people's deserts instead in terms of what they would receive under a just scheme that generally requires people to bear the costs of their choices and allows them to enjoy the benefits of those choices. I suggest that the principled reason for appointing the best-qualified candidates might derive from the requirement of respect for persons. Drawing upon George Sher's work, I argue that in most cases respect for persons requires that we select candidates for jobs solely on the basis of their ability to perform well at them. When we select candidates for different reasons, this tends to be disrespectful, to both those who fail and those who succeed. This does not establish the conclusion that respect for persons always requires selectors to choose the best-qualified candidates, but it does justify a presumption to that effect which is defeasible but nevertheless principled.

In Chapter 3, I move on to consider Rawls' account of fair equality of opportunity, which can be conceived as a way of addressing the respects in which the simple view is incomplete whilst eschewing pre-justicial notions of desert. Rawls argues that fair equality of opportunity requires not only 'careers to be open to talents' but also that those with the same level of talent and ability and willingness to use them should have equal chances of success. Whilst defending Rawls' account against some influential criticisms that have been levelled against it, I argue that it is unable to justify the idea that fair equality of opportunity is lexically prior to the difference principle. If we suppose that the principle of fair equality of opportunity aims to counteract the effects of differences in social circumstances, whilst the difference principle is intended to counteract the effects of differences in natural potential, then it might seem that what we need instead is an approach which declines to give lexical priority to either one of these principles and which acknowledges the need for each to be balanced against the other. It is a relatively short step from here to a position which takes 'counteract' to mean 'neutralize', and maintains that justice requires us to prevent differences in people's circumstances from affecting their relative access to advantage but allow their choices to do so. I refer to this as 'the neutralization approach'.

Chapter 4 focuses on the neutralization approach and raises a difficulty for it. In particular, I argue that the aim of neutralizing the effects of differences in people's circumstances runs counter to some widely held moral intuitions. For if we suppose that justice or equality of opportunity requires the neutralization of these effects, then it would seem that each of us has a reason to refrain from behaving in any way that would advantage our children relative to others. Yet that in turn would entail that we have a reason (even if that reason is inconclusive) not to pass on our skills and experience to our children, or even spend 'quality time' with them, when we know that doing so would advantage them. This is strongly counter-intuitive. It goes well beyond the idea that there are ways in which we can purchase advantages for our children, such as private education, that threaten equality of opportunity, for it would govern all our personal interactions with our children. In place of the neutralization approach, I argue that justice requires us to mitigate the effects of differences in people's circumstances, not the more demanding goal of neutralizing them. This is merely to label a contrasting approach, however—one that I refer to as the mitigation approach—rather than to offer a determinate alternative. Indeed, unlike the neutralization approach, the mitigation approach is not itself a theory, or even a sketch of one, in the absence of an independent defence of a set of principles. The mitigation approach aims to limit the effects of differences in people's social circumstances and natural endowments, maintaining that these differences should not unduly affect their relative access to advantage, but it requires principles which spell out what it is for this to be the case. Different versions of the mitigation approach can be generated by different sets of principles.

It might seem that the neutralization approach is a form of egalitarianism, strictly conceived, whereas the mitigation approach is best understood in terms of a sufficiency view which holds that justice requires us to ensure that everyone is in a position to lead a decent life, or perhaps in terms of a priority view which maintains that justice requires us to give extra weight to the interests of the worse off. This is too simplistic, however. In Chapter 5, I argue that particular versions of the mitigation approach may also incorporate what I call 'quasi-egalitarian principles'—principles which hold that certain kinds or degrees of inequality are objectionable as such. I also maintain that a defensible version of the mitigation approach might incorporate more than one kind of principle—it need not consist entirely of quasi-egalitarian principles, nor need it be exhausted by a prioritarian or sufficiency principle—and, furthermore, that different kinds of principles might be appropriate for different goods or different aspects of people's circumstances.

Chapter 6 is spent identifying and defending a set of such principles, starting with those that are required to govern access to qualifications. Here, I advocate a basic skills principle, which holds that each child is entitled to receive an education that enables him to acquire a set of skills which will give him an adequate range of options, and an educational access principle designed to rule out the possibility that some might have access to levels of education (or indeed standards of education) which are denied to others simply as a result of differences in their social circumstances. The former principle is grounded in a sufficiency view, which holds that justice requires us to promote the conditions necessary for each person to be in a position to lead a decent life, whereas the latter principle is quasi-egalitarian because it draws limits to justifiable inequality and maintains that inequalities which have a particular character are objectionable as such because they are incompatible with treating people as equals. The basic skills principle and the educational access principle are then combined with other principles, including ones which govern gifts and bequests, and differences in natural endowment, in order to give content to a particular interpretation of what it is to level the playing field in the way that justice requires.

In developing this vision, the mitigation approach can, in effect, incorporate a meritocratic ideal of equal opportunity because not only can it provide us with an account of what constitutes fair access to qualifications, it can also embody a principled commitment to open competition. Indeed, the presumption that the best-qualified candidates should be selected for advantaged social positions, which I defend in Chapter 2 by appealing to the idea of respect for persons, can be built into the mitigation approach: it has the implication that differences in people's natural endowments may legitimately have some impact on their access to the internal and external goods that jobs carry with them, though the presumption I defend works in tandem with other principles that serve to limit the degree and kind of inequality that may legitimately result from such differences.

The mitigation approach, like the neutralization approach, draws a distinction between people's circumstances and their choices that it regards as normatively significant. According to these approaches, differences in the choices that people make can justify inequalities of outcome; levelling the playing field in the way that justice requires does not entail counteracting the effects of choice. Since both approaches give weight to choice in this way, I regard them as versions of what I call 'responsibility-sensitive egalitarianism'. In Chapter 7, I explore this form of egalitarianism further by asking when justice requires us to hold people responsible for their behaviour by requiring them to bear its costs. Some maintain that people can legitimately be required to bear the costs of their behaviour if and only if they could have acted otherwise and no excusing conditions apply. Against this formulation, some would argue that what matters is whether an agent's behaviour is responsive to his reasons in the right way, and whether there are any excusing conditions, but not whether he could have acted otherwise. I maintain that both of these accounts are inadequate because they do not recognize the full range of reasons we might have for not requiring a person to bear the full costs of his behaviour. In developing this argument, I discuss the case of mothers who decide to give up their careers to bring up their children, even though they are not forced to do so. This case need not be taken as an illustration of the way in which women's socialization deprives them of their ability to make autonomous choices, yet there is a strong argument for saying that they should not be required to bear the costs of their choices, such as the shortfalls that may be created in their pensions. They make these choices against the background of a widely accepted norm that mothers should look after their children personally. Even though they may reject that norm, when they nevertheless act in accordance with it, fairness requires that they should not be required to bear the full costs of doing so.

Some have argued that responsibility-sensitive egalitarianism is objectionably individualist. In Chapter 8, I respond to different forms of this criticism. In the second half of the chapter, I focus in particular on the question of whether responsibility-sensitive egalitarianism can provide us with an adequate account of how the costs of caring for those who cannot meet their own needs should be allocated. If a person's needs are self-inflicted, do others have any obligations of justice to help meet those needs? Some forms of responsibility-sensitive egalitarianism will maintain that when it is possible for a person to insure against infirmity but he declines to do so, then others cannot legitimately be required to help meet his needs if he becomes unable to do so himself. In response I argue that this form of egalitarianism does not have to be so unfeeling in its approach to those with self-inflicted needs. Indeed, I argue that it can consistently incorporate a commitment to ensuring that everyone is in a position to lead a decent life, regardless of any foolish risks they might have taken.

II. *Sceptical Attacks*

I defend the idea that equality of opportunity is part of what is required to level the playing field in the way that justice requires. But the idea that equality of opportunity is a component of justice, and that (in general) it requires selectors to appoint the best-qualified candidates, is open to challenge from different ends of the ideological spectrum. Some on the Left will argue that equality of opportunity is simply a device the purpose of which is to legitimate inequalities of wealth and income that are inherently unjust. No doubt the idea of equality of opportunity does play this role more often than political philosophers care to acknowledge, but it seems to me that a proper understanding of it can also be the basis for a critique of real world inequalities of wealth and income. Indeed, the account of equality of opportunity that I defend maintains that although a meritocratic version of this ideal should govern the allocation of jobs and access to the qualifications required for them, it should be combined with a more robust form of egalitarianism that requires us to mitigate the effects of circumstances that are beyond the individual's control, thereby offering a vision of what it is to level the playing field that would require significant redistribution of wealth and income.

A more fundamental challenge to the idea that equality of opportunity is a component of justice comes from a libertarian perspective. Libertarians argue that employers are entitled to fill vacant positions within their workforce with whoever they want, for whatever reason they want. Influenced by this libertarian critique, there are others who argue that although justice places some constraints on the reasons for which employers can legitimately reject applicants, these constraints do not require them to select the best-qualified candidates.

According to the pure libertarian position, the entitlement of employers to decide who should work for them on whatever basis they choose is grounded in their property rights.[7] (Managers acting on behalf of their employer might be regarded as having a similar entitlement that derives from the employer's property rights.) I do not propose to give an extended response to this challenge here or indeed at any place in the book. But let me indicate the broad outlines of such a response. Any reasonable account of property rights must recognize that they are limited by the rights or entitlements of others: I may own a car but I am not in general entitled to use that car to run you over. Even if a person may in many cases have a right to do wrong, they do not have a right to violate the rights of others or to act unjustly. So the most obvious strategy for defending the idea that equality of opportunity is a component of justice will

[7] See, e.g. J. Narveson, *The Libertarian Idea* (Philadelphia, PA: Temple University Press, 1988), 315–8; S. Kershnar, 'Why Equal Opportunity is not a Valuable Goal', *Journal of Applied Philosophy* 21 (2004), 168.

involve showing that applicants for jobs have rights or entitlements that restrict the reasons for which selectors can legitimately reject them. (This does not by itself show that the decisions of employers should be subject to legislative constraints. Such constraints might be regarded as ineffective or counterproductive.)

Even if such a conclusion can be established, however, the other position I described remains undefeated. Influenced by a libertarian perspective, some will argue that the rights or entitlements of applicants for jobs are not such as to impose a duty on employers to select the best-qualified candidates. Matt Cavanagh, for example, maintains that candidates have a right not to be treated with unwarranted contempt but argues that this does not entail that the best-qualified candidates have a right to be selected, for employers may have a variety of reasons for rejecting them that do not express unwarranted contempt.[8] My defence of equality of opportunity will make some concessions to Cavanagh's position; I do not think it can be shown that the best-qualified candidate for a job always has a right to it, nor that he or she is always entitled to it. But I maintain that Cavanagh's position is flawed because there is good reason to suppose that in the process of selecting for jobs (or advantaged social positions more generally) candidates are entitled to be treated with respect. Many of the reasons an employer might have for rejecting the best-qualified candidates express disrespect for them, even if that disrespect does not amount to unwarranted contempt. Unwarranted contempt is a particularly serious form of disrespect, and for that reason is more objectionable than some other forms, but it is not the only form.

[8] See M. Cavanagh, *Against Equality of Opportunity* (Oxford: Oxford University Press, 2002), Pt 3.

CHAPTER 1

The Simple View

Equality of opportunity is a complex ideal. Not only does it involve a number of different components but also we cannot understand it fully without situating it in the context of a more general account of justice. Or so I argue, for this is not obviously true. From the perspective of what I call 'the simple view', equality of opportunity can seem a straightforward ideal, intelligible even in the absence of any more general theory of justice, and concerned exclusively with the idea that selection processes which allocate jobs and scarce educational places should involve open competition. But even that idea is much less straightforward than it might seem. In order to reveal some of its complexities, I unpack the notion of an open competition, consider how it relates to the possession of an opportunity, analyse the notion of a qualification it employs, and explore the conception of unfair discrimination it involves. I argue that some of these elements cannot be properly analysed or assessed without reference to a fuller theory of justice, and that the simple view is incomplete even as an account of equality of opportunity.

I. *Open Competition and Its Implications*

According to the simple view, equality of opportunity is a component of justice which requires open competition for a range of scarce opportunities. But what makes a competition open in the relevant sense? According to Antony Flew, a competition is open only if all those who enter are treated the same, that is, the same criteria of selection are applied to all candidates.[1] This does not quite capture

[1] See Flew, *The Politics of Procrustes*, pp. 45, 113.

the idea, however. It is not enough to say that the same criteria should apply to all candidates, for a competition run according to the rule that any competent man should be chosen in preference to any woman, no matter how well qualified, meets that condition. If such a rule were in operation, then all applicants, men and women, would be treated in the same way in the same sense that the qualified and the unqualified are treated in the same way when the rule applied is that the best-qualified applicant should be chosen. In order to avoid this difficulty we need to characterize the idea of an open competition in something like the following way: a competition is open if and only if no one is prevented from entering it, the competition is widely advertised, and the rules of the competition are well-designed to select the best-qualified applicant.

What is the scope of the simple view? What 'scarce opportunities' does it suppose should be governed by open competition? It would be implausible to maintain that all such opportunities should be allocated by open competition. Some of these opportunities are quite properly left to particular individuals to allocate as they choose, for example, the scarce opportunity to marry a particular woman may be properly hers to distribute how she sees fit.[2] We might introduce the idea of 'an advantaged social position' to identify a subset of scarce opportunities which defenders of the simple view believe should be governed by open competition.[3] These might be characterized as positions which meet one or more of the following conditions: first, they carry with them material benefits; second, they bring with them prestige or social status; third, fulfilling their responsibilities is in itself rewarding; fourth, they are a means to secure positions that carry material benefits, or prestige or social status, or which are such that fulfilling their responsibilities is in itself rewarding.

So understood, the category of advantaged social positions includes jobs of all varieties and educational or training places of all kinds. (Characterizing a social position as 'advantaged' in this

[2] I say 'may be' in order to allow diversity in the way that marriage partners are legitimately selected. There need be nothing unjust, for example, in a practice of arranged marriage. My point is simply that justice does not require the scarce opportunity to marry a particular woman to be subject to open competition.

[3] I take the notion of an advantaged social position from John Rawls' work although the characterization I go on to give may not capture precisely the same idea.

sense need not imply that it is particularly privileged, for it covers even jobs with low salaries, little or no prestige and few if any internal rewards.) But the position of spouse would also fall under it, so it does not enable us to answer the objection which it was designed to meet. After all, being married to a person can carry with it prestige or social status, material benefits, and even be fulfilling. If the phrase 'advantaged social position' is intended to pick out the class of opportunities which are properly subject to open competition, and only that class, then it would seem that there is no way of doing so without reference to individual rights or entitlements to offer these opportunities without being constrained by principles of just allocation. We have to say that advantaged social positions are, in part, positions that no particular individual or group has a right or entitlement to distribute without regard to such principles. Understood in these terms, the notion of an advantaged social position is itself moralized and cannot be fully unpacked in the absence of a wider theory of justice. Indeed different theories of justice will draw the boundaries of the set of advantaged social positions in different ways. Libertarians, for instance, will argue that many jobs are not advantaged social positions in the relevant sense because the employer has the right to allocate them without regard to qualifications, whereas left liberals and socialists will deny that this is the case. There will also be disagreements between liberals, multiculturalists, and others concerning whether religious offices, for example, are advantaged social positions in the relevant sense. Should religious groups be allowed to use criteria for who can legitimately fill a religious office that are derived from its own doctrines? Suppose, for example, that these doctrines stipulate that this office can permissibly be filled only by men. Different theories of justice will diverge on this question.[4] (In what follows, I simply assume that

[4] For relevant discussion, see B. Barry, *Culture and Equality: An Egalitarian Critique of Multiculturalism* (Oxford: Polity, 2001), 165–76. It might be argued that being male counts as a qualification for the religious office in the example I have described because of the religious doctrines involved. So even if they do constitute advantaged social positions in the relevant sense, there need be no violation of open competition when men are selected in preference to women. This is problematic, however. Even if the duties associated with the office could only be carried out by women because of the attitude of those to whom they are ministering, this raises the issue of when the attitudes of others may legitimately shape what is to count as a qualification. See S. V of this chapter for further discussion.

the vast majority of jobs and educational places are advantaged social positions in the relevant sense without defending the broader theory of justice that would be required to underwrite this view.)

Does the simple view allow that equality of opportunity may require open competition to be extended beyond advantaged social positions? This will depend in part on whether there are other scarce opportunities that justice requires us to allocate by open competition rather than, say, permitting them to be distributed by unconstrained individual decisions. Left liberals and socialists might argue that the allocation of public housing and the distribution of medical care should be done on the basis of open competition. Here the idea of the best-qualified applicant becomes strained, as does the idea of competition, but the motivation behind the extension of equal opportunity to these areas is often clear. In the context of publicly funded health care, the claim that when transplant organs are in short supply, decisions about who should receive them should be made on the basis of equal opportunity, usually amounts to roughly the idea that they should be distributed on the basis of need and that when need is equal, the amount of time spent waiting for a transplant should be decisive. In other words, need and waiting time are thought to 'qualify' a person for the treatment. The point of demanding equality of opportunity in the allocation of health care is to insist that patients should not be allowed to jump the queue simply because they have the ability to pay or because they know the surgeon. In a related way, the claim that decisions about who should receive public housing should be governed by equality of opportunity usually amounts to the idea that it should be distributed on the basis of greatest need, and when needs are equal, on a first come first served basis. In both of these cases, however, we need to be careful to distinguish between competitive and non-competitive equality of opportunity. Sometimes when people say that the distribution of some good should be governed by equality of opportunity, they mean that this good ought to be available to anyone who needs it. (It would be less misleading here simply to drop the language of equality of opportunity and speak instead in terms of justice.) This is to be contrasted with the ideal of competitive equality of opportunity which the notion of open competition is used to express.[5]

[5] K. Nielsen, *Equality and Liberty: A Defense of Radical Egalitarianism* (Totowa, NJ: Rowman and Allanheld, 1985), 166; Lloyd Thomas, 'Competitive Equality of Opportunity', esp. 389–91.

The simple view implies that a policy of favouring or discounting applicants for advantaged social positions on the basis of considerations that have nothing to do with their qualifications is inconsistent with full and complete equality of opportunity. If a candidate is favoured merely because he is white, or male, or from the right background, then this is a violation of open competition.[6] So according to the simple view it marks a departure from equality of opportunity. It does not follow, however, that defenders of the simple view must suppose that it is *unjust* to reserve a proportion of jobs for a particular group of people irrespective of whether they are the best-qualified. There is more to justice than equality of opportunity; forms of positive discrimination or affirmative action would be just if they were mandated by some other principle of justice which takes priority over equality of opportunity.[7] For example, a defender of the simple view might consistently allow that a proportion of places in Law or Medicine should be reserved for members of previously disadvantaged groups, on the grounds that this is required to compensate them for past injustice.

By virtue of their commitment to open competition, defenders of the simple view are suspicious of headhunting, that is, the practice of filling a vacancy without advertising by approaching a suitable candidate and offering him or her the position. When vacancies are filled without advertising in this way, by definition, there is no open competition. Must the simple view always regard this practice as a transgression of equality of opportunity, however?

Addressing this question brings into sharp relief two different variants of the simple view. According to one variant, open competition matters only in so far as it is conducive to identifying the best qualified amongst those actually or potentially interested in this position,[8] whereas according to the other variant it is intrinsic to any

[6] Unless a case can be made for saying that race, sex, or background count as a qualification: see Ss III and V of this chapter.

[7] In Ch. 2, S. IV, I also suggest that there may be ways of justifying open competition that are compatible with a practice of positive discrimination. See also note 29 of this chapter.

[8] This formulation does not quite capture the view I have in mind. Suppose that some people's preferences were manipulated so that they did not want to occupy particular advantaged social positions. Defenders of the view I have in mind might want to say that these people are denied equality of opportunity even though they do not apply for these positions and are aware of them. Apart from a brief discussion in Section II, I bracket this issue in what follows.

fair procedure for filling it, not merely a means of identifying the best qualified. According to this conception, if some other, less costly, method of filling the position were equally well suited to identifying the best qualified amongst those actually or potentially interested in the position, then there would be no reason to insist on open competition. Indeed, if some other method was better able to secure the appointment of the best qualified amongst those potentially or actually interested, then open competition might be objectionable. According to the second conception, in contrast, there may be sufficient reason to favour open competition even if it results in the appointment of a less well-qualified candidate than some alternative method. The fairness involved in giving everyone the chance to apply for the position in a competition that aims to select the best-qualified applicant is accorded independent moral weight.

In practice, these two variants of the simple view are likely to converge in their judgements about which procedures violate equality of opportunity and which are required by it. In most cases it is difficult to know in advance what application pool there would be for a position were it to be advertised widely, and as a result, identifying the best-qualified applicant will require open competition. In some cases, however, selectors can have a very good idea of what candidates there will be, perhaps because a similar position has been advertized in the recent past or perhaps because the potential applicant pool is just very small. In such cases, provided selectors are justified in believing that the person they want to appoint is as well qualified as anyone who would emerge as a result of advertising it, headhunting may be a more efficient way of identifying the best-qualified among those potentially interested in the position. In these cases, the first variant of the simple view will maintain that there is no objection to headhunting, whereas the second variant will hold that there is at least one reason to think that it violates equality of opportunity.

The differences between these two views are even more pronounced in circumstances where someone would not apply for a job were it advertised even if he was formally invited to do so. (He might fear being rejected, not only because of the immediate damage that would cause to his self-esteem but also because of the consequent loss of face if others were to become aware that he had been rejected.) Such a person might nevertheless be the best qualified of all of those who are interested in the job or would be interested in it. In these circumstances, the first variant of the simple view would maintain that equality of opportunity is not merely consistent with headhunting the individual in question but actually requires it, whereas the second variant would hold that equality of opportunity still provides a reason for insisting upon open competition.

These two conceptions differ crucially on the issue of whether equality of opportunity is, at the root, a property of procedures or a property of outcomes. The second conception insists that it is, at the root, a property of procedures, so it can allow that, for example, equality of opportunity may obtain even when a procedure results on occasion in the appointment of a less well-qualified candidate, provided that the procedure is as well-designed as practically possible to result in the appointment of the best-qualified candidates. The first conception, in contrast, regards equality of opportunity as primarily a property of outcomes—equality of opportunity obtains when those best qualified for a position from the pool of people who are, or would be, interested in filling it are selected—and procedures are judged in terms of their conduciveness to promoting such outcomes. Although the second conception may seem attractive, it is hard to defend. For if we ask the question, 'Why should advantaged social positions be allocated on the basis of an open competition?' then it is difficult to see how we can resist the answer, 'Because this is likely to result in the appointment of the best-qualified candidate amongst those who are, or would be, interested in filling the position'. (The response, 'Because such a procedure is the fairest way of allocating these positions', would only delay the need to provide a deeper answer of this sort.)

It is a consequence of the simple view that a particular procedure may meet the requirements of equality of opportunity irrespective of whether other such procedures in the same society do so. Furthermore, the simple view does not maintain that for a society to provide equal opportunity across its full range of institutions and practices, the total set of opportunities available to different individuals must be identical or equivalent in some sense, unless all that is meant by this requirement is that scarce opportunities, such as the opportunity of securing a job or an educational place, should be subject to open competition.

Note that the simple view is not necessarily committed to the idea that rewards for jobs should be assigned by a free, or even relatively free, market. The issue of extrinsic rewards could be regarded as separate, to be governed by an independent principle of justice. In consequence, a commitment to open competition is compatible with support for a high degree of redistributive taxation. There is, however, a tension between a commitment to open competition and a commitment to strict equality of outcome, for many suppose that part of the point of advocating open competition is to justify some measure of inequality of outcome.[9] It is not obvious, however, that there is necessarily a logical inconsistency here. The simple view is concerned primarily with the allocation of jobs and educational or training places. In the absence of further argument we should not rule out the possibility that there might be reasons for allocating them by open competition even if winning or losing made no difference to the *overall* distribution of benefits and burdens.

II. *Possessing an Opportunity*

The relationship between equality of opportunity, as the simple view conceives it, and the possession of an opportunity is far from transparent. It is clear that there can be open competition for a scarce opportunity even if not everyone who enters that competition has a genuine chance of success. Indeed, some applicants, such as those who are not even minimally qualified for it, might have no chance of success whatsoever. Someone who applies for a position of translator but cannot speak or read the language that he will be required to translate, and has no ability to acquire that language, has no chance of being selected, barring a radical mistake on the part of the selectors. It follows that in the context of unpacking the ideal of equal opportunity, the simple view must distinguish between 'possessing an opportunity' in the relevant sense and 'having an available option', where having an available option to do or attain something means that one has a realistic chance of success if one attempts to do or attain that thing.[10]

[9] See Flew, *The Politics of Procrustes*, 48–9.

[10] Brian Barry seems to identify 'having an opportunity' with 'having an available option': see Barry, *Culture and Equality*, 105.

Nor can the simple view equate 'possessing an opportunity' with 'having a reasonable choice'. Consider a range of cases where a person could in principle enter a competition for a job and would have a good chance of success but is unwilling to do so for that job would require her to violate commitments that are central to her identity. Falling under this description would be the case of a pacifist who is qualified for a job in a munitions factory, or the case of someone who is a vegetarian on moral grounds faced with the prospect of applying for a job in an abattoir. There is a clear sense in which working in a munitions factory is not a reasonable choice for the pacifist; nor is working in an abattoir a reasonable choice for the vegetarian.[11] Yet, according to the simple view, equality of opportunity is secured in relation to these positions provided that they are subject to open competition.

In the context of considering what it is for those with different cultural identities to possess equality of opportunity, Bhikhu Parekh maintains that:

> ... the concept of equal opportunity ... needs to be interpreted in a culturally sensitive manner. Opportunity is a subject-dependent concept in the sense that a facility, or resource, or a course of action is only a mute and passive possibility for an individual if she lacks the capacity, the cultural disposition or the necessary cultural background to take advantage of it.[12]

Defenders of the simple view would reject Parekh's conception of equality of opportunity. According to the simple view, if someone lacks the cultural background or cultural disposition which others possess that is needed to take advantage of a job, it will not necessarily follow that there is a failure of equality of opportunity.[13] In taking this stand, defenders of the simple view need not deny that if someone lacks the cultural background to take advantage of a job, then it is not a reasonable choice for her and hence not a genuine option for her. But they will maintain that it does not follow,

[11] This point does not rely on the vegetarian's having a moral objection to killing animals for food; even if his reluctance to work in an abattoir stemmed from the fact that he cannot stand the sight of blood, it is plausible to hold that working there is not a reasonable choice for him.

[12] B. Parekh, *Rethinking Multiculturalism: Cultural Diversity and Political Theory* (Basingstoke, UK: Macmillan, 2000), 241.

[13] See Barry, *Culture and Equality*, 37–8, 105, although Barry is not offering a defence of the simple view.

without adducing further considerations, that she lacks equality of opportunity. For in their view 'possessing an opportunity' should not be treated as equivalent to 'having a reasonable choice'.

The simple view can still allow that there is a sense in which 'opportunity is a subject dependent concept', however. Suppose that some groups of people are indoctrinated so that they do not want to fill particular kinds of prestigious advantaged social positions that carry with them higher than average extrinsic rewards. The reason they do not apply for these positions, is not because they are unaware of them, but because they think that they are not for them. In cases such as these a defender of the simple view might still want to say that they are denied equality of opportunity. From this perspective, open competition is insufficient for equality of opportunity because it also requires the absence of this kind of indoctrination.

What meaning does the simple view attach to 'possessing an opportunity'? In assessing whether a person has equality of opportunity in relation to some social position, the simple view treats 'possessing an opportunity to fill it' as roughly equivalent to 'having the possibility of entering an open competition for it'[14] (perhaps with the proviso that this must take place in a context where no one is subject to systematic indoctrination or manipulation of a kind that makes him not want to occupy such positions). According to the simple view, equality of opportunity requires open competition for advantaged social positions, such as jobs and scarce educational places, but it does not follow that a person must have some chance of success in these competitions, nor that occupying these positions must be a reasonable choice for her given her commitments.

But does the simple view give an adequate account of what it is to possess an opportunity? In my view this question cannot be settled in the absence of a justification for the idea that advantaged social positions should be allocated through open competitions, which itself would require an account of the role of this idea within an overall theory of justice.[15] Without this we do not know what significance to attach to a person's 'having the possibility of entering an open competition for an advantaged social position'; nor do we know whether this way of interpreting what

[14] See Flew, *Politics of Procrustes*, 46–7.

[15] Or, at least, an account of its role within a fuller theory of equality of opportunity: see S. VI of this chapter.

it is to possess an opportunity is better adapted to its role of providing a defensible theory of equality of opportunity than, say, the idea of having an available option or having a reasonable choice.

III. *Being Qualified*

In order for a competition for a job or educational place to be open, the rules of that competition must be well-designed to select the best-qualified candidate. But clarifying what it is to be qualified for such a position, or indeed to be the best-qualified for it, is not an easy matter.

One might think that some progress could be made on this issue by specifying a list of characteristics that could *never* count as a qualification for a position. It would follow that to select on the basis of these characteristics would always be to violate the terms of open competition and hence (according to the simple view) to offend against equality of opportunity. Sex, race, and religion would be the obvious candidates here (though no doubt there are others as well). But on further reflection, this approach seems implausible, for a person's race, sex or religion may sometimes count as a qualification for a position. For example, when a part in a play is for a man or woman in particular, being a man or a woman may count as a qualification. When a religious office within a church is being filled, a commitment to that particular religion is itself a qualification for it.

Of course, this does not make the notion of a qualification vacuous. An employer is not at liberty to insist that any characteristic that pleases him is a genuine qualification for a job. In assessing whether a characteristic qualifies a person for a job, we need to ask whether that characteristic is relevant to that person's ability, or potential ability, to do the job or do it well (and perhaps ask whether it contributes to promoting the overall aims of the organization). If not, then it cannot count as a genuine qualification for it. To treat it as one would be to violate the terms of open competition. For example, suppose that an advertisement for the job of office clerk specifies that the successful applicant should not possess a beard, even though there is no reason why someone should not be able to do the tasks that the job involves with facial hair. In this case, the requirement of open competition has been violated, for something that is not a genuine qualification is being treated as one in judging between candidates.

The case described is fairly trivial but other relevantly similar ones are not. Suppose for example that an employer requires female employees to wear skirts to work, even though the wearing of skirts does not enable them to do their jobs any better.[16] In this case, the requirement disadvantages those Moslem women who cannot be true to their religion, as they understand it, and comply with the regulation. In order for competitions for jobs to be genuinely open, the requirements of the job should be connected in an appropriate way with the capacity to perform it or perform it well.

This does not imply that whenever some condition that a group of people cannot meet without betraying one of their commitments is specified as a requirement for a job, it cannot be a genuine qualification for it. Contrast the case of a job in the construction industry which requires employees to wear protective head gear. This disadvantages those Sikhs who believe that their religion requires them to wear a turban in public. But a construction company may have strong reasons, connected with the job that they need doing, for wanting employees to wear protective headgear. The company may point to 'the greater risk that work will be disrupted due to injury if not all workers are protected, and the danger that somebody who incurs a head injury poses to fellow workers by falling on them or dropping things on them from a height'.[17] For this reason, the company may legitimately regard willingness to wear protective headgear as a qualification for jobs on site, even though this may in effect exclude Sikhs who are unwilling to do so on the grounds that it would require them to remove their turbans at work.

Some critics have thought that the notion of a qualification on which the simple view relies is deeply problematic. Iris Young, for example, attacks 'the principle of merit' to which the simple view is committed. This principle maintains that 'positions should be awarded to the most qualified individuals, that is those who have the

[16] What if the job is to work as a waitress in a café that attracts male customers who come to admire women's legs? The general issue of whether it is legitimate for what counts as a qualification to be influenced by the desires, prejudices and dispositions of customers, clients and other members of a workforce is discussed in S. V, p. 32.

[17] Barry, *Culture and Equality*, 54.

greatest aptitude and skill for performing the tasks those positions require'.[18] Young objects to the principle on the grounds that it presupposes that the qualifications for a position can be defined in value neutral and culturally neutral ways, which she believes is impossible. Young may be right that it is impossible to define the qualifications for a job in value neutral or culturally neutral ways. It is certainly true that many of the characteristics and abilities that are regarded as qualifications for a job will be more easily gained by members of one culture rather than another, and indeed by people with one set of values rather than another, and that may be enough to establish her conclusion. But it is unclear why Young should suppose that this provides an argument against the principle of merit or against the simple view of equality of opportunity that I have been unpacking.

She does give one reason why the merit principle requires qualifications to be specified in a way that is value neutral and culturally neutral:

> If merit criteria do not distinguish between technical skills and normative or cultural attributes, there is no way to separate being a 'good' worker of a certain sort from being the sort kind [sic] of person—with the right background, way of life, and so on.[19]

Defenders of the simple view will be unimpressed by this argument, however. To support their view all they require is the assumption that we can distinguish between those qualities, characteristics, and capacities which enable a person to do a job and do it well (and perhaps those qualities which promote the overall aims of the organization) from those which are irrelevant to doing that job and doing it well (and those which do not promote the overall aims of the organization).[20] From this perspective, it does not matter whether or not qualifications are defined in neutral ways. (I do not wish to deny that there are difficulties here for the simple view. In particular, there is the difficult issue of whether or when the attitudes of clients, customers, and fellow workers can legitimately affect what counts as a genuine qualification for a job. For example, it does

[18] I. Young, *Justice and the Politics of Difference* (Princeton, NJ; Princeton University Press, 1990), 200.

[19] Young, *Justice and the Politics of Difference*, p. 201.

[20] D. Miller, *Principles of Social Justice* (Cambridge, MA: Harvard University Press, 1999), 190–1; Barry, *Culture and Equality*, 99–102.

seem that whether a person will fit in with other employees may at least sometimes count as a qualification for a job given its potential impact upon harmony and productivity in the workplace, but this raises serious worries about the way in which, say, racist or sexist attitudes amongst a workforce may count against black or women applications. However, these difficulties arise for any view of equality of opportunity that is concerned with the fairness of procedures for filling advantaged social position, and the issues involved are discussed in Section V of this chapter.)

Of course, Young is correct to observe that what counts as a qualification for a job may be a matter of reasonable disagreement, as indeed the judgement that a particular individual is the best qualified for it may be. This latter sort of judgement will often involve a complex balancing of a variety of different considerations. For example, in some cases a person may be qualified for a position even though she does not already possess the ability to do it; the mere potential to develop that ability over time may itself be a qualification. In such cases, when the employer has reason to think that an applicant will be able to do that job better, after having undergone training, than some other candidate who has already been trained, he or she may legitimately regard the former as better qualified than the latter. Evidence concerning whether the person is likely to remain in the job once she has been trained may then properly be regarded as relevant to the judgement of whether she is the best-qualified candidate. The question of whether a person is the best-qualified applicant for a job may also be complicated by the fact that it is sometimes impossible to give a list of the particular qualifications that are required for a particular job: it may be the case that within a workplace, certain kinds of skills are required but it may not matter precisely how these skills are distributed between the occupants of particular jobs within it. So a workplace may need someone who is good at negotiating, someone who can speak French, and someone who is able to construct a database, without it mattering much how these skills are parcelled out in relation to other features of the division of labour within it.

Given the wide scope that exists for reasonable disagreement over what counts as a genuine qualification for a job, and over which of a number of candidates for it is the best-qualified, this raises the question of how, in the face of this disagreement, some set of purported qualifications should be specified as the qualifications required for a job. Any full specification of the simple view would need to take a stand on this issue. But the simple view, considered on its own, is not committed to any particular answer to it. Indeed, it need not reject Young's preferred solution, which involves subjecting the writing of job descriptions to democratic control and opposing the hierarchical nature of the division of labour.[21]

IV. *Discrimination*

It might be argued that the simple view appears plausible because it is easily confused with a principle of non-discrimination, which shares some of its implications but is more restricted in scope. The principle of non-discrimination opposes rules, procedures, and decisions which deny people access to advantaged social positions because of, say, their race, sex, religion, or nationality but stops short of advancing the idea that selectors should appoint the best-qualified candidates for these positions. But it is not clear that it is possible to defend a principle of non-discrimination without committing oneself to some such idea. In spelling out what constitutes unfair discrimination, some account will need to be given of what makes something a qualification, for otherwise we will be unable to explain why being male, or having a particular religious faith, may sometimes count as a qualification, such that selecting people partly on this basis would not involve unfair discrimination. (Recall my earlier examples: being male is a qualification for playing a male character in a production; having a particular religious faith may be a qualification for a religious office.)

It does not follow straightforwardly from this that a principle of non-discrimination must entail the principle that the best-qualified candidates should be appointed. Defenders of the principle of non-discrimination may provide an account of what constitutes a qualification and then maintain that unfair discrimination occurs whenever some property from a given list (sex, race, religion, ethnicity, nationality, say) is treated as a qualification, or a lack of qualification, when it is not. But that merely invites the question: why not say that unfair discrimination occurs whenever a property is treated

[21] Young, *Justice and the Politics of Difference*, 213.

as a qualification or a lack of qualification when it is not? Why restrict the list of properties here? Once we endorse a principle of non-discrimination which maintains that unfair discrimination occurs whenever a property is treated as a qualification (or lack of qualification) for an advantaged social position when it is not, we are a short step away from embracing some version of the simple view.[22]

The simple view goes hand in hand with a particular account of what constitutes unfair discrimination, or what constitutes a form of discrimination that violates equality of opportunity. According to the simple view, unfair discrimination is a property of decisions, procedures, or rules that do not fulfil the requirement of open competition, or more fundamentally, it is a property of decisions, procedures, or rules that are not conducive to the aim of selecting the best qualified from those who are interested in filling the position (or would be interested in filling it were they not subject to manipulation or indoctrination). So, in general, unfair discrimination arises when some are barred from the competition for an opportunity, or when the rules of the competition are designed so that they do not select the best-qualified applicant but favour members of some particular group, or when selectors break the rules.

From the perspective of the simple view, the paradigm cases of unfair discrimination are intentional; they arise when prejudiced selectors violate the conditions of open competition in full knowledge that they are doing so. But the simple view can allow for cases of unintentional unfair discrimination as well. For example, it can acknowledge the way in which the best-qualified may be denied jobs or educational places because of stereotypes that are operating subconsciously in the minds of selectors. Secondary sexism of this sort occurs when, for example, a woman is passed over because selectors think that women are less committed to their careers, and more likely than men to sacrifice their careers to raise children, even though she is in fact as committed as, or more committed than, the other candidates, including the male ones.

The simple view can also acknowledge some forms of what might be termed 'institutional discrimination'. The expressions

[22] Matt Cavanagh thinks that there is a way of defending a principle of non-discrimination which prevents it from collapsing into the principle that the best qualified candidates should be appointed: see M. Cavanagh, *Against Equality of Opportunity*, Pt 3. I consider his argument in Ch. 2, S. IV.

'institutional racism' and 'institutional sexism' are sometimes used merely to refer to institutions where there is a pervasive ethos which allows the prejudices of those who work within those institutions, including those in positions of power and authority, to influence decisions (such as those concerning who gets promoted), procedures and rules, and behaviour in general. But there are other more specific phenomena that this expression can be used to capture. Suppose, for example, that an institution defines the qualifications for its positions in sex-biased or race-biased ways. Qualities which are not strictly needed to carry out the duties constitutive of these positions are included in the job descriptions and used as selection criteria, with the result that, say, women or blacks or Moslems or Sikhs are disadvantaged. To return to the earlier example, the dress code with which an institution operates may require women to wear skirts at work, for reasons which are not intrinsic to the tasks that need to be carried out, with the result that Moslem women are disadvantaged. The simple view can regard this phenomenon as a form of unfair institutional discrimination.

According to the simple view, determining with certainty whether selectors give applicants equality of opportunity, or unfairly discriminate against some group of them, will often require a detailed examination of the process of selection to discover the reasons why someone was excluded from the competition or why one candidate was chosen in preference to another. For only then can one demonstrate that, as a result of prejudice, some applicants were discouraged from applying or were not seriously considered; or that the criteria of selection were designed to favour members of one particular group rather than pick out the best-qualified applicants; or that the qualifications for a job were defined in discriminatory ways.

In order to show that members of some group have been unfairly discriminated against it is insufficient (and unnecessary) to show that they are not proportionately represented in employment or higher education.[23] Indeed, given the range of possible explanations for inequalities of outcome, it is not clear that the relative absence of members of some groups in various sought-after positions by itself provides even prima facie evidence of unfair discrimination on this

[23] See, e.g. Flew, *Politics of Procrustes*, 48ff; Barry, 'Equality of Opportunity and Moral Arbitariness', 39–40.

view. For example, inequalities of outcome between different groups may reflect the different values to which members of those groups are committed, and these different values in turn might be explained in terms of the different practices of these groups.

Is the account of unfair discrimination that is implicit in the simple view adequate? Again this is a question that cannot be properly addressed without giving the simple view a deeper theoretical grounding. We need to know the role of the simple view within an overall theory of justice (or, alternatively, within a fuller account of equality of opportunity), for without this we cannot determine whether there are more instances of unfair discrimination than it is able to acknowledge. (In Chapter 3, Section II, I suggest that there may be.)

V. *Revisiting the Notion of a Qualification*

So far I have tried to unpack the simple view as sympathetically as possible, in some cases indicating the resources it has to answer criticisms that might be levelled at it, but in the course of doing so showing that it is more complex than it might appear and that it stands in need of deeper theoretical grounding. In the remaining sections of this chapter I consider two ways in which the simple view, as I have specified it, must be regarded as incomplete. In the next section I raise doubts about whether open competition can legitimately be regarded as sufficient for equality of opportunity. In the remainder of this section I explain how a complexity that is involved in the notion of what it is to be qualified for a position provides an additional reason for thinking that the simple view needs to draw upon further principles of justice for it to be fully intelligible. This complexity has to do with the difficulty of finding a satisfactory way of explaining what a qualification is, without appealing to prior intuitions about justice.[24] Let me explain this difficulty more fully.

There are a number of circumstances in which an employer might increase the productivity of his enterprise by appointing whites in preference to blacks with comparable talents, skills, motivation, and experience (let us say that collectively these constitute a person's

[24] My discussion draws upon material from A. Mason, 'Equality of Opportunity, Old and New', *Ethics*, 111 (2001), 760–81.

aptitude), or by appointing men in preference to women with a comparable aptitude. By appointing whites in preference to blacks who possess a comparable aptitude, an employer with a racist workforce can avoid the friction and disharmony which would otherwise be created among them. By appointing whites in preference to blacks who possess a comparable aptitude, an employer with racist customers or clients can avoid a loss of business.

In each of these cases, though the employer has a reason to appoint a white person in preference to a black, it seems misconceived to suppose that being white is a qualification for the job. But why should this be? One possible explanation might be that the qualifications for a job are constituted by the abilities and dispositions needed to do that job effectively, considered in isolation from the abilities, and dispositions of the workforce, customers, and clients. Indeed in the case I described it is tempting to say that it is not the black applicant who lacks the ability to fit in with members of the existing workforce, but rather they who lack the ability to accommodate him. From this perspective he is qualified for the vacancy in a way that the current employees are not for the posts they already hold.

The problem with this response is that there is no plausible way in general of specifying the various things that may count as qualifications for jobs, including abilities, potential to develop abilities, and dispositions, independently of the abilities and dispositions of others such as customers, clients, or members of the workforce.[25] The qualifications for a job often do include abilities that are heavily dependent on the abilities or dispositions of these others. Consider some uncontroversial cases in which this is so. If someone is needed to negotiate a compromise on an issue that is acceptable to different parties, then their ability to perform that role successfully, and hence whether they are qualified for it, will depend on how they are regarded by those with whom they will be negotiating. If the members of a workforce speak only Gujarati, then a qualification for a new job in it would be the ability to speak Gujarati. If customers

[25] In this respect I agree with Alan Wertheimer: see his 'Jobs, Qualifications, and Preferences', *Ethics*, 94 (1983), 99–112. Wertheimer calls those qualifications for a job which depend upon the dispositions of others 'reaction qualifications' and argues that at least some of them may be legitimate grounds for selecting candidates.

like an easy smile, then a qualification for the role of salesperson would be a cheerful disposition.

There are also cases in which race or sex is often thought legitimately to count as a qualification because of the attitudes of others. Consider some examples. If there is a need for gynaecologists in an area where women are uncomfortable with male doctors, or have moral or religious objections to men other than their husbands seeing them unclothed, then it seems that being a woman is a qualification for that post. If a university has very few female academics, and as a result its pastoral care for female students suffers because some of these students would on occasion prefer to speak to another woman about their difficulties, then being a woman may legitimately count as a qualification for an academic post in it. It is often supposed that being black may be a qualification for the role of community policeman in a black neighbourhood. Sometimes this is justified on the grounds that a black person will have knowledge and experience lacked by white applicants, so that being black is not in itself being treated as a qualification for the job but rather the relevant knowledge and experience. Most of the time, however, it is justified on the grounds that a black person will be the object of less suspicion and animosity, and hence be in a better position to develop the trust required to police the community effectively than a white counterpart. If this is the justification, then it seems that blackness is being treated as a qualification for the post.[26]

These considerations suggest that any adequate account of 'qualifications' has to meet two conditions. First, it needs to be able to accommodate the idea that the dispositions, beliefs, and abilities of (for example) customers, clients, and members of the workforce can in some cases crucially affect what counts as a qualification for a job. Second, it needs to be able to accommodate the idea that prejudice against members of a group cannot legitimately make it the case that

[26] There may seem to be a difficulty here in individuating the relevant property which counts as a qualification. In the first example, why regard being female as a qualification for the post of gynaecologist rather than the ability to make female patients feel at ease? In the second example, why regard being black as a qualification to the job of community policeman rather than possessing the capacity not to give rise to animosity? I think that the relevant qualifications can be described in different ways, but one legitimate way of describing them in the first example involves reference to sex, and in the second example one legitimate way of describing them involves reference to skin colour.

not being a member of that group counts as a qualification for a job. So, for example, prejudice against blacks in the workplace cannot make it the case that being white is a qualification for a job in it, even though employers may have a prudential or efficiency-related ground for appointing whites. As far as I can see, only a moralized account of qualifications will be able to meet these conditions. Such an account would need to appeal to further principles of justice (perhaps other principles of equality of opportunity) which draw limits to what can be a qualification by determining what constitutes a just reason for selecting or discounting a candidate in an appointments procedure.[27]

The general picture would need to be something like the following. Being white when a workforce is prejudiced against blacks cannot legitimately be treated as a qualification for a job in it, for that would be unjust. A qualification for a job is any performance-related characteristic or feature that constitutes a good reason for appointing a person to it, partly in virtue of its not being unjust to select someone on the basis of that characteristic or feature. But if this is the correct picture, we cannot provide a defence of the simple view that does not draw upon further principles of justice. For the notion of what it is for a candidate to be qualified for a job is being shaped by intuitions concerning what kind of factors may justly influence selection decisions.

VI. *The Insufficiency of Open Competition*

Even though defenders of the simple view hold that open competition is a requirement of equality of opportunity, it would be implausible to maintain that it is a *sufficient* condition of equal opportunity.

[27] This is also the conclusion that Wertheimer seems to reach: see 'Jobs, Qualifications, and Preferences', 112. Miller comes close to accepting it when he maintains that we need some way of distinguishing legitimate and illegitimate reaction qualifications: see D. Miller, 'Deserving Jobs', *Philosophical Quarterly*, 42 (1992), p. 175. In discussing the related issue of how we are to distinguish legitimate from illegitimate methods of predicting performance, Sher maintains that we need to employ the considerations which underwrite the ideal of equality of opportunity itself. See G. Sher, *Approximate Justice: Studies in Non-Ideal Theory* (Lanham, Maryland: Rowman and Littlefield, 1997), 128–31. For relevant discussion, see also J. Fishkin, *Justice, Equal Opportunity, and the Family* (New Haven: Yale University Press, 1983), 25–30.

Consider two cases, which unavoidably raise questions about the sufficiency of open competition for equality of opportunity. The first is the case of someone who lacks basic numeracy and literacy and, therefore, lacks the qualifications needed for the vast majority of jobs and training opportunities that are available in his or her society. The second is the case of an individual living in a multicultural society who cannot speak the language of the dominant community and, therefore, lacks the qualifications required for most of the jobs in the mainstream economy, for these require the ability to communicate with members of that community.

In the absence of a more detailed specification of these cases, they do not demonstrate that open competition cannot be sufficient for equality of opportunity. But they unavoidably raise questions about *access to qualifications*. For it would be implausible to suppose that equality of opportunity could be secured irrespective of what differences there were in terms of people's access to the qualifications which are prerequisites for a wide range of jobs and training places, even if scarce educational opportunities were distributed on the basis of open competition. In a multicultural society if children born into minority cultural communities do not have available to them schools which assist them in becoming fluent in the language necessary for participating in the mainstream economy, then they cannot possess equality of opportunity. If as a result of poor schooling some children fail to acquire the basic numeracy and literacy that is needed for most jobs in the economy, then they can hardly be said to possess equality of opportunity.

More generally, if we were to suppose that open competition is sufficient for equality of opportunity, this would imply that a society might secure equality of opportunity for its members provided that there was open competition for scarce educational opportunities, even when the social circumstances of some (such as the class into which they were born or the education which they happened to receive) effectively prevented them from obtaining the qualifications which were necessary for success in these competitions. In this context, Bernard Williams gives the example of a society in which members of a prestigious warrior class had previously been selected solely from wealthy families but which is reformed so that selection is done by open competition. However, the wealthy families continue to supply virtually all the warriors since the rest of the populace is undernourished as a result of their poverty.[28]

We must conclude that open competition is at best a necessary condition of equality of opportunity. The simple view, as I have specified it, provides us with at most only a *partial* account of the nature of equality of opportunity. Any full account of equality of opportunity that is plausible must place some conditions on what kind of access to qualifications is needed for the ideal to be realized. Those sympathetic to the simple view might preserve the idea that equality of opportunity requires scarce opportunities (or some designated set of them) to be subject to open competition, but maintain that this must take place against a background which ensures fair access to the qualifications required for success in those competitions if there is to be full equality of opportunity. Such a view could continue to allow that it is intelligible to say that an individual selection procedure realizes equality of opportunity even though the other such procedures in a society do not. However, it would have to insist that a particular procedure could realize it fully only if the background against which it operated ensured fair access to the qualifications on the basis of which individuals were assessed in the context of that procedure.

VII. *Conclusion*

Many difficulties could be raised with the simple view. The problems which I have highlighted do not question the idea that open competition is, in general, necessary for equality of opportunity. Apart from pointing out that the underlying motivation for this condition may be consistent with acknowledging a class of exceptions to it, namely, some cases of headhunting, and arguing that open competition may simply be instrumental to the deeper goal of appointing the best-qualified candidates, I have not challenged it in this chapter.

If we understand the simple view as specifying a necessary but not sufficient condition of equality of opportunity, the issues I have raised do not pose a fundamental challenge for it. Instead they give

[28] See B. Williams, 'The Idea of Equality', in his *Problems of the Self* (Cambridge: Cambridge University Press, 1973), 244–5.

reason to conclude that the simple view is incomplete and that when its missing components are supplied it will be more complex than its label would suggest. It needs to be embedded in a broader view of equality of opportunity or justice that enables us to identify the class of scarce opportunities which should be governed by equality of opportunity, to unpack the notion of a qualification fully, and to provide the deeper theoretical grounding that is required to justify its vision (or partial vision) of what it means to level the playing field.

Any adequate version of the simple view needs to place various conditions on access to qualifications. Indeed, it is plausible to suppose that it must have at least two components: the condition that the best-qualified candidates should be selected to fill advantaged social positions and the condition that there should be fair access to the qualifications required for success in competitions for these positions. Let me stipulate that any account of equality of opportunity which is fundamentally committed to these two elements is a meritocratic theory.[29] (By 'fundamentally committed', I mean endorses these two elements in a way that does not involve deriving them from other principles through the addition of empirical premises.) In Chapters 2 and 3, I explore in some depth two different ways of justifying a theory of this kind. In the next chapter I focus on one which appeals to the idea of desert by maintaining that when there is fair access to qualifications, the best-qualified applicants for advantaged social positions deserve those positions.

[29] It immediately follows that meritocratic views have the potential to justify some forms of positive discrimination or affirmative action. For in a society that has failed to provide its members with fair access to qualifications, equality of opportunity, so understood, is an unrealizable ideal, for one of its necessary conditions is unfulfilled. Under these circumstances it may be that this ideal is better promoted by allocating positions to those who lack qualifications through being deprived of access to them (and then giving them appropriate training) than by selecting the best-qualified candidates. So there need be no straightforward inconsistency between a meritocratic account and positive discrimination or affirmative action: the latter may be regarded as the best means of promoting equality of opportunity when it is impossible to realize this ideal fully in practice. See also Ch. 3, S. IV, for relevant discussion.

CHAPTER 2

The Desert of the Best Qualified

If the simple view is to be transformed into a meritocratic theory, the idea of desert might seem to provide the way forward: the best-qualified candidates for advantaged social positions *deserve* those positions provided there is fair access to qualifications. Although this approach has considerable intuitive appeal, it is hard to defend in a convincing fashion. Indeed the most obvious way of developing it, in terms of the idea that the best-qualified candidate deserves the job as a reward for past performance, runs into insuperable problems. This chapter focuses on what seems to me to be the most sophisticated alternative:[1] David Miller's argument that the best-qualified candidates deserve the jobs because they are the candidates most likely to deserve the incomes assigned by a market that is appropriately constrained by the need to provide fair access to qualifications. This argument employs a 'pre-justicial' notion of economic desert which treats contribution as its sole basis. I contend that it is ultimately unsuccessful.

I. *Markets, Desert, and the Best-Qualified Candidate*

In circumstances when there is fair access to qualifications, why should it be thought that the best-qualified applicant for a job deserves to be appointed? One obvious possibility would be that on the basis of his past achievements, the best-qualified applicant deserves the rewards he will receive from that job. Successful

[1] Here I bracket George Sher's argument for why the best-qualified candidate should be given the job, largely because I doubt that it is best understood in terms of desert. I discuss his argument in S. IV.

applicants are rewarded for past performance with various benefits that are intrinsic to the jobs they secure, such as the opportunity to obtain job-related satisfaction and self-realization, as well as extrinsic rewards, such as the salary assigned to it or the prestige it attracts.

On reflection, however, this approach faces considerable difficulties. There is a gap between a person's past achievements and his present qualifications for a job that makes it hard to ground the deservingness of the best-qualified candidate in his past achievements. The person who has achieved the most in the past, along the dimensions relevant to how well he can be expected to do the job, may not be the best-qualified person for it even if he is the most deserving of it. Consider, for example, an applicant for a job who, despite a superb track record—and indeed a better record in terms of relevant past achievement than any of the other candidates—has suffered a serious accident which means that he will no longer be able to perform at the same level. If we look solely at his past achievements, and base our judgements of desert on these, then we shall have to conclude that he, of all the candidates, deserves the job, but because of his accident he is no longer the best qualified for it. This serves to emphasize the point that selection for jobs (and educational places) is forward not backward looking: selectors are concerned with the qualifications of candidates mainly because they want to pick out those who are likely to perform the job well (or derive the most from the course). This makes it hard to see how the idea that the best-qualified candidate deserves the job can be grounded in their past achievements.

Against the idea that the best-qualified applicant for a job deserves it as a reward for past performance, David Miller also points out that the salary a person receives for a job is a reward for performing its duties. It does not represent a reward for what he did prior to being appointed to it:

> Jobs are properly rewarded in the course of performing them . . . When selecting the best-qualified candidate to hold a job, the employer is not in the business of rectifying a shortfall in the rewards that person received in previous employment.[2]

[2] Miller, 'Deserving Jobs', 166. See also Miller, *Principles of Social Justice*, 160.

Miller, however, thinks we can nevertheless justify the idea that the best-qualified candidate for a job deserves it when there is fair access to qualifications, and that we can do so by appealing to widely shared intuitions about desert, intuitions which he thinks a number of influential theories of justice have neglected. His argument has two main parts. First, he maintains that by appointing the best-qualified candidate 'we bring about a situation in which rewards are as closely as possible aligned with deserts'.[3] The best-qualified candidate is the person most likely to deserve the rewards, such as the income the job brings with it, at least in an appropriately designed market economy. Second, he argues that the best-qualified candidate deserves the job because they deserve the opportunity to obtain the rewards they will deserve if they perform at the level we can reasonably expect.

Although there may be concerns about the second part of Miller's argument, in particular whether the idea that the best qualified are likely to come to deserve the income they will receive could be the basis for saying that they deserve their jobs, I focus exclusively on the first part of the argument.[4] Here Miller draws a connection between the income that an appropriately designed market assigns to jobs and the deservingness of the people performing these jobs to receive that income given the contribution they make in the course of performing them. (In this way Miller in effect brackets the issue of intrinsic rewards, focusing instead on one kind of extrinsic reward.) In the remainder of this section, I raise doubts about whether markets can be expected to reward contribution appropriately. This may not seem to get to the heart of the matter, however, for it does not question whether contribution can properly be considered the sole basis of economic desert. This is the issue that I address in Section II.

Miller's argument is premised on the idea that actual markets can reward contribution of the relevant kind, at least approximately. Only if markets can reward contributions of the relevant kind, or track them in some rough and ready way, does it make sense for

[3] Miller, 'Deserving Jobs', 170; Miller, *Principles of Social Justice*, 164.

[4] I raise some difficulties with the second part of Miller's argument in my 'Meritocracy, Desert and the Moral Force of Intuitions', in D. Bell and A. de-Shalit (eds), *Forms of Justice: Critical Perspectives on David Miller's Political Philosophy* (Lanham, MD: Rowman and Littlefield, 2003), 57–60. My discussion of the first part of Miller's argument also draws upon this article.

him to suppose that the salary which an appropriately designed market assigns a job can properly reward the contribution made in the course of performing it. We should not underestimate the difficulties involved in the idea that markets reward contribution of a kind that is relevant to desert. Miller is clear that not every contribution deserves reward; in his view a contribution deserves reward only if it is connected in the right way to the agent's purposes. If an achievement is accidental, that is, if it is an example of what he calls 'integral luck',[5] then it does not deserve reward, or at least not the same reward that it would deserve had such luck not been involved. But the problem here is that markets do not, and cannot be designed to, factor out integral luck. They reward contributions regardless of whether or not they depend on integral luck.[6]

Market outcomes are also deeply affected by what Miller calls 'circumstantial luck' in a way that might seem to undermine the idea that markets can track contribution of a kind relevant to desert. (Circumstantial luck is luck which affects the opportunity to put in the kind of performance that would make them deserving of reward. Someone who lacks any skill at archery but enters an archery competition and shoots three arrows which happen to hit the centre of the target experiences good integral luck, whereas a superb archer whose car breaks down on the way to the competition and is therefore unable to compete experiences bad circumstantial luck.) Market rewards reflect facts about supply and demand, for example, how many others are producing the same kind of goods, or offering the same kind of service, and how many people are interested in obtaining this good or service. Given fluctuations in supply and demand, some of which are in practice wholly unpredictable, those offering a good or service in the marketplace are susceptible to large doses of circumstantial luck, sometimes to their benefit and sometimes to their detriment.[7]

Even if we bracket the issue of whether the kinds of luck that affect market outcomes undermine the idea that the rewards assigned by the market can be deserved, the very idea that actual markets can track desert will seem plausible only if it is assumed that the

[5] Miller, *Principles of Social Justice*, 143.

[6] See S. Olsaretti, *Liberty, Desert and the Market: A Philosophical Study* (Cambridge: Cambridge University Press, 2004), 81.

[7] See Olsaretti, *Liberty, Desert and the Market*, 82–3.

size of the (economic) contribution a person makes is a function of the demand he satisfies through his productive activity. Yet some product or service might fail to make a real contribution, even if it meets a demand, if that demand is constituted by preferences based on false beliefs, or it might make a less significant contribution than the demand for it would imply when people's preferences are distorted by lack of information. Miller gives little weight to these sorts of objection. He insists that actual (or present) contribution, as opposed to potential (or future) contribution, has to be measured by looking at the actual demand that is met by a good, or the actual benefits people receive from it, rather than by making judgements about what the demand for it would be, or how it would benefit people, if it were properly understood or truly appreciated, or immune to the effects of circumstantial luck in general.[8] In short, producing an item or providing a service makes an economic contribution to society if and only if that item or service benefits individuals, and it benefits individuals if and only if it satisfies their desires. But any plausible account of well-being must allow that people may want something which does not benefit them, for example, because of false beliefs about it, or which does not benefit them as much as they think because they lack information about the alternatives. Once this point is given due weight, it will be hard to sustain the idea that 'the benefit that someone derives from a good or service is measured by the amount she is willing to pay for it',[9] and it will be correspondingly hard to resist the conclusion that actual markets provide a highly imperfect measure of contribution.

Even if we put aside this particular doubt about the extent to which markets measure contribution, there are plenty of other reasons for denying that markets are likely to secure an exact correspondence between contribution and reward.[10] As Miller seems to

[8] See Miller, *Principles of Social Justice*, 185.

[9] Miller, *Principles of Social Justice*, 184–5.

[10] For some of these worries, see Nien-He Hsieh, 'Moral Desert, Fairness and Legitimate Expectations in the Market', *Journal of Political Philosophy* 8 (2000), esp. 95–9. Hsieh argues that even if we accept the assumptions of neoclassical economics, the equilibrium price of a good or service does not always reflect the contribution made by that good or service because the benefit it provides to an individual is sometimes greater than its equilibrium price. For example, the equilibrium price of a loaf of bread may be $2, but if a baker sells that loaf to someone who would have been willing to pay $10, then his contribution is worth $10 not $2.

acknowledge there will be many cases in practice where jobs are underpaid or overpaid relative to the contribution they involve. It is not clear, however, that the desert of the best-qualified candidate, or the idea that the best-qualified candidate ought to be appointed, is sensitive to this fact in the way that it should be if Miller were right about the relationship between them. If some job were undervalued by actual markets, then less well-qualified candidates might be as well placed as the best-qualified candidate to deserve the income it provides. In such cases, it would appear that Miller has to concede that appointing a less well qualified candidate would not involve failing to give the best-qualified candidate the opportunity she deserves. Miller's response is to argue that '[i]t is not possible to move towards a situation of overall justice through a series of such individual decisions. At best, what happens is that one arbitrary injustice is corrected at the expense of creating another'.[11]

This may be an adequate defence of the idea that hiring the best-qualified candidate is the best way of minimizing the injustices which occur as a result of jobs being overpaid or underpaid relative to the actual contributions they involve. But it is striking that employers do not even entertain the possibility of appointing a less well-qualified candidate to a job in order to correct for the fact that it is underpaid. This is not just because this would be irrational from the point of view of the efficiency of their enterprises. We simply do not suppose that the moral correctness of appointing the best-qualified candidate is affected in any way by whether or not the job concerned receives its proper remuneration. Given his commitment to taking common opinion seriously, Miller ought to be bothered by this counter-intuitive feature of his strategy. This draws attention to a general feature of his approach which might seem to be at odds with our intuitions: namely, the justice of appointing the best-qualified candidate to an advantaged social position is made conditional upon its being likely to secure a particular outcome, an outcome in which the person appointed comes to deserve the rewards attached to that position. Our commitment to the principle that justice requires the appointment of the best-qualified candidate does not seem to be conditional in the way that this approach would require. (I develop this kind of point further in Chapter 6, Section IV.)

[11] Miller, 'Deserving Jobs', 172; Miller, *Principles of Social Justice*, 166.

II. *Desert and Effort*

Even if markets were able to reward contributions of the relevant kind (i.e. contributions that were intended, unaffected by integral luck, and not too heavily influenced by circumstantial luck), we might still wonder whether in doing so they were rewarding desert. To the extent that people may deserve reward for effort that, through no fault of their own, does not result in a contribution, then there is little reason to suppose that the market will allocate either jobs or incomes in a way that satisfies all legitimate desert claims. But is effort a legitimate basis for deserving jobs or the income they provide?

Miller emphasizes that desert is a complex notion. For a start, 'the basis of desert—the characteristics in virtue of which people are said to deserve this or that—appears to change according to the kind of benefit in question'.[12] Moreover, 'the range of possible desert bases and the different kinds of benefits that people can deserve depend to some extent on existing institutions and may be expected to vary from place to place'.[13] Notwithstanding these points, it does seem that across a range of benefits, desert depends in part upon effort expended (at least in so far as that effort is directed at something worthwhile and not wholly misplaced), not only purposeful achievement. We often think that effort properly directed at something worthwhile deserves reward even when it does not result in achievement. This is reflected in both the comparative and non-comparative judgements we make. We often judge that someone who works hard on a worthwhile project, but through no fault of his own has little of the talent required to complete it successfully, deserves some reward, even if his achievement is negligible.[14] And some would judge that he deserves the same reward as (or even greater reward than) another with more of the relevant talent, who whilst working on a similar project puts in little effort but completes it successfully. So in a range of cases, whether a person deserves reward might seem to depend not only on the contribution he makes

[12] D. Miller, *Market, State and Community: Theoretical Foundations of Market Socialism* (Oxford: Oxford University Press, 1989), 157.

[13] Miller, *Principles of Social Justice*, 149.

[14] See G. A. Cohen, 'David Miller on Market Socialism and Distributive Justice', unpublished paper.

but also the effort he expends, even when that effort is unsuccessful. Indeed, turning to the case of employment, we might legitimately suppose that in some cases a less well-qualified candidate for a job will be more likely to deserve the salary attached to it because of the greater effort he will put in, even if we anticipate that he will be less productive or achieve less.

It should be conceded, however, that the judgements we make about effort, achievement, and desert are complex. It would be a mistake to assume that effort and achievement are mutually exclusive categories. The effort a person makes can sometimes be a kind of achievement. For example, the effort a severely depressed person succeeds in making despite their feelings of despair may in itself constitute an achievement. In the context of jobs, effort-making may itself be part of an achievement because of the way in which it can serve as a model for others, inspiring them to make more effort and as a result perform better. Furthermore, effort must be directed in some minimal way towards a valuable goal for it to make sense to say that it deserves reward; someone who sets himself the project of counting all the blades of grass in a field hardly deserves reward for his efforts, let alone his 'achievement' if he succeeds. But although these observations complicate the story we should tell about the relations between effort, achievement, and desert, they do not undermine the point that effort and achievement can come apart and that, when they do, sometimes at least effort deserves independent reward.

To clarify the discussion so far we can distinguish some different positions that might be advanced on the relationship between desert, effort, and achievement in the performance of jobs:

(a) A person's efforts, and only their efforts, deserve reward but they do so only when they are directed towards achieving something valuable.[15]
(b) A person's achievements, and only their achievements, deserve reward. Effort merits reward only in so far as it constitutes an achievement, or is part of an achievement.

[15] Wojceich Sadurski seems to accept (a), or something close to it, when he says that 'effort is the only legitimate basis and measure of desert' (W. Sadurski, *Giving Desert its Due* (Dordrecht, The Netherlands: Reidel, 1985), 116).

(c) A person's achievements deserve reward, and their efforts sometimes do so too, but only when those efforts are directed towards achieving something valuable.

Position (a) has potentially counter-intuitive consequences. For it implies that what a person actually achieves in the course of performing a job makes no difference to what he deserves, but our intuitions seem to favour the idea that his achievement is relevant at least to determining what he deserves. We might at this point move to (a*), where (a*) maintains that a person's efforts in the course of performing a job, and only those efforts, deserve reward but only when these efforts achieve something valuable (rather than merely being directed towards achieving something valuable).[16] But this rules out a possibility that we seem to allow, namely, that effort directed towards achieving something valuable might deserve some reward even if it is unsuccessful. So both (a) and (a*) are problematic.

Position (b) seems to be Miller's position. In support of it, it might be argued that when we reward effort in the course of performing a job, we do so not because we think it deserves reward, but to provide incentives for others and indeed for the agent himself to continue making an effort, in the hope that his effectiveness will improve. If we thought that the effort he expends was likely to have no impact upon his achievements or the achievements of others, then we would suppose that he should stop wasting his time rather than be rewarded for his effort. In response, it can be argued that it is implausible to believe that when we reward job related effort, we do so solely for the incentives a general practice of doing so provides. Indeed (b) is problematic precisely because it implies that the effort a person expends in doing a job never makes a difference, in itself, to what he deserves, unless it constitutes an achievement (or part of one).[17] It seems to me that our intuitions make that hard to swallow. They lend support to the idea that both effort without achievement and

[16] This would constitute what is sometimes called a 'realised-virtue theory': see J. Wolff, 'The Dilemma of Desert' in S. Olsaretti (ed.), *Desert and Justice* (Oxford: Oxford University Press, 2003), 221. (a) corresponds to what Wolff calls a pure effort theory, whereas (b) corresponds to what he calls a pure achievement theory.

[17] Note that (b) is importantly vague: it is consistent with the idea that achievement (and only achievement) deserves some reward and with the more demanding idea that it deserves reward in proportion to the size of the achievement. See Olsaretti, *Liberty, Desert and the Market*, 64–5.

achievement in the course of performing a job may deserve reward. If this is so, they favour (c), or some refined version of it, rather than (a), (a*), or (b).

There are, of course, a host of questions about what (c) implies, or what the correct version of it would be. In fact, it picks out a family of different conceptions of the relationship between desert, effort, and achievement in the performance of jobs. Members of this family will give different roles and weights to effort and achievement because they give different answers to questions such as: Under what circumstances does effort alone deserve reward? When a person deserves reward for some achievement, do their efforts also deserve reward? Some versions might coherently maintain that effort deserves independent reward *only* when it does not result in achievement. This would avoid a conclusion that may seem counterintuitive, namely, that the clumsy deserve more reward than the skilful for making the same object since the effort expended by the former is greater.[18]

Some members of the family of conceptions that fall under (c) will maintain that the effect of differences in natural endowments should be counteracted by placing limits on the extrinsic rewards people receive when their achievements relative to others are due in significant part to the natural talents they possess. Indeed, some might go so far as to maintain that one person can deserve more reward than another for his efforts and achievements only to the extent that those efforts and achievements were under his voluntary control. Miller argues that this voluntarist conception of desert verges on incoherence, for 'desert shrinks to within a tiny fraction of its normal range',[19] since even choice-making and effort-making depend on contingencies that are not within the agent's control.[20] Miller's conception of desert, in contrast, allows that luck may have a substantial impact upon people's deserts. The fact that someone

[18] See Miller, *Principles of Social Justice*, 183.

[19] Miller, *Principles of Social Justice*, 148.

[20] Rawls also seems to endorse this sort of argument but as a general critique of the very idea of desert: see Rawls, *A Theory of Justice*, 104. He is often supposed to be appealing to a principle which maintains that in order to justifiably deserve something, it is necessary to deserve the grounds on which one deserves. See Nozick, *Anarchy, State and Utopia* (Oxford: Blackwell, 1974), 224; A. Zaitchick, 'One Deserving to Deserve', *Philosophy and Public Affairs* 6 (1977), 370–88. For relevant discussion, see Olsaretti, *Liberty, Desert and the Market*, 24ff; and G. Sher, 'Effort, Ability and Desert', *Philosophy and Public Affairs* 8 (1979), 361–76.

happens to have been born with the potential to develop a talent whilst others have not does not, in Miller's view, undermine the claim that he deserves extra reward for the successful exercise of that talent, even if those others have put in the same amount of effort. In order to make this idea plausible, Miller again invokes the distinction between integral and circumstantial luck in relation to a performance. He argues that integral luck nullifies desert but insists that circumstantial luck always lies in the background of human performances and undermines desert only when it affects in a clear and direct way what different people achieve relative to one another.[21]

But even if the voluntarist conception of desert that Miller rejects really does suffer from the problem that he identifies, there is a variant of it which can avoid this problem and which provides a challenge to his own account. For it might be maintained that one person can deserve more reward than another for his efforts or achievements only if those efforts and achievements are the result of different choices they have made, without denying that the possession of a capacity for effort-making and choice-making depends on contingencies that are beyond the agent's control.[22] Or it might be maintained that making judgements of comparative desert requires us to compensate partially, rather than fully, for the effect of differences between individuals that are beyond their control. From each of these two perspectives, Miller's distinction between circumstantial and integral luck might be accorded little normative significance when it comes to making judgements of comparative desert, on the grounds that the presence of either kind of luck may make a difference to people's deserts.[23]

In defence of (b), Miller might maintain that there are some benefits, such as prizes, which are deserved solely on the basis of achievement. Then he might simply insist that salaries, when they

[21] Miller, *Principles of Social Justice*, 146.

[22] For relevant discussion, see Olsaretti, *Liberty, Desert and the Market*, 26–8.

[23] I would not deny, however, that Miller's view of the relationship between circumstantial luck and desert has some foundation in ordinary thought. That said, widely held views on this matter may pull in a highly inegalitarian direction to which he is not sympathetic. For example, it often seems to be accepted that sportspersons with rare natural gifts that are in high demand, such as Thierry Henry and Tiger Woods, deserve the enormous incomes they earn relative to others.

are set at the appropriate level, are in this respect similar.[24] Effort made in the course of one's employment may deserve gratitude or congratulation when it does not result in achievement (or is not part of an achievement), but it does not deserve monetary reward; giving effort of this sort monetary reward may be justified on the grounds that incentives are needed to persuade everyone to work harder but it cannot be justified on grounds of desert. If we focus on the actual practice of giving rewards in market contexts, and the rhetoric of desert that sometimes accompanies this practice, then Miller's claims may seem plausible, for effort tends to be rewarded only if it is either part of an achievement, or likely to lead to greater achievement in the future. But outside of market contexts, there are many cases where we think effort deserves material reward even when it is unconnected to achievement in these ways: the child who works hard, but whose school results are poor, is nevertheless deemed to deserve reward rather than mere praise (perhaps the same holiday that they were promised they would receive if they were to pass their exams), not merely as a way of encouraging future endeavour. It is precisely these sorts of examples that may lead us to think that markets, though they may reward contribution, do not reward in accordance with desert.

Of course we do employ notions of desert which give no weight to effort except in so far as it issues in achievement, or constitutes an achievement, for example, when determining the degree class a student deserves, we look solely at the quality of their coursework and their examination performance. But these are generally institutional notions of desert which are used to signify a person's legitimate entitlements as a result of their performance, judged in the light of the rules of the relevant institution. They are not fundamental, morally speaking, since these rules are subject to evaluation in terms of principles of justice (and the social purposes served by the institutions) and do not provide content to them. As Miller himself argues, the idea that the best-qualified candidate for a job deserves it cannot

[24] This seems to be the line he takes against Hayek. He points out that prizes are often deserved purely on the basis of achievement, and argues that economic desert also has this character: see Miller, *Principles of Social Justice*, 183–4. I am not convinced that this is a strategy that Miller can live with, however, given his deference to popular beliefs and his acceptance of the fact that people do often give weight to effort in an economic context even when it does not result in achievement: see Miller, *Principles of Social Justice*, Chs 3–4, esp. 66–7.

be underwritten by an institutional notion of desert of this kind, for institutions might operate with selection procedures which tracked something other than the qualifications of the applicants, perhaps because of the social purposes selectors believed these institutions should serve.

Miller could of course reply that when we attempt to reward people on the basis of their contribution, and give no independent weight to effort, we may still be seeking to reward desert in some pre-institutional sense. Indeed he could argue that it is precisely this pre-institutional sense which allows us to criticize our institutions and practices for failing to reward people in proportion to the contributions they have made (e.g. when we say that the two different jobs involve equivalent contributions and therefore should receive the same rewards), or failing to track contributions of the right kind (e.g. when we say that excellence in teaching as well as in research should be rewarded by universities).[25] But unless Miller can show that contribution alone deserves reward in these cases, institutions are at best being assessed in terms of some surrogate of desert or one aspect of desert, namely, a person's contributions, not desert itself. It is not enough here to argue that rewarding people on the basis of contribution is the best practical approximation to rewarding desert in its ordinary sense. For giving people the rewards they deserve requires tracking the efforts they have made not just their achievements. Although there is some correlation between contribution and effort, it is sufficiently tenuous that it would be grossly inaccurate to say that when we reward contribution we are rewarding effort and therefore desert in the ordinary sense.[26] Miller is, at best, proposing a revisionist account.

III. *Methodological Questions*

We seem to be faced with a clash of differing intuitions about desert. Miller's intuition, which he thinks has a basis in popular opinion, is that in the performance of jobs at least, achievement and achievement alone provides the relevant desert basis. The different (and indeed

[25] Miller, *Principles of Social Justice*, 142–3.

[26] See G. Sher, 'Qualifications, Fairness, and Desert', in N. Bowie (ed.), *Equal Opportunity* (Boulder, CO: Westview Press, 1988), 118.

inconsistent) intuition to which I have appealed, which I think also has a basis in popular opinion, is that effort in the performance of jobs may also deserve reward even when it does not result in achievement or constitute part of an achievement. This raises some difficult questions concerning moral methodology, regarding the significance that should be given to the fact that a conviction is widely shared. These questions also emerge in Miller's work on nationality, where he is most explicit about his method.[27] He claims that his approach

> rather than dismissing ordinary beliefs and sentiments out of hand unless they can be shown to have a rational foundation, leaves them in place until strong arguments are produced for rejecting them ... [W]e build upon existing sentiments and judgements, correcting them only when they are inconsistent or plainly flawed in some other way.[28]

Miller does not elaborate upon these remarks but they invoke the seemingly innocuous principle that we should not reject widely shared views without good reason.

This principle can be understood in different ways, however. How does Miller understand it? Does he take it to imply that there is always a reason for believing that widely shared views are true or justifiably held or, more specifically, that a view being widely shared is evidence of its truth or of its being justifiably held?[29] Miller does seem to hold a view such as the latter. For instance, he maintains that 'a theory of justice needs to be grounded in evidence about how ordinary people understand distributive justice'.[30] But why should we suppose that a view being widely held gives it special credibility? The most plausible answer that Miller can give to this

[27] See S. Caney, 'Individuals, Nations and Obligations', in S. Caney, D. George, and P. Jones (eds), *National Rights, International Obligations* (Oxford: Westview, 1996), 125, for criticism of the way in which Miller employs intuitions about nationality in his defence of special obligations to fellow nationals. See also D. Weinstock, 'National Partiality: Confronting the Intuitions', *The Monist* 82 (1999), esp. 518–24.

[28] D. Miller, 'In Defence of Nationality', *Journal of Applied Philosophy* 10 (1993), 4.

[29] Could the principle that widely shared views should not be rejected without good reason be derived from the more general principle that we should not reject any view unless there is good reason to do so? If it were derived from this more general principle, then it would not imply that there is any reason for believing that widely shared views are true. Indeed it would be purely formal and would not imply that there is any presumption in favour of widely shared views being justifiably held. This is not Miller's way of understanding his principle.

[30] Miller, *Principles of Social Justice*, 61.

question is to maintain that there are reliable methods of reaching the truth on moral questions, and that the fact a large number of people have converged upon the same views gives a reason for thinking that they have employed those methods.[31] (This is consistent with acknowledging that in some cases convergence might have occurred for other reasons, for example, because people were disposed to reason in a faulty way[32] or simply because they have all made certain factual errors.[33])

But Miller's version of the principle that we should not reject widely-held beliefs without good reason seems to presuppose a further epistemological position that some will find much more contentious: that we are entitled to hold a normative or moral belief that is *unsupported* by reason or argument so long as there is no good reason to reject it. Can this epistemological position be defended? Consider what a defender of a coherentist theory of justification would say in response to this question. According to a coherentist theory of justification, one's belief that *p* is justified in so far as *p* is part of a coherent set of beliefs.[34] Defenders of such a theory will be inclined to argue that even beliefs not directly supported by reasons may receive *indirect* support simply in virtue of being part of a coherent set of beliefs, and thereby count as justified. They can therefore accept that we are entitled to subscribe to a belief that has no direct support provided it coheres with other beliefs we hold.

There is another epistemological position that is also congenial to Miller's position, which some of Wittgenstein's remarks gesture towards. This maintains that one can be entitled to hold a belief (i.e. not be *unjustified* in holding it) even though it is not, and cannot be, justified.[35] This position makes space for the existence of beliefs which are neither justified nor unjustified. This sort of

[31] Is this Miller's reason for endorsing the principle, however? He does maintain that common opinion endorses various methods of inquiry; and he rejects the idea that 'philosophers can discover truth by means not available to lay-persons' (Miller, *Principles of Social Justice*, 52–3).

[32] See G. Gaus, *Justificatory Liberalism: An Essay on Epistemology and Political Theory* (Oxford: Oxford University Press, 1996), 133.

[33] See Miller, *Principles of Social Justice*, 53.

[34] See D. Brink, *Moral Realism and the Foundations of Ethics* (Cambridge: Cambridge University Press, 1989), 124.

[35] Compare, for example, Wittgenstein's claim that 'To use a word without a justification does not mean to use it without right' (L. Wittgenstein, *Philosophical Investigations*, trans. by G. E. M. Anscombe (Oxford: Blackwell, 1953), section 289).

epistemological picture is attractive, but not unproblematic as the following question reveals: Can a belief that rests upon other beliefs, that are neither justified nor unjustified, legitimately be regarded in itself as justified? If we answer this question in the negative, then a very large number of our beliefs will turn out not to be justified (though it will not follow that they are unjustified). On the other hand, if we answer the question in the affirmative, we seem to be violating a widely-held epistemological principle that 'justifying beliefs must themselves be justified'.[36]

I do not propose to adjudicate between the coherence theory of justification and the Wittgenstein-inspired alternative I have described, for this is not necessary for my purposes. The idea that there can be beliefs which cannot be given direct support (whether or not they are regarded as justified in virtue of belonging to a coherent set, or as occupying some middle ground between the justified and the unjustified), gives some reason to be cautious, like Miller, in seeking systematic unity in ethics. The danger of trying to systematize our ethical judgements is that we may misunderstand the basis of our settled convictions. For example, we may suppose that one principle can be derived from another, failing to appreciate that it has an independent basis. If principles and values are genuinely plural, then our reasons in defence of those principles and values are likely to run out, fairly quickly in some cases, leaving us with beliefs that can be given no direct support. Miller can fruitfully draw upon the idea that there may be beliefs of this kind in his discussion of desert. Indeed it helps explain the potential legitimacy of what he calls 'intuitive arguments' that simply express brute intuitions about desert. (Intuitive arguments are contrasted with indirect arguments which try to underpin the idea that a person deserves reward for some performance by appealing to the way in which the presence of the desert basis contributes to the realization of some other value that justifies the reward.[37]) Intuitive arguments have potential force only because it can be legitimate to subscribe to beliefs about desert for which no direct support can be given.

[36] David Brink makes use of this principle to argue against epistemological foundationalism: see Brink, *Moral Realism and the Foundations of Ethics*, 116–22.

[37] See D. Miller, 'Recent Theories of Social Justice', *British Journal of Political Science* 21 (1991), 379–80.

If I have understood Miller's methodology properly, it seems to me to be defensible.[38] My main doubt over his treatment of desert concerns how he applies this methodology to ordinary convictions about desert, rather than the methodology itself. He maintains that theories of justice need to be grounded in evidence about how ordinary people understand distributive justice, yet contends that common opinion is 'torn between the view that we deserve reward for what we achieve and the view that we deserve reward only for what is within our control, that is, our efforts and choices'.[39] Miller cannot consistently maintain that theories of justice need to be grounded in evidence about people's ordinary convictions yet simply discount a large part of that evidence in holding that people deserve reward only for their achievements. Indeed, the evidence Miller cites might be interpreted differently and in a way that creates even greater difficulties for his position. For the evidence to which he appeals does not, as he suggests, unambiguously support the conclusion that common opinion is *torn* between the view that we deserve reward for the contribution we make and the view that we deserve reward only for our efforts and choices. Rather, it can be read as supporting the conclusion that common opinion accepts that effort and achievement may both merit reward, so that effort may merit reward even when it does not result in, or constitute, achievement and achievement may merit reward even when it is effortless, but is divided over the relative significance of each.[40] It is not enough

[38] But see A. Swift, 'Social Justice: Does It Matter What the People Think?', in D. Bell and A. de Shalit (eds), *Forms of Justice* (Lanham, MA: Rowman and Littlefield, 2003), for further discussion.

[39] Miller, *Principles of Social Justice*, 71.

[40] Miller draws his conclusion after considering the views of Pamela, who invokes compensation, skill, responsibility, effort, and training as justifications for large rewards, but when these criteria clash maintains that 'productivity supersedes effort'. However, what Pamela says is consistent with the idea that we deserve reward for both our efforts and our achievements. More generally, Miller seems to accept the point that people's intuitions support the idea that we deserve reward for both our efforts and achievements in the context of contributions to small groups: 'people judge that the appropriate reward depends on what each person achieves, but they qualify this to some degree when presented with data about effort so that it is possible for a person who achieves less but tries harder to deserve more than another who tries less but achieves more' (Miller, *Principles of Social Justice*, 66).

in this context to maintain that common opinion supports the idea that people deserve monetary or economic reward for purposeful achievement but only gratitude for effort unsuccessfully directed towards the same achievement, for there is no evidence that common opinion makes any systematic distinction of this kind.

IV. *Respect for Persons*

David Miller's argument that the best-qualified candidates deserve the jobs because they are the candidates most likely to deserve the incomes assigned by an appropriately constrained market has encountered a number of difficulties. But the prominence in our practices of the idea that justice requires selecting the best-qualified candidates for jobs and educational places gives us good reason to search elsewhere for a satisfying justification of it. If that idea cannot plausibly be underwritten by the notion of desert, how might it be justified? It seems unlikely that its status as a weighty component of justice could be defended by any approach which saw it as the best means of realizing some independently specifiable conception of justice, or as the most socially efficient means of allocating jobs and educational or training places. There is an alternative strategy available, however, which in my view offers more promise, which appeals to the idea of respect for persons.

Matt Cavanagh has argued that some cases of selecting or rejecting people on grounds of their sex or race involve a specific kind of disrespect, namely, unwarranted contempt. But he maintains that this account of what is wrong with discrimination is unable to justify the meritocratic idea that employers should select the best-qualified candidates. Indeed, he argues that there may be cases when a person is rejected on grounds of their race or sex that do not involve any injustice because the decision to reject does not involve unwarranted contempt. For example, a black person might be rejected because the selectors have a sheer dislike of his race without holding any views about racial inferiority and in that case no contempt would be shown towards him. In Cavanagh's view, discrimination of this sort is not unjust, but he does not think this conclusion reveals a flaw in his account. Indeed he maintains that the principle that it is wrong to treat people with unwarranted contempt does the best job of explaining and justifying 'our deepest convictions about which kinds of discrimination are wrong while at the same time not having unacceptable implications in other areas'.[41] But he cannot escape the fact that it is a counter-intuitive consequence of his account that it sees nothing unjust or wrong in selectors rejecting a person because they simply dislike the race to which he belongs. A broader account of what it is to respect persons might be able to avoid such a consequence by acknowledging that other failures of respect can be wrong even when they do not involve contempt. (Indeed it is not obviously true that those who believe that black or female applicants are mentally or morally inferior must necessarily have *contempt* for them, yet Cavanagh assumes that these are the clearest cases of unjust discrimination.)

A number of theorists have thought that there are significant connections between the idea that we should appoint the best-qualified candidates for advantaged social positions, and hence object to discrimination on grounds of race or sex, and the demand that we respect agency or autonomy.[42] What is the precise nature of these connections supposed to be and can they justify that idea?

In defending the idea that the best-qualified candidates should be appointed, George Sher writes:

> When we hire by merit, we abstract from all facts about the applicants except their ability to perform well at the relevant tasks. By thus concentrating on their ability to perform, we treat them as agents whose purposeful acts are capable of making a difference in the world.... [S]electing by merit is a way of taking seriously the potential agency of both the successful and the unsuccessful applicants.[43]

Sher argues that when someone is hired because he is the nephew of the director, or because he is a member of some group or other, or

[41] Cavanagh, *Against Equality of Opportunity*, 166.

[42] The connection between equality of opportunity and autonomy has often been noted, though it has not been worked out to the depth it deserves. See G. Sher, *Approximate Justice: Studies in Non-Ideal Theory* (Lanham, MD: Rowman and Littlefield, 1997), 128; A. Goldman, 'The Justification of Equal Opportunity', 96. See also Richards, 'Equality of Opportunity', 73. Allen Buchanan argues that equal opportunity when it is understood as comprehensive non-discrimination is grounded in the principle of equal respect for persons: see A. Buchanan, 'Equal Opportunity and Genetic Intervention', in E. F. Paul, F. D. Miller, and J. Paul (eds), *The Just Society* (Cambridge: Cambridge University Press, 1995), 121.

[43] Sher, 'Qualifications, Fairness, and Desert', 119–20.

because of his needs, the potential agency of the applicants is ignored and they are not accorded respect as rational agents. Candidates are treated 'as mere bearers of needs or claims, as passive links in causal chains, or as interchangeable specimens of larger groups or classes'.[44] (Although Sher thinks that his argument is grounded in the idea of desert, I doubt that this is the best way of understanding it. It seems to appeal directly to the idea of respect for persons as agents and the notion of desert plays no genuine role.[45]) In Sher's view, it is only if candidates are selected or rejected on the basis of their qualifications to do the job that their agency is truly respected.

There does seem to be a way in which the agency of applicants is not treated with respect when, for example, selectors allow their racial or sexual prejudices to influence their decisions. When, say, a selector regards blacks as stupid or lazy and discounts black applicants as a result, there is a clear way in which their agency is treated with disrespect. This approach is also able to explain why some failures to appoint the best-qualified candidates are worse than others.[46] It is worse, for example, for a black person to be rejected because a selector has contempt for his race than for him to be rejected because the selector happens to dislike the red tie he is wearing. Rejecting a candidate because he is black or because she is a woman is, in general, worse than rejecting him or her in preference to the boss' son as a favour to him. Although in both cases the decision is disrespectful, in the latter case it is nothing about her that leads to her being rejected (except that she is not related to the boss) whereas in the former case it is a positive feature of her (that she is a woman or that she is black) that leads to her rejection. Sher's approach can accommodate these observations by maintaining that the nature of the injustice perpetrated will depend on the kind of failure of respect involved.

[44] Sher, 'Qualifications, Fairness, and Desert', 123. Sher's approach here is an extension of one which maintains that selection for advantaged social positions should be done on the basis of relevant reasons. See Williams, 'The Idea of Equality', 232–3.

[45] The kind of respect with which Sher is concerned is what Stephen Darwall calls 'recognition respect', which 'consists in giving appropriate consideration or recognition of its object in deliberating about what to do' (S. L. Darwall, 'Two Kinds of Respect', *Ethics* 88 (1977), 38).

[46] See Cavanagh, *Against Equality of Opportunity*, 156.

I also want to suggest that whether a selection policy or practice is disrespectful depends in part on the message conveyed by it, not just its rationale.[47] A policy or practice may be disrespectful even if its official or actual rationale is not. How do we decide what message is conveyed by a policy or practice? Often the message conveyed simply derives from its publicly stated rationale or justification, or the known intentions of those responsible for it. For example, prejudice usually conveys a straightforwardly disrespectful message. When racism overtly influences selection decisions, the applicants receive the message that it is not what you are able to do that matters but the colour of your skin. Sometimes, however, the message that is conveyed reflects what is, under the circumstances, a natural way of interpreting the policy or practice even though that interpretation ignores, or even contradicts, the publicly stated justification and the intentions of those responsible for it. In cases of this sort whether the policy or practice is itself disrespectful depends on whether the way in which it is interpreted could reasonably be foreseen and countered. So, for example, affirmative action programmes may give members of disadvantaged groups the message that the wider society believes they need to be given a head start because they are unable to compete effectively in a fair competition, even if that is not the publicly stated rationale of these programmes or the intended message. If this message can be foreseen and countered but no steps are taken to do so, then the policy or practice may itself be disrespectful.

This way of developing Sher's argument is strengthened by being considered in the light of how those candidates who are selected or rejected for reasons that have nothing to do with their ability to do the job well (or their potential to acquire that ability) experience their success or failure. Those who are denied jobs as a result of racial or sexual prejudice generally feel demeaned or insulted at being rejected on this basis because of the message it intentionally conveys. Even those who are the beneficiaries of affirmative action programmes in societies which employ quotas for disadvantaged groups sometimes suffer low self-esteem and feelings of inadequacy that can to some extent be traced back to the thought that they owe their positions to membership of a social group rather than their

[47] See T. E. Hill, *Autonomy and Self-Respect* (Cambridge: Cambridge University Press, 1991), ch. 13, for relevant discussion of the way in which policies and practices can convey messages.

abilities or potential abilities. Those who benefit from affirmative action programmes may receive the message: 'It is not your abilities that matter but the fact that you are a member of a disadvantaged group'. And they may receive that message whether it is intended or not, and irrespective of whether it is part of the publicly stated rationale of the programme.

This appeal to the importance of the message conveyed by a policy in deciding whether agency is being respected does not reduce the argument to the idea that an established practice of appointing the best-qualified candidate creates a legitimate expectation that the best-qualified candidates will be successful in the future. Rather, it points to the existence of meanings that can transcend the rationale, publicly stated or not, for a selection process. The mere expectation that the best-qualified candidate will be appointed could be changed in particular cases simply by announcing publicly that different selection rules are going to apply and that as a result the process may not have this outcome.[48] But even if there were such an announcement, a sense of grievance might arise amongst unsuccessful candidates because of the message conveyed by the new practice of selection, for example, that what matters is not a person's ability or agency but some other fact about them.

Clearly these points do not provide a case against every affirmative action programme. Sometimes the intentions of those responsible for these programmes, the rationales they give for them, and the efforts they make to avoid misunderstanding, may justify the insistence that these programmes involve no disrespect to the agency of the applicants. For example, as Sher himself argues, a practice of appointing less well-qualified applicants need involve no disrespect to the agency of the various candidates when it is clear that those who are successful would have been the best-qualified had they not been the victims of past discrimination.[49]

This argument indicates that the 'respect for persons' approach will allow exceptions to the principle that the best-qualified candidates should be appointed to advantaged social positions. The class of exceptions seems to be much more extensive, however, in a way that might seem damaging to the idea that there is any straightforward connection between respecting persons and selecting the

[48] Miller, 'Deserving Jobs', 165.

[49] See Sher, *Approximate Justice*, ch. 3.

best-qualified candidate. There is a range of cases where taking into account considerations other than the candidates' abilities to perform the job does not appear to be disrespectful to their agency. Surely, we might sometimes respect the agency of the candidates by attending to their needs as well as their ability to perform the relevant tasks well, since in general it is impossible to be an effective agent unless one's needs have been met; to act in this way would not be to treat candidates as 'mere bearers of needs'.

In response Sher might argue that jobs serve social purposes; there are various tasks created by the division of labour that exists in a society. Given these purposes, respect for persons in the process of selection requires us to attend to the candidates' qualifications, and only those qualifications. The candidates' needs are relevant in other contexts, for example, in the provision of welfare benefits, but not in the process of selecting for jobs. Respect for persons as agents imposes different requirements in different areas. (Indeed the notion of respect for persons may seem indeterminate precisely because we are inclined to ask what it requires in general rather than what it requires in particular contexts.) In the process of selecting for a job, it requires us to consider the candidates' abilities to perform well the tasks that are constitutive of that job (and their potential to develop those abilities), whereas in distributing welfare payments it requires us to consider people's needs.

This response has some force but it is not wholly persuasive. It is hard to see how it could establish the conclusion that it is *always* disrespectful to take into account people's needs in the process of selection.[50] A person may sometimes need a job not merely for the income it would provide, but also in order to boost his levels of self-esteem and self-respect given his experience of failure in the past, and it may be that this could not be secured by welfare payments, nor, say, by taking part in a training scheme. (More generally, appointing the best-qualified applicants may in various ways be demeaning to those who lack qualifications for a job, or indeed lack qualifications for any job that is sought after.) So we should leave open the possibility that respect for persons as agents may occasionally permit or even require selectors to take into account not only the person's aptitude to do the job in filling advantaged social positions, but also

[50] See Cavanagh, *Against Equality of Opportunity*, 70–1.

their needs. (Of course, when respect for persons does permit or require the selector to take into account an applicant's need for the job, this consideration will have to be weighed against the interests of those who are affected by how well that job is performed, such as the employer, or the customers and clients, which will give an independent reason to favour the best-qualified candidate. This independent reason is likely to take priority except when respect for persons requires, rather than merely permits, the appointment of a less well-qualified candidate.)

There are also other cases when not giving absolute priority to the goal of selecting the best-qualified candidates involves no disrespect, for example, when doing so would be massively inefficient. Selectors faced with an enormous field of candidates may decide that they will generate a short list simply by picking out the first half dozen or so that are sufficiently well qualified; there seems no good reason to insist that we should regard this practice as disrespectful. A similar point applies to a selection policy that allows the use of statistical inferences, that is, a policy which allows candidates to be selected at least partly because they have some characteristic that is correlated with the aptitude to perform the tasks that are constitutive of the job or educational place in question. Selectors who employ statistical data know that this will not always result in the appointment of the best-qualified candidates, but their use of it need not be disrespectful if the costs of obtaining the information that would enable a more reliable identification of these candidates would be high (or indeed if such information would be impossible to obtain).[51]

I do not think that the various exceptions I have described defeat the idea that there is a strong connection between respecting persons and appointing the best-qualified candidate. The respect for persons approach I have been outlining should allow these exceptions to the principle that selection procedures should be designed to result in the appointment of the best-qualified candidates. But this principle still serves as a good rule of thumb; there is a presumption that respect for persons requires selectors to design selection procedures in this way, even though that presumption is defeasible.

A respect for persons approach also helps us to resolve a difficulty left over from Chapter 1, concerning how we are to characterize

[51] For relevant discussion, see Sher, *Approximate Justice*, ch. 9; Cavanagh, *Against Equality of Opportunity*, 180–93.

the notion of a qualification.[52] There I argued that an adequate account of what constitutes a qualification for a job has to satisfy two conditions. First, it must be able to accommodate the idea that the dispositions, beliefs, and abilities of those affected by who is appointed to a post can in some cases crucially influence what counts as a qualification for it, for example, if customers like sales assistants have a cheerful disposition, then having such a disposition may legitimately be regarded as a qualification for that post. Second, an adequate account needs to be able to accommodate the idea that prejudice against members of a group cannot make it the case that not being a member of that group counts as a qualification, so, for example, racist attitudes in the workplace cannot legitimately make it the case that being white is a qualification for a job in it. I concluded that only a moralized account of qualifications could meet these two conditions. A respect for persons approach can help to provide such an account, for it can allow that the attitudes of customers, clients, and members of the workforce may crucially affect what counts as a qualification but insist that these attitudes can do so only if they do not display a failure to respect others. This would prevent racist attitudes in a workplace from making it the case that being white is a qualification for a job in it, since these attitudes involve a failure of respect, but it would allow that being black could be a qualification for the job of community policeman in a black neighbourhood, and that being female could be a qualification for the role of gynaecologist in an area where women have religious objections to being seen unclothed by male doctors, on the grounds that the attitudes which would make race or sex a qualification in these cases can be appropriately respectful.

Some maintain the respect for persons is a purely formal notion, a placeholder for whatever moral principles we should use to govern our relations with each other. Richard Arneson, for example, argues that:

> One expresses due respect for persons and treats them respectfully by acting towards persons in accordance with the moral principles that are best supported by reasons. In this sense respect for persons looks to be ... a purely formal idea, neither a clue to what principles are best supported by moral reasons nor a constraint on what principles might be chosen.[53]

[52] See Ch. 1, S. V.

[53] R. Arneson, 'Luck Egalitarianism and Prioritarianism', *Ethics* 110 (2000), 344.

But in ordinary discourse 'respect for persons' also has a narrower usage which does not presuppose that each and every failure to comply with the moral principles best supported by reason in one's dealings with others automatically counts as a failure of respect. Sher's argument, and my adaptation of it, involves this narrower usage. We should not understand it as appealing to some *independent* idea of respect for persons from which moral demands are derived. Rather we should see the relevant demands as expressing, in a constitutive way, what it is to respect persons. Understood in this way Sher's proposal is that respect for persons in the process of selection is expressed by considering candidates solely on the basis of their ability to do the relevant tasks. This sort of appeal to the idea of respect for persons in justifying the selection of the best-qualified candidates is not one that Miller must necessarily find uncongenial. He acknowledges that what it is to treat people as equals, to respect their dignity, varies historically, and from one place to another: for example, it means one thing in an aristocratic society, quite another in democratic societies.[54] He also insists that an aristocratic society, with its hierarchical notion of what it is to treat people with dignity and respect, is not a real option for us, given our commitment to democratic notions of social equality. Similarly, questions might be raised about whether we could become the kind of creatures who did not feel that there had been a failure of respect when we were accepted or rejected on grounds other than our ability to do the job.

V. *Conclusion*

The meritocratic ideal's commitment to the idea that the best-qualified applicants should be appointed to advantaged social positions is not only widely shared but also independently appealing. However, it is not adequately grounded in the claim that the best-qualified applicant deserves the position. A better argument for it appeals to the different idea that respect for persons requires us to consider their abilities in selecting for advantaged social positions, not simply because this promotes efficiency or utility or whatever, but because, in general, a failure to do so is disrespectful to the candidates.

[54] Miller, *Principles of Social Justice*, 241.

Where does this leave us in relation to the notion of desert? Intuitions about desert are divided concerning the precise roles of effort and achievement in determining economic desert, and concerning whether one person may deserve more reward than another when the greater effort or achievement he produced was unavailable to the other, so it would be unrealistic to expect an appeal to intuition alone to be able to resolve disputes of these kinds. We are also left with some difficult questions about the proper structure of any adequate theory of justice within which some notion of desert plays a role, questions which again our intuitions seem unable to provide much help in answering. As we have seen, desert theorists distinguish between pre-institutional notions of desert, which maintain that desert judgements are prior to, and independent of, actual institutions, and institutional notions which analyse desert in terms of the entitlements to goods that are created by satisfying the institutional rules governing their distribution. Our intuitions about desert are hard to reconcile with the latter alone and seem to favour pre-institutional notions. We do, for example, think that it may make sense to hold that an employee is receiving less pay than he deserves even though he is being rewarded in accordance with his employer's rules governing salaries and promotions (and even if these rules are compatible with wider state institutions that monitor and enforce a policy of non-discrimination). It is not so clear, however, that our intuitions favour a pre-justicial notion in the sense identified by Samuel Scheffler.

What makes a notion of desert pre-justicial? Pre-justicial notions deny that desert claims are derived from an independently formulated conception of justice;[55] they hold that we cannot characterize a person's deserts in terms of what he would receive from a just scheme, where what counts as a just scheme is specified in some way that is wholly independent of the concept of desert. It might appear that an approach of the kind that has been the focus of this chapter, which maintains that the best-qualified candidates for jobs deserve them provided there is fair access to qualifications, cannot be pre-justicial on the grounds that it requires some set of principles

[55] S. Scheffler, *Boundaries and Allegiances: Problems of Justice and Responsibility in Liberal Thought* (Oxford: Oxford University Press, 2001), 176–7, 185, S. Scheffler, 'Distributive Justice and Economic Desert', in S. Olsaretti (ed.), *Desert and Justice* (Oxford: Oxford University Press, 2003), 69, n. 2.

to determine what is to count as fair access to qualifications. This does not follow, however, for an account of what people deserve may be pre-justicial even if it invokes principles of justice, provided that these principles are not independent of the concept of desert or, if they are independent of it, desert claims are not derived from them alone but utilize further principles that employ the concept of desert. The approach I have been evaluating does require some set of principles to determine what is to count as fair access to qualifications—and these principles need to be satisfied before any of the desert claims it makes can be justified—but they may be conceived either as spelling out the conditions under which the best-qualified candidate deserves the job, these conditions being extracted from the concept of desert itself, in which case they are not independent of it, or as providing only part of an account of what constitutes a just scheme such that desert claims can be derived from them only in conjunction with further principles which invoke the concept of desert.

Indeed some might think that the position I have ended up defending is *committed* to a pre-justicial notion according to which justice involves giving people what they deserve, and that in the course of performing jobs, they deserve to be rewarded for their efforts and achievements. But in fact this is not the only way in which a position of this sort might be understood. For we might maintain instead that people deserve the distributive shares they receive when those shares arise from a just scheme, where a just scheme involves rewarding differential effort and achievement. The principles for rewarding effort and achievement might then be defended by appealing to ideas about the importance of holding people responsible for their choices, or respecting their capacity for autonomy, that are deeply embedded in our thought and practice but relatively independent of pre-justicial ideas about desert. As T. M. Scanlon has argued, there are a variety of reasons 'for wanting what happens to us to depend on our choices and other forms of response to alternatives',[56] and these reasons may play a role in justifying various choice-sensitive principles. Eschewing a pre-justicial notion of desert, it might then be said that people receive what they deserve only when these principles are satisfied.

[56] T. M. Scanlon, *What We Owe to Each Other* (Cambridge, MA: Harvard University Press, 1998), 256. See *ibid*., ch. 6, Ss 2–3 for relevant discussion.

It seems to me that our intuitions are insufficient to enable us to decide between a pre-justicial theory which maintains that justice requires giving people what they deserve, and that they deserve to be rewarded for their effort and contribution, and the alternative I have outlined. Further considerations, including the overall power of the competing theories within which these very different notions of desert are embedded, will need to play a role in assessing them. Whether the theory I have outlined, which gives desert a role but does not regard it as a pre-justicial notion, is the most powerful will depend on how it is elaborated. In the next chapter I propose to explore one way in which it might be developed that can be found in the work of John Rawls. Although Rawls distances himself from the notion of desert, his doubts are best understood as directed at pre-justicial understandings of it. He argues that equality of opportunity, properly understood, requires careers to be open to talents and that those with the same level of talent and ability and willingness to use them should have the same prospects of occupying advantaged social positions. Rawls need not object to the idea that people *deserve* the rewards that they would receive from a just scheme in which, *inter alia*, careers are open to talents and those with the same level of talent and ability, and willingness to use them, have the same chances of success. Understood in this way, his account would seem to preserve the structure of a meritocratic theory. For the principle that careers should be open to talents is closely related to the idea that the best-qualified candidates for advantaged social positions should be appointed to them, and the idea that those with the same level of talent and ability and willingness to use them should have equal chances of success offers an interpretation of what it is for there to be fair access to qualifications.

CHAPTER 3

Rawlsian Fair Equality of Opportunity

Although Rawls' account of fair equality of opportunity has received less attention than some other parts of his theory of justice, it merits careful consideration.[1] Rawls in effect arrives at his account after noting one of the respects in which the simple view is incomplete. Whilst insisting on the importance of 'careers being open to talents', Rawls maintains that this by itself is insufficient for genuine equality of opportunity on the familiar ground that it would permit a variety of differences in people's social circumstances to have a deep impact upon their relative life chances. His account promises to accommodate the view that the best-qualified candidates should be appointed to advantaged social positions whilst providing a justification for the idea that everyone, regardless of their social circumstances, should have access to the qualifications that are required to be successful in these competitions. He thus appears to be offering what is, in my terms, a meritocratic theory but not one that is rooted in a pre-justicial notion of desert.

I. *Rawls' Theory of Justice: A Very Brief Sketch*

Rawls' principle of fair equality of opportunity is but one part of his theory of justice and to understand it properly we need to be clear about its role in that theory. Since Rawls' work is familiar, I propose to give the briefest possible sketch of his theory for the uninitiated, drawing mainly upon his original statement of it in

[1] This chapter incorporates material from my 'Social Justice: The Place of Equal Opportunity', in R. Bellamy and A. Mason (eds), *Political Concepts* (Manchester, UK: Manchester University Press, 2003).

A Theory of Justice. Readers already familiar with it would be best advised to go straight to the next section.

The guiding idea behind Rawls' theory is that the principles of justice which should be adopted are those which rational persons, concerned to further their own interests, would agree upon in an initial position of equality. In order to model this initial position, he employs a device that he calls the veil of ignorance, behind which the parties are presumed to be unaware of various facts about themselves, such as their class or status, race and wealth, and their conception of the good, that is, their views about what is of value and importance. This veil of ignorance is intended to secure a kind of impartiality: if the parties are in ignorance of these facts, they cannot seek to benefit themselves by arguing for principles that are congenial to (say) their class, race, or conception of the good.

Although they are behind a veil of ignorance, the parties are to make various assumptions and we are to make some assumptions about them. First, each is to assume that they have some conception of the good, even though they do not know its content. Second, each is assumed to be rational, and because they are rational they are assumed to want the means to realize their conception of the good, whatever its content. Since liberty and opportunity, wealth and income, and self-respect are likely to make it easier for a person to realize his own conception of the good, it is assumed that the parties in the original position will want as much of them as possible. Rawls calls these the primary goods.

Rawls argues that the parties in this original position of equality, behind the veil of ignorance, will choose two main principles. According to the first principle, each person is to have an equal right to the most extensive basic liberty compatible with a similar liberty for all. Basic liberties include political liberty, freedom of speech and assembly, liberty of conscience and freedom of thought, freedom of the person along with the right to hold personal property, and freedom from arbitrary arrest and seizure.[2] The second principle comes in two parts. According to it, social and economic inequalities are to be arranged so that they are open to all, which he develops

[2] In his later work, Rawls refines his statement of the first principle so it reads that 'Each person has an equal right to a fully adequate scheme of equal basic liberties which is compatible with a similar scheme of liberties for all' (J. Rawls, *Political Liberalism* (New York: Columbia University Press, 1993), 291).

into the principle of fair equality of opportunity, and so that they are to the greatest benefit of the least advantaged, which he calls the difference principle. Rawls argues that when entertaining the possibility of conflict between these principles, the parties in the original position will rank the first principle above the second, and the principle of fair equality of opportunity above the difference principle.

Although the original position is the centrepiece of Rawls' theory as he presents it, he also gives a further argument for both the principle of fair equality of opportunity and the difference principle that is sometimes referred to as 'the intuitive argument'. This starts from the premise that distributive shares should not be improperly influenced by factors arbitrary from the moral point of view, and concludes that the difference principle, constrained by the principle of fair equality of opportunity, is what is needed to prevent this from happening.

This is the briefest possible sketch of Rawls' theory and the place of his principle of fair equality of opportunity within it. In the next two sections I explore this principle further before considering various difficulties it faces (in Sections IV and V).

II. *The Principle of Fair Equality of Opportunity in the Context of the Simple View*

Rawls begins his discussion of equality of opportunity by endorsing the principle that careers should be open to talents and noting its historical significance. According to this principle, everyone should have 'the same legal rights of access to all advantaged social positions'.[3] Minimally, this must imply that there should be no legislation that requires selectors to discriminate, and no legislation that requires different treatment of different groups. Rawls does not say anything more to clarify the notion of careers being open to talents, and as a result it is amenable to different interpretations. But I assume that careers would not genuinely be open to talents if selectors chose to exclude certain groups from consideration, for otherwise that would make the notion consistent with an informal system of apartheid. Even if selectors are not legally obliged to do

[3] Rawls, *A Theory of Justice*, 72.

so, they must by and large practise non-discrimination if there is to be equality of opportunity. The idea that careers should be open to talents is perhaps not strictly equivalent to the idea that advantaged social positions should be subject to open competition, or to the idea that the best-qualified candidates should be selected for these positions, but it is a close relative of them.[4] In other words it is closely connected to what I have been calling the simple view.

Rawls argues that the principle of careers open to talents is insufficient for fair equality of opportunity by appealing to the major premise in what I referred to earlier as the intuitive argument. In his view the principle of careers open to talents is insufficient because it permits 'distributive shares to be improperly influenced by... factors ... arbitrary from a moral point of view'.[5] For example, the social class into which a person happens to be born is 'arbitrary from a moral point of view' but might detrimentally affect a person's chances in life even in the presence of open competition for advantaged social positions. He argues that a principle of fair equality of opportunity can correct for this by requiring that positions be open to all not only formally, but also in such a way that each has a fair chance of attaining them.[6] He treats this as equivalent to the idea that

> those who are at the same level of talent and ability, and have the same willingness to use them, should have the same prospects of success regardless of their initial place in the social system, that is, irrespective of the income class into which they are born.[7]

Although Rawls does not explicitly say so, he presumably also means that those with a higher level of talent and ability and a greater willingness to use them should have greater prospects of success than those with lower levels of talent and ability or less willingness to use them. Rawls' principle of fair equality of opportunity promises to complete the simple view by recovering what he takes to be its underlying rationale, namely, to counteract the effects of differences in people's social circumstances on their access to advantaged social positions.

[4] Thomas Pogge offers an interpretation of this idea which falls short of open competition. See T. Pogge, *Realizing Rawls* (Ithaca, NY: Cornell University Press, 1989), 165.

[5] Rawls, *A Theory of Justice*, 72.

[6] Rawls, *A Theory of Justice*, 73.

[7] Rawls, *A Theory of Justice*, 73.

Rawls intends the principle of fair equality of opportunity, like each of the principles of justice he defends, to govern the basic structure of society. Institutions need to be designed so that advantaged social positions are subject to open competition and so that the qualifications required for success in these competitions are accessible to people regardless of their social circumstances, with the result that those with the same level of talent and ability and willingness to use them have equal chances of success. So equality of opportunity, as Rawls conceives it, is primarily a property of society's basic institutions, rather than of individual selection procedures. (It can nevertheless be attributed to particular selection procedures but only on condition that these procedures operate in the context of a set of institutions which ensures that those with the same level of talent and ability and willingness to use them have equal chances of filling positions.)

Note that the principle of fair equality of opportunity can potentially accommodate a more radical notion of institutional discrimination than we canvassed earlier in the context of discussing the simple view.[8] Suppose, for example, that a workplace could be structured in one of several equally efficient ways, but the way that is chosen results in the creation of a range of jobs the qualifications for which disadvantage members of some group. The job specifications pick out qualities and abilities which are genuinely required to do these jobs well, but the workplace could have been structured in a way that created a different range of jobs, requiring different qualifications that would not have disadvantaged this or any other group. According to the principle of fair equality of opportunity, we may be entitled to conclude that the workplace is practising institutional discrimination, for those with the same level of talent and ability, and willingness to use them, are not being given equal chances of success.

Although this kind of institutional discrimination is a theoretical possibility from the perspective of the principle of fair equality of opportunity, clear examples of it are hard to find. Consider a potential case, however. Suppose that a workplace is structured so that one of the qualifications for a range of jobs is the ability to work extra hours at short notice, or the ability to work sixty hours a week when necessary. But the workplace could have been structured differently

[8] See S. IV of Ch. 1.

so that much fewer jobs required these abilities, perhaps by creating part-time positions or perhaps by instituting some kind of shift system. When a range of jobs require employees to be able to work extra hours at short notice, or to be able to work a sixty-hour week when necessary, this will have a disproportionate impact upon those (in practice, mainly women) with childcare commitments who, because of those commitments, are unable to work long hours or extra hours without prior warning. If we were to treat 'raising children' as a morally arbitrary aspect of a person's situation,[9] then the principle of fair equality of opportunity would license the conclusion that the employers are guilty of institutional discrimination but in a way that goes beyond how we understood this form of discrimination in Chapter 1. This illustrates the way in which the principle of fair equality of opportunity attends to the network of selection decisions that are made within an institution and across a society, rather than focusing narrowly on individual selection procedures.

III. *Levels of Talent and Ability and Differences in Social Circumstances*

The principle of fair equality of opportunity requires that those with the same level of talent and ability and the same degree of willingness to use them should have equal chances of success. But this principle does not specify at what point in people's lives the comparison between their levels of talent and ability, and motivation to use them, is to be made for the purposes of applying the principle. To make matters worse, we are not even told what it means to say that two individuals possess the same level of talent and ability.

One proposal might be that the relevant point of comparison is when individuals reach the age of reason. Yet this seems to be in conflict with the spirit of the principle, for taking this as the relevant point would appear to allow differences in people's social circumstances to have too great an impact upon their chances of success. By the time that individuals have reached the age of reason,

[9] This is the controversial assumption. For in most cases the issue of whether to have children is within the control of the parents, and hence it might be argued that raising children is not in general a morally arbitrary feature of a person's situation. For further discussion of these issues, see Ch. 7, S. IV, and Ch. 8, S. V.

they may already have experienced very different kinds of education and upbringing and as a result developed the potential with which they were born to vastly differing extents and acquired very different levels of motivation. It is hard to believe that these differences will always be irrelevant from the point of view of fair equality of opportunity, as Rawls understands it.

An obvious alternative would be to take birth as the appropriate reference point. But if we go this far back, it seems odd to attribute talents and powers at all to newborn babies. Perhaps this infelicity can be avoided by referring instead to their potential to develop talents and powers given favourable social circumstances. Even birth, however, may seem too late a point at which to compare potential if we are concerned with fair equality of opportunity, with its underlying aim of counteracting differences in people's social circumstances. For potential at birth can also be deeply affected by social relations during pregnancy.[10] Poverty, for example, may mean that the mother has had such a poor diet that the potential of the newborn baby has already been stunted in a way that is relevant for fair equality of opportunity. If we follow the logic of this reasoning, we seem to be forced back to the point of conception. But even here similar problems may arise. For example, there may be defects in an embryo that are the direct product of social relations, or the choices of the mother (e.g. the inability or unwillingness of the mother to take supplements that may lead to disabilities in the child). Rawls himself seems to be exercised by these problems when he notes that:

> [t]he consistent application of the principle of fair opportunity requires us to view persons independently from the influences of their social position. But how far should this tendency be carried? It seems that even when fair opportunity (as it has been defined) is satisfied, the family will lead to unequal chances between individuals.[11]

We shall consider the relationship between fair equality of opportunity and the institution of the family in the next section. For now my interest in this passage concerns Rawls' apparent acknowledgement of the theoretical difficulty involved in selecting a particular point at which to compare life chances and levels of talent, ability or potential for the purposes of the principle. It seems to me that his solution is

[10] See B. Barry, *Why Social Justice Matters* (Cambridge: Polity, 2005), 47–9.

[11] Rawls, *A Theory of Justice*, 511.

to put the theoretical difficulty to one side, by in effect regarding the principle of fair equality of opportunity as a *practical* principle of justice. For even if we were to resolve the theoretical difficulty by finding a convincing argument for saying that conception, or birth, is the right point to compare life chances and levels of potential for the purpose of counteracting the effects of differences in people's social circumstances, we would still be left with the overwhelming practical problem of how we are to make judgements about these levels at conception or birth, even with the benefit of hindsight. Furthermore, the need to find a practical principle for governing the basic structure of society makes it unnecessary to resolve the theoretical problem of whether conception, birth, or some point after these but prior to adulthood, should be regarded as the appropriate reference point. If the principle of fair equality of opportunity is to be capable of implementation, the point at which it requires us to compare people's levels of talent, ability, or potential must occur at some time after birth when they are more readily detectable. As a result the principle may depart to some extent from its underlying theoretical rationale, to counteract the effects of differences in people's social circumstances. (This may be part of the reason why Rawls remarks that even when fair opportunity, as he defines it, is satisfied, the family will still generate unequal chances between individuals. Those with the same level of talent, ability, or potential may have equal chances at the point at which the principle of fair equality of opportunity requires us to make comparisons, but unequal chances when judged from the perspective of some earlier time, such as birth, which the deeper underlying theory might regard as the relevant point for the purpose of comparison.)[12]

[12] Rawls, *A Theory of Justice*, 511. But cf., ibid., 301, which seems to offer an alternative account of how similarly endowed and motivated individuals may have unequal chances of success despite the principle of fair equality of opportunity being satisfied. This account appeals, rather confusingly, to the idea that the principle applies to 'sectors of society' (such as income classes) rather than individuals, so that fair equality of opportunity may obtain between different sectors even though similarly endowed and motivated individuals within the same sector have unequal chances of success. For an interpretation of the relevant passages that differs from mine, and which holds that Rawls is simply trading on an ambiguity in the idea of being similarly motivated and endowed, rather than (as I suggest) moving from a theoretical to a practical perspective, see D. Miller, 'Equality of Opportunity and the Family', a paper presented to the workshop on Equality of Opportunity at the ECPR Joint Sessions, Granada, 14–19 April 2005.

Even if we accept that we must take some stage of development in childhood as the relevant point of comparison for practical purposes, there is still a further theoretical issue that needs addressing. For how are we to assess levels of talent and ability and willingness to use them at this point? One proposal would be that we should assess these levels in terms of what price the talents and abilities (perhaps when they are more fully developed) would command in a free market where careers are open to talents. According to this view, one person's talents and abilities and willingness to use them are at a higher level than another's if they would command a higher price in a free market where careers are open to talents. This way of assessing levels of talent and ability has the consequence that these levels will depend to some degree on the demand for the relevant talents and abilities. So what constitutes a higher level of talent and ability will be determined partly by social attitudes, and indeed by the social forms present in a given society. It follows that the principle of fair equality of opportunity allows a person's chances in life to be influenced by the attitudes of others regarding what activities are important or worthwhile, and by the 'accident' of being born into a society that has a particular set of social forms—a set that may not be favourable to one's talents and abilities, or indeed the potential with which one was born. This is not a problem for Rawls, however, for it does not undermine the aim of the principle, namely, to counteract the effects of *differences* in people's social circumstances, for when the principle is realized those from the same generation face the same set of such circumstances. (It does, however, raise questions about the extent to which defenders of the principle can coherently aspire to achieve fair equality of opportunity between members of different generations.)

IV. *Two Further Objections Considered and Rejected*

I consider two influential objections to Rawls' notion of fair equality of opportunity which I think can be answered before moving on (in the next section) to discuss another one that in my view creates more serious difficulties for it. The first of these arguments maintains that Rawls' conception of fair equality of opportunity has an implication which is fatal to it: it would appear that what Rawls seeks to achieve from fair equality of opportunity—that is, equal life chances for those similarly endowed and motivated—could be secured simply by randomly re-assigning babies to different parents at birth.[13] Indeed, as Brian Barry points out, if equality of life chances at birth were a sufficient condition for fair equality of opportunity, then a caste system which randomly re-assigned babies shortly afterwards would qualify.[14] This might seem enough to refute the idea that equality of life chances is a sufficient condition of fair equality of opportunity.[15]

In reply it might be pointed out that if we suppose Rawls is maintaining that equality of life chances is a sufficient condition of fair equality of opportunity, we are ignoring one of the two elements of fair equality of opportunity. He is clear that careers must be open to talents, and that would immediately rule out a caste system. This response does not wholly defeat the objection, however, for the status of 'careers open to talents' within Rawls' account of fair equality of opportunity is problematic. The difficulties in understanding its proper role come into view once we recognize that there are potential conflicts between it and the idea that similarly endowed and motivated individuals should have equal chances of success.[16] Suppose that employers tend to devalue women. As a result of discrimination women's life chances may be less good than the life chances of men with a similar level of talent, ability, and motivation. Given the complexity of selection decisions, sexism may operate in subtle and even unintentional ways, and as a result it may be hard

[13] See Fishkin, *Justice, Equal Opportunity, and the Famil* 57. Fishkin does not present this as an argument against Rawls or others. He merely observes that a principle committed to equal life chances at birth could be satisfied by the random re-assignment of babies.

[14] Barry, 'Equal Opportunity and Moral Arbitrariness', 32. Note that this argument must assume that there are no structures in place in such a society which disadvantage people on the basis of their race or sex.

[15] It would be too easy to reply to Barry by maintaining that Rawls' principle of fair equality of opportunity does not suppose that birth is the appropriate point at which to compare levels of talent and ability for the purpose of determining whether they have equal chances of success. For even if this is so, Barry's argument could be reformulated in terms of whatever reference point short of adulthood is chosen.

[16] See also R. Arneson, 'Against Rawlsian Equality of Opportunity', *Philosophical Studies* 93 (1999), 81.

to detect or prevent.[17] For example, it may be hard to know when gender stereotypes, such as the idea that women are less committed to their careers, are influencing selection decisions. So in some circumstances the most effective way of promoting equal chances of success for similarly endowed and motivated men and women, overall and in the long term, may be to enforce a quota system by means of the law. In this way promoting equal life chances would require abandoning the requirement that appointments be made on the basis of qualifications alone. In Rawls' terms, an enforced quota system is a clear violation of the principle of careers open to talents for it would mean that potential applicants no longer possessed 'the same legal rights of access to all advantaged social positions'.[18]

If careers being open to talents and equal life chances for the similarly endowed and motivated are *each* necessary conditions of fair equality of opportunity, it follows that in some circumstances equality of opportunity may be impossible in practice. Given Rawls' aspiration to provide us with a theory in which conflicts within and between principles are resolved by priority rules, he at least owes us an account of which of these two necessary conditions should take priority when they come into conflict. The point cuts deeper than this, however. When we reflect upon the issue of which of these two elements should take priority in Rawls' theory, it starts to become unclear why he should give the idea of open competition any independent role at all.[19] What drives his account of fair equality of opportunity is that it requires us to counteract the effects of differences in social circumstances since these are arbitrary from the moral point of view, and that idea is cashed out in terms of equal chances of success for those with the same level of talent and ability and willingness to use them. But if equal chances of success for people thus situated is what really matters for fair equality of opportunity, the idea that the best-qualified candidates should be appointed appears to play at best a derivative role. Appointing the best-qualified candidates is in most circumstances the best means of ensuring that those with the same level of talent and ability

[17] See L. W. Sumner, 'Positive Sexism', *Social Philosophy and Policy* 5 (1987), esp. 213–4.

[18] Rawls, *A Theory of Justice*, 72.

[19] This issue is explored by Arneson in 'Against Rawlsian Equality of Opportunity'.

and willingness to use them have the same chances of success. But when that goal could be better realized by some other means, then fair equality of opportunity does not require us to select the best-qualified candidates.

Understood in this way, Rawls' account of fair equality of opportunity is best conceived in terms of the following structure. First, an underlying rationale, namely, to counteract the effects of different social circumstances, on the grounds that these are morally arbitrary. (In the next chapter I distinguish between an approach which aims to neutralize the effects of differences in social circumstances, and one which merely aims to mitigate these effects. In this chapter, however I use the term 'counteract' in a way that is ambiguous between neutralizing and mitigating because it is hard to determine which Rawls favours.) Second, a principle to govern the design of social institutions that is intended to define what, for practical purposes, should be taken to constitute counteracting the effects of differences in social circumstances. That is to say, that those with the same level of talent and ability and willingness to use them, judged at some point after birth but before adulthood, should have equal chances of success. Third, a specification of the best means in general of realizing this principle, that is, selecting the best-qualified candidates and providing everyone with an adequate education. (If this is its real structure, fair equality of opportunity is not, in my terms, a genuine example of a meritocratic theory, for it is not fundamentally committed, in the required way, to selecting the best-qualified applicants. Its commitment to selecting the best qualified rests, in part, upon empirical premises.)

Once we acknowledge this structure, however, we can respond to Barry's objection on Rawls' behalf. Even though it seems that the principle of fair equality of opportunity, as Rawls understands it, could be realized in any social system simply by randomly re-assigning babies at birth since this would ensure equal chances of success for those with the same level of talent and ability and willingness to use them, this would not fulfil its underlying rationale. For the underlying aim of the principle of fair equality of opportunity is to counteract the effects of differences in people's social circumstances, and that could not be achieved simply by randomly re-assigning babies at birth. If one's life chances were a function of the family to which one happened to be re-assigned, they would be deeply affected by differences in their social circumstances. At worst, Rawls' attempt to capture what, in practice, would constitute counteracting the effect of these differences is flawed, not this underlying aim.

The second objection I propose to address in this section maintains that fair equality of opportunity can be realized only by abolishing the family and that this is an unacceptable price to pay.[20] Similarly motivated and endowed individuals will have unequal prospects of success (at any point after birth and before they reach adulthood) so long as they experience different family environments and belong to different cultural communities. For example, some parents may value educational achievement, and encourage their children in this direction, whilst others do not. Rawls recognizes this difficulty, but his response to it is weak.[21] He moves from the claim that 'the principle of fair equality of opportunity can be only imperfectly carried out, at least as long as the institution of the family exists' to the claim that '[i]t is impossible in practice to secure equal chances of achievement ... for those similarly endowed and motivated'[22] and from there to the conclusion that all we can do is mitigate the morally arbitrary effects of 'the natural lottery' by implementing the difference principle. But if fair equality of opportunity requires abolishing the family, Rawls needs to give us some reason for not doing so. It is not enough for him to reply that fair equality of opportunity can never be fully realized in practice, for the objection is that it could be more fully realized by abolishing the family.[23]

Does Rawls have the resources to construct a better response to the argument that fair equality of opportunity, as he understands it, would require abolishing the family? He could point out that in his theory the basic liberties take priority over fair equality of opportunity, and then argue that these basic liberties entail that people be allowed to form families and raise any children that they beget, provided that they do not harm them. This would require him to add to his list of basic liberties, for they do not, as they

[20] See Flew, *The Politics of Procrustes*, 55–6.

[21] See Rawls, *A Theory of Justice*, 511–2, 74.

[22] Rawls, *A Theory of Justice*, 74.

[23] See V. Munoz-Dardé, 'Is the Family to be Abolished Then?', *Proceedings of the Aristotelian Society* 99 (1999), 37–56.

stand, appear to justify a right to raise one's children. He could then concede that, strictly speaking, fair equality of opportunity would require abolishing the family, but maintain that this is ruled out by the priority given to the (conditional) liberty to raise one's children.[24]

This line of argument is not without difficulty, however. In his later work, Rawls employs a conception of citizens as reasonable and rational, which requires them to possess two moral powers, namely, the capacity for a sense of justice, and the capacity to form and revise a conception of the good. The basic liberties are then conceived as 'essential social conditions for the adequate development and full exercise of the two powers of moral personality over a complete life'.[25] Yet, as Véronique Munoz-Dardé points out, it is not obvious that a right to raise one's children, of the kind which would be required to justify the traditional family or something similar, is an essential condition for the adequate development and full exercise of the two moral powers that Rawls identifies.[26] The best case which can be made here is that even if the family is not strictly an essential condition for the adequate development of these two powers, in practice over time other institutions, such as compulsory state provision of childcare of various kinds, would be likely to fare worse in developing these powers than some suitably constrained form of the family, given the dangers of vesting the state with that amount of power in the upbringing of children.[27] Of course, this case for the family is consistent with acknowledging that fair equality of opportunity would require extensive regulation of family practices.

[24] See A. Gutmann and D. Thompson, *Democracy and Disagreement* (Cambridge, MA: Harvard University Press, 1996), 310.

[25] Rawls, *Political Liberalism*, 293.

[26] See Munoz-Dardé, 'Is the Family to be Abolished Then?', 41. Munoz-Dardé maintains that Rawls' defence of the family appeals to the idea that the family is necessary for moral development and hence for citizens to have a sense of justice (ibid., 41). But I don't think that he does in fact see himself as making this argument, for in his discussion of moral development he says that he is simply taking the family for granted and exploring its role in moral development and concedes that 'in a broader inquiry the institution of the family might be questioned, and other arrangements might indeed prove to be preferable' (Rawls, *A Theory of Justice*, 463).

[27] See Munoz-Dardé, 'Is the Family to be Abolished Then?', 48–9.

V. *Can Rawls Justify the Priority He Gives to Fair Equality of Opportunity?*

The criticisms of Rawls' principle of fair equality of opportunity I have so far considered are ones that I believe his theory, properly understood, is equipped to answer. In this section, however, I examine an objection which leads to serious difficulties for it. This objection focuses on the underlying rationale for the principle of fair equality of opportunity and argues that, given this rationale, the principle does not go far enough. Rawls' move from careers open to talents to fair equality of opportunity is driven by the idea that the distribution of advantaged social positions should not be improperly influenced by factors that are arbitrary from the moral point of view. Yet fair equality of opportunity permits access to positions to be affected by natural endowments (i.e. those talents and abilities, or parts of them, which are due to one's genetic inheritance), which Rawls also accepts are arbitrary from the moral point of view. Therefore, if he is to be fully consistent it seems he must concede that fair equality of opportunity, properly thought out, requires all persons to have an equal chance of occupying advantaged social positions, irrespective of natural endowment.[28] If Rawls' theory were implicitly committed to the idea that advantaged social positions should be distributed in such a way that people's natural abilities have no bearing on who gets them, it would be hard to imagine a notion that is more fundamentally at odds with our intuitive understanding of equality of opportunity.

Rawls' reply to this objection would be to argue that we have to understand the way in which the principle of fair equality of opportunity is intended to combine with the difference principle to counteract the effects of both differences in social circumstances and differences in natural endowments. The principle of fair equality of opportunity allows unequal natural endowments to affect access to advantaged social positions, but the difference principle limits the inequalities, especially of wealth and income, that may permissibly result.[29] In this way Rawls permits higher levels of talent and ability to attract greater reward but only if such a practice benefits the worst off. Understood in this way, in effect the principle of fair

[28] See Barry, 'Equal Opportunity and Moral Arbitrariness'.

[29] See Rawls, *A Theory of Justice*, 74–5.

equality of opportunity governs access to advantaged social positions whereas the difference principle governs the distribution of wealth and income. What I want to suggest in response is that this approach cannot justify the lexical priority that Rawls gives to the principle of fair equality of opportunity. In his ordering of principles, he ranks the principle of fair equality of opportunity above the difference principle, requiring the former to be satisfied before the latter in the event of conflict between them. But if the principle of fair equality of opportunity governs access to advantaged social positions, whilst the difference principle governs wealth and income, why should we suppose that the former should be given lexical priority over the latter? For the effect of giving the principle of fair equality of opportunity priority over the difference principle is to insist that equality of access to advantaged social positions cannot legitimately be sacrificed for greater material benefits for the worst off group.[30]

Is there a good reason that can be given from within Rawls' theory for attaching this kind of weight or importance to a principle governing access to advantaged social positions? Consider this question from the point of view of the original position. Access to advantaged social positions is a primary good: it is a good that it is rational for a person to assume they want when they do not know the content of their conception of the good. But why would persons in the original position give priority to a principle that governs access to advantaged social positions over one that governs access to wealth and income? Rawls hints that the kind of reasons which would lead the parties in the original position to give the principle of liberty priority over the difference principle will also lead them to give fair equality of opportunity priority over the difference principle.[31] He maintains that in the original position, when a person knows that society has reached a point where everyone's basic needs can be met, it is rational for him to give priority to the principle of liberty.[32] It is rational for someone in the original position to assume that once his basic needs have been met, the basic liberties will be more beneficial for pursuing his own conception of the good, whatever that turns out to be, than, say, greater wealth or income. Even if this is a good argument for the

[30] See Rawls, *A Theory of Justice*, 302–3.
[31] See Rawls, *A Theory of Justice*, 301.
[32] See Rawls, *A Theory of Justice*, 542–3.

priority of liberty,[33] it is hard to see how the analogous argument in relation to opportunity is supposed to work. The initial question in effect resurfaces in a new form: why is it supposed to be rationally required from the standpoint of the original position to refuse to trade-off access to advantaged social positions in favour of greater wealth and income *if* the basic liberties are in place?[34]

Rawls develops his argument for the priority of liberty in a way that might seem to promise an explanation of why he thinks the principle of fair equality of opportunity should take priority over the difference principle. He argues that in a just society the basis of self-respect for all is secured by the public affirmation of equal citizenship, which requires enshrining the basic liberties in public institutions.[35] Might it be argued in a parallel way that the basis for self-respect can be secured only if the principle of fair equality of opportunity is also enshrined in society's basic institutions? It is hard to see how this position could be sustained. Rawls faces a dilemma. Either the social basis of self-respect can be secured simply by institutionalizing the principle of equal liberty or it cannot. If it can, then the social basis of self-respect does not rely upon institutionalizing the principle of fair equality of opportunity. On the other hand, if the social basis of self-respect cannot be secured simply by institutionalizing the principle of equal liberty, the question immediately arises of why we should think it will be best secured by enshrining the principle of fair equality of opportunity and giving it lexical priority over the difference principle. For once we have moved away from the assumption that the principle of equal liberty suffices, it is hard to see how we could justifiably rule out the possibility that the basis for the self-respect of the worst off group might sometimes be better secured by giving priority to the difference principle rather than the principle of fair equality of opportunity in matters of institutional

[33] See H. L. A. Hart, 'Rawls on Liberty and its Priority', in N. Daniels (ed.), *Reading Rawls* (Oxford: Blackwell, 1975), esp. 249–52, for some doubts about this argument. See Rawls, *Political Liberalism*, Lecture VIII, esp. 310–24, for Rawls' response.

[34] Let me concede, however, that in practice fair equality of opportunity, as Rawls understands it, is in general likely to provide more wealth and income for members of the worst off group so the issue of what should be done when greater access to advantaged social goods comes into conflict with greater wealth and income will arise only in a limited range of cases.

[35] See Rawls, *A Theory of Justice*, section 82.

design.[36] Why is access to advantaged social positions, understood in Rawls' terms, supposed to be so much more important for securing self-respect than making the worst-off as well of as it is possible for them to be?

Rawls does present a further reason for thinking that access to advantaged social positions is of particular importance. He points out that they may be valuable not just as a means of securing material goods but also as a means of securing rewarding jobs and hence self-realization:

> if some places were not open on a fair basis to all, those kept out would be right in feeling unjustly treated even though they benefited from the greater efforts of those who were allowed to hold them. They would be justified in their complaint not only because they were excluded from certain external rewards of office such as wealth and privilege, but because they were debarred from experiencing the realization of self which comes from a skilful and devoted exercise of social duties. They would be deprived of one of the main forms of human good.[37]

The idea that access to advantaged social positions is important (at least in part) because of the internal goods they supply is plausible but it is of limited help in justifying the priority of fair equality of opportunity over the difference principle. For a start, there is no reason to think that when the better qualified are prevented from obtaining the goods internal to advantaged social positions, their deprivation is in general greater than that of the less well qualified who are denied that good by a practice of selecting the best qualified. Provided a person is sufficiently well qualified that he can secure these internal rewards, when he is denied the possibility of doing so, he is deprived of potential goods. At best Rawls' observations warrant the conclusion that access to advantaged social positions should be given special weight. But that could be done in two ways, neither of which would justify giving the principle of fair equality of opportunity lexical priority over the difference principle. First, freedom of occupation could be treated as a basic liberty, to be protected by the first principle of justice, the principle of liberty. Second, access to advantaged social positions could be added to the

[36] See Arneson, 'Against Rawlsian Equality of Opportunity', 104–5.

[37] Rawls, *A Theory of Justice*, 84.

list of primary goods that the difference principle is supposed to cover.[38]

Consider the first of these suggestions. Rawls himself seems to treat freedom of occupation as a basic liberty in his later book *Political Liberalism*.[39] But he accepts that freedom of occupation can be secured without the principle of fair equality of opportunity being satisfied.[40] Freedom of occupation, when it is conceived as a negative liberty in Rawls' preferred way, in effect as the absence of state-directed labour, does not seem to require equal chances of success for the similarly endowed and motivated. (Nor does it seem to require careers to be open to talents, as Rawls conceives it, for there are ways of regulating access to jobs which fall short of a policy of state-directed labour but which nevertheless mean that people do not have the same legal rights of access to them. An enforced quota system of the kind described earlier would be an example.)

Consider the second proposal, namely, that access to advantaged social positions might be included in the list of primary goods that the difference principle covers. As Rawls deploys the difference principle, it is primarily concerned with the distribution of wealth and income but there is no reason in principle why it could not be extended to cover opportunity, if opportunity were regarded as a separate primary good. In this context, opportunity would be best conceived as a genuine chance of occupying an advantaged social position that enables self-realization, rather than the mere possibility of entering an open competition for one.[41] In practice, of course, including opportunity, so understood, as a separate primary good would raise various difficult questions concerning the relative weight to accord to wealth, income, and opportunity. But these difficulties are not resolved by insisting that opportunity is much more significant than wealth and income, which in effect is the assumption behind ranking the principle of fair equality of opportunity above the difference principle. If the scope of the difference principle was extended to cover opportunity understood as a separate primary good, it would still have implications for the distribution of

[38] See Arneson, 'Against Rawlsian Equality of Opportunity', 98–9.

[39] See Rawls, *Political Liberalism*, 228, 230, 308. See also Rawls, *A Theory of Justice*, 275; B. Barry, *Theories of Justice: A Treatise on Social Justice, Vol. I* (Hemel Hempstead, UK: Harvester-Wheatsheaf, 1989), 398–400.

[40] See Rawls, *Political Liberalism*, 228.

[41] See Ch. 1, S. II.

advantaged social positions. If institutions are to ensure that the worst off group is as well off as possible (in terms of their shares of opportunity, wealth, and income), these positions must be distributed in such a way that the talents and powers of individuals are utilized to good effect.

So the importance of access to advantaged social positions cannot justify the lexical priority given to the principle of fair equality of opportunity. It is in any case misleading to suppose that the principle of fair equality of opportunity and the difference principle are to be distinguished solely in terms of the goods that they govern. They also differ in terms of what aspects of people's circumstances they address. The principle of fair equality of opportunity aims to counteract the effects of differences in people's social circumstances on their access to advantage, whereas the difference principle is intended to counteract the effects of differences in natural endowments on access to advantage. Does this provide any insight into the way in which the two principles combine together that might serve to justify their lexical priority? It is hard to see how it could do so. For why should we think that when the goal of counteracting the effects of differences in social circumstances comes into conflict with the goal of counteracting the effects of differences in natural endowments, the latter should take priority? Rawls' theory has no obvious answer available to it.

VI. *Conclusion*

Rawls' principle of fair equality of opportunity held out the promise of completing the simple view whilst his overall theory provided the grounding for it; however, on further investigation it is hard to see how his theory could justify giving that principle lexical priority over the difference principle. If we regard the principle of fair equality of opportunity as primarily concerned with distributing a particular good, namely, the opportunity to occupy advantaged social positions, then in giving priority to this principle over the difference principle, we are in effect attaching overriding importance to the opportunity to occupy advantaged social positions in a way that is implausible. If, on the other hand, we see the principle of fair equality of opportunity as primarily concerned with counteracting the effects of differences in social circumstances on access to overall advantage, whilst the difference principle is primarily concerned with counteracting the effects of differences in natural endowments on that access, it is again hard to see why the first goal should take priority. These problems with Rawls' account might suggest that we should reject the simple view altogether, not merely add to it, and that we should pursue a more radical conception of equality of opportunity which would require us to counteract both the effects of differences in people's social circumstances and differences in their natural endowments on their access to advantage. On the surface at least, this would appear to provide a conception of what it is to level the playing field that is rather different from a meritocratic theory, even though it has continuities with Rawls' own theory of democratic equality. It is to this possibility that I turn in the next chapter.

CHAPTER 4

Counteracting Circumstances

The priority that Rawls gives to the principle of fair equality of opportunity over the difference principle is hard to justify. Rawls, it might seem, would be better advised to think of these principles as working together to prevent differences in people's social circumstances, and differences in the potential with which they happen to be conceived, from improperly influencing their access to advantage, with neither principle being given lexical priority over the other. A theory of this sort could offer a radical view of what it is to level the playing field, one that can be expressed in terms of the idea that we should counteract the effects of differences in both social circumstances and natural endowments. It would in some respects mark a departure from Rawls' theory, but it might be thought that in other ways it fulfils the ambitions of that theory rather better.

Instances of this general approach might permit unequal outcomes to emerge from the different choices people make when their choices possess the appropriate kind of independence from their circumstances. For there is good reason to deny that these choices are 'arbitrary from the moral point of view' and to regard them as having the kind of moral authority that can justify inequality. Indeed Rawls' own theory is vulnerable on precisely this issue, for it faces the charge that it does not give an appropriate role to personal responsibility because it does not acknowledge a principled reason for allowing people to enjoy the benefits of their choices. The principle of fair equality of opportunity, considered by itself, without the difference principle in the frame, would allow inequalities that were the product of the choices people make rather than the social circumstances in which they find themselves. But combining the principle of fair equality of opportunity with the difference principle seems to jeopardize this possibility, for the latter holds that inequalities are justified only if they benefit the worst off group. Hence it would seem that inequalities which are due, in effect, to the choices people make will be allowed to persist only if they benefit the worst off group.[1]

If we are to take seriously the ambition of counteracting the effects of differences in people's social circumstances and natural endowments, we need to do so in a way that does not at the same time counteract the effects of their different choices, so that we give due weight to personal responsibility. In the remainder of the book I propose to explore in more depth this sort of radical vision of what it would mean to level the playing field, which I refer to as 'responsibility-sensitive egalitarianism'. In this chapter I focus in particular on what is involved in supposing that justice requires us to *counteract* the effects of differences in social circumstances and natural endowments. Earlier I noted that the idea we should counteract these effects is ambiguous between neutralizing them (so that differences in people's social circumstances and natural endowments do not in any way affect their relative access to advantage) and merely mitigating these effects. I clarify what is at issue here and argue that there may be reason to favour an approach which, even at the level of fundamental principle, is committed to mitigating the effects of differences in circumstances rather than neutralizing them.

[1] Will Kymlicka gives an example, adapted from Ronald Dworkin's work, to illustrate this point, involving two people of equal talent who share the same social background and who start with equal shares of resources: 'One wants to play tennis all day, and so only works long enough at a nearby farm to earn enough money to buy a tennis court, and to sustain his desired lifestyle.... The other person wants a similar amount of land to plant a garden, in order to produce and sell vegetables for herself and others.... The gardener will quickly come to have more resources than the tennis-player, if we allow the market to work freely. While they began with equal shares of resources, he will rapidly use up his initial share, and his occasional farm work only brings in enough to sustain his tennis-playing. The gardener, however, uses her initial share in such a way as to generate a larger income through longer hours of work. The difference principle would only allow this inequality if it benefits the least well off—i.e. if it benefits the tennis-player who now lacks much of an income' (Will Kymlicka, *Contemporary Political Philosophy*, 2nd edn (Oxford: Oxford University Press, 2002), 72–3).

I. *Choice and Circumstance*

Responsibility-sensitive egalitarianism is often formulated in terms of a distinction between choice and circumstance. According to this way of expressing the general doctrine, justice requires us to counteract the effects of differences in people's circumstances on their relative access to advantage, but there is a presumption that inequalities, which are due to the different choices people make, are permissible. As it stands, however, the distinction between choice and circumstance is too vague and underdeveloped to be of much help. After all, there are many outcomes that are, in some sense, unchosen, the costs of which we nevertheless are inclined to think that it is fair to require a person to bear, for example, the costs of unsuccessful gambles. Some, such as Ronald Dworkin, have taken this into account by drawing a further distinction between brute luck and option luck, where 'option luck is a matter of how deliberate and calculated gambles turn out—whether someone gains or loses through accepting an isolated risk he or she should have anticipated and might have declined', whereas '[b]rute luck is a matter of how risks fall out that are not in that sense deliberate gambles'.[2] If counteract is then taken to mean 'neutralize', we might suppose that people are entitled to full compensation for bad brute luck (but are not entitled to reap the benefits of good brute luck) and are entitled to reap the benefits of good option luck (but are not entitled to any compensation for bad option luck). According to this specific form of responsibility-sensitive egalitarianism, which sometimes goes by the name of luck egalitarianism, inequalities of outcome are just if and only if they are the product of requiring people to bear the costs of their bad option luck or of allowing them to enjoy the benefits of their good option luck, whereas such inequalities are unjust if they are the product of requiring people to bear the costs of their bad brute luck or of allowing them to enjoy the benefits of their good brute luck.

Dworkin's distinction between brute luck and option luck needs more work, however. As Peter Vallentyne has argued, clarifying it is far from easy. For example, we cannot say that 'the occurrence

[2] R. Dworkin, *Sovereign Virtue: The Theory and Practice of Equality* (Cambridge, MA: Harvard University Press, 2000), 73); R. Dworkin, 'What is Equality? Part 2: Equality of Resources', *Philosophy and Public Affairs* 10 (1981), 293.

of an event is due to brute luck for an agent if and only if the possibility of its occurrence was not (for the agent) a (reasonably) foreseeable outcome of his or her choices'[3] because this definition would cover events which could not be avoided even though they were still the product of choice and foreseeable. For instance, when a person makes the decision to drive on through a storm with the result that his car is hit by lightning but where we assume that the probability of being hit by lightning when driving is no different from the probability of being hit whilst stationary and that the agent knows this. Perhaps progress can be made by tinkering with the definition of brute luck in the face of apparent counterexamples such as this, but it is important to recognize what is guiding our intuitions. What we are doing is tailoring our account of brute luck so that it is made directly relevant to answering the question 'Under what conditions is it fair to require people to bear the costs of their behaviour and under what conditions is that unfair?' In other words, our account of the distinction between brute luck and option luck is being guided by a particular conception of when it is fair and when it is unfair to hold people responsible for their behaviour by requiring them to bear its costs.

What this means is that the distinction between choice and circumstances (and the further distinction between brute luck and option luck) is not being treated as foundational in the way that it might seem.[4] On the surface, it might seem that these distinctions are being drawn independently of the issue of when it is fair to require people to bear the costs of their behaviour and then being used to argue for a particular answer to that question, namely, that people can legitimately be required to bear the costs of their choices, of their option luck, but not of their circumstances, their brute luck. But that is not what is really going on. Rather, an answer (or set of answers) to the question of when it is fair to require people to bear the costs of their behaviour is being used to draw the distinctions in the first

[3] P. Vallentyne, 'Brute Luck, Option Luck, and Equality of Initial Opportunities', *Ethics* 112 (2002), 531.

[4] Matt Matravers argues that there is a tension in Dworkin's own account of when people should be held responsible for their behaviour concerning the role of the distinction between choice and chance, in particular whether or not it is meant to be foundational: see M. Matravers, 'Luck, Responsibility, and "The Jumble of Lotteries that Constitutes Human Life"', *Imprints* 6 (2002), esp. 36.

place. I prefer to employ a partly different strategy. I simply stipulate an account of 'circumstances' which, defenders of responsibility-sensitive egalitarianism would all agree, correctly identifies features of people's condition the differential effects of which should be counteracted. But I intend to leave open the question of whether justice permits people to enjoy the benefits of their choices (or requires them to bear the costs of their choices), when 'choice' is understood as what is left over by this account of their circumstances.

I suppose that a person's circumstances are what happens to him 'outside the space of his rational agency', whereas a person's choices pertain to what takes place within that space. An aspect of a person's condition lies within the space of his rational agency if and only if it is intelligible, at least in principle, to ask him to justify it or evaluate it in terms of his reasons either because it is something he could have influenced or prevented or because, even though he could not influence it, it falls within the space of his reasons because it is governed by relations of consistency, coherence, and the like.[5] The class, family, or culture into which a person is born, and his race and sex, are clearly part of his circumstances. So too is the potential with which a person is born, that is, his natural endowment. Behaviour—what a person does or fails to do, and the foreseeable consequences of his actions and omissions—generally falls into the category of choice because it is intelligible to ask a person to give his reasons for behaving as he did, except in extreme cases, for instance, when he is sleepwalking or hypnotized. A person's beliefs also fall into the category of choice. They lie within the space of his reasons for we may sensibly ask a person to give his reasons for holding some particular belief; so too his desires and preferences fall within this space if it makes sense to ask him to give his reasons for why he desires what he does, or why he prefers one thing to another. Indeed, it may be intelligible to ask someone to give his reasons why he has some particular desire or preference even if it is not under his control: even if someone has been brought up in such a way that he cannot help having expensive tastes, we can nevertheless intelligibly ask him to give his reasons why (say) he prefers some particular claret to another, or indeed why he prefers good wine to

[5] I borrow the phrase 'the space of reasons' from John McDowell, who in turn takes it from Wilfrid Sellars: see J. McDowell, *Mind and World* (Cambridge, MA: Harvard University Press, 1994), 5ff.

good beer, and he may be able to give reasons in response that appeal to some aspect or other of its flavour. When a person would rather not have a particular desire, it may also make sense to ask him why he would rather not have it, and thereby invite him to evaluate it. So preferences that are beyond a person's control may nevertheless lie within the space of his rational agency and hence be included as choices according to my stipulated definition.

Responsibility-sensitive egalitarianism holds that justice requires us to counteract the effects of differences in people's circumstances on their access to advantage. In what follows I simply take this position for granted; my aim is merely to explore what it means to say that justice requires 'counteracting the effects of differences in people's circumstances'. I also bracket the issue of how, precisely, a responsibility-sensitive egalitarianism should deal with the issue of when people can legitimately be required to bear the costs of their choices when choice is understood in accordance with my stipulated definition. I take up this issue in Chapter 7. As we see there, competing versions of responsibility-sensitive egalitarianism tackle it differently and they will need to draw at least some normatively relevant distinctions between kinds or contexts of choice.

II. *Neutralization Compared to Mitigation*

According to what I call 'the neutralization approach', justice requires us to neutralize the effects of differences in people's circumstances (except perhaps when this would make some worse off and no one better off), and maintains that these effects are neutralized if and only if they do not create any inequalities in their access to advantage. If circumstances are understood in the way I have stipulated, this implies that neither the social relations into which we are born nor the natural endowments we happen to inherit should create any inequalities of access to advantage. But, we might ask, why think that justice requires us to *neutralize* the effects of differences in people's circumstances rather than merely to *mitigate* these effects, that is, prevent them from unduly affecting people's access to advantage? Let us call this position 'the mitigation approach'. The impulse behind it is to limit inequalities that are the product of differences in people's circumstances but not to eradicate them entirely.

It might be thought that the mitigation approach makes sense only as a practical compromise: when we are unable to neutralize the effects of differences in people's circumstances we should aim to mitigate these effects instead. Understood in this way, the neutralization approach and the mitigation approach would not be competitors. They would not be mutually exclusive, for theorists may favour mitigating the effects of differences in circumstances because they believe that in practice this is the closest we can come to neutralizing them. This is not the way in which I understand these two approaches, however. According to my way of framing the distinction, they are competitors because they differ at the most fundamental theoretical level. Even at this level, however, there is still a problem keeping the approaches apart, for as it stands the neutralization approach is simply a version of the mitigation approach: one which maintains that whenever differences in people's circumstances create an inequality of access to advantage, they unduly affect it. In order to solve this problem, I simply stipulate that the mitigation approach permits differences in people's circumstances to generate at least some inequalities of access to advantage (and not merely when these inequalities make some better off and none worse off).

My characterization of the mitigation approach is still seriously incomplete, however, for it does not tell us what is to count as 'an undue effect' on people's access to advantage.[6] Indeed, the mitigation approach as specified so far, unlike the neutralization approach, is not really a *theory* of egalitarian justice at all since it gives no guidance on which inequalities are just and which are unjust. So if the mitigation approach is to be an alternative theory of egalitarian justice, it needs further development. It can be developed in different ways (and competing versions may display greater or lesser divergence from the neutralization approach in their policy implications). In terms of its structure, some versions might consist

[6] Both the mitigation approach and the neutralization approach also require some account of how 'advantage' should be understood for the purposes of comparing how well off people are. The main candidates in the literature are primary goods, welfare, resources, capabilities, or some combination of these. My assessment of the neutralization approach, and the case I develop for a mitigation approach, is independent of the issue of which of these, if any, is the appropriate metric, so I do not propose to explore it here.

of a single fundamental principle that determined what kind or degree of inequality of access could justly arise from differences in circumstances. (By 'fundamental' here, I mean 'not derived from any other principle'.) This fundamental principle, in conjunction with empirical assumptions, might then yield various more concrete principles that governed different goods (e.g. educational qualifications, health care) or mitigated the effects of different aspects of people's circumstances (e.g. natural abilities, the family or culture into which they are born). Other versions of the mitigation approach might provide us with an irreducible plurality of fundamental principles, perhaps distributing different goods or governing different aspects of people's circumstances, these principles combining together to determine what it is for people's circumstances to have an undue effect on their access to advantage.

Whatever form the mitigation approach takes, the principles it offers give content to what it is for people's circumstances to have an undue effect on their access to advantage. As a result, it would be wrong to think of the fulfilment of these principles as providing the means to achieve some independently specifiable goal, such as the goal of preventing differences in people's circumstances from unduly affecting their access to advantage. Here there is a disanalogy with the neutralization approach, for when it provides further principles their fulfilment is to be regarded as the best means of realizing the goal of preventing differences in people's circumstances from creating any inequalities of access to advantage.

It will be possible to seek justification for the principles that are advocated by a version of the mitigation approach. We can always ask, 'Why is it just to allow people's circumstances to have the degree and kind of impact upon their access to advantage that these principles permit?' and 'Why would allowing these circumstances to have any more impact, or a different kind of impact, be unjust?' It may be that a stage is reached where these questions admit of no further answers, and defenders of the mitigation approach will be reduced merely to asserting their view that to allow differences in people's circumstances to have any greater impact, or a different kind of impact, on their access to advantage would be unjust. This does not create any serious disanalogy with the neutralization approach, however. For defenders of it can also be called upon to explain why differences in people's circumstances should not be allowed to create *any* inequalities of access to advantage and their reasons may run out as well.

III. *Evaluating the Approaches*

Are there any arguments which might reveal the superiority of the neutralization approach over the mitigation approach, or vice versa, even before we have identified a specific set of principles to constitute the latter? One of Rawls' central arguments in favour of what he calls Democratic Equality might be thought to provide a reason to endorse the neutralization approach rather than some version of the mitigation approach. He maintains that the circumstances in which people find themselves, such as the family into which they are born and the natural endowments they happen to possess, are arbitrary from the moral point of view. It might seem a short step from here to the conclusion that justice requires us to neutralize the effects of differences in these circumstances. Regardless of whether this is Rawls' own argument, is it any good? [7]

For a number of reasons, I think that the conclusion does not follow from the relevant premises. The fact that a person happens to be born into a particular set of social relations or born with a particular set of natural endowments, and the claim that these circumstances are in some sense morally arbitrary, does not in itself determine whether we should, at the level of fundamental principle, aspire to neutralize their effects or merely mitigate them. (Indeed, as critics of egalitarianism would argue, it does not give us any reason on its own to worry about the effects of differences in people's circumstances

[7] It has often been assumed that Rawls is a defender of the neutralization approach but this has been challenged. For relevant discussion, see N. Daniels, 'Democratic Equality: Rawls' Complex Egalitarianism', in S. Freeman (ed.), *The Cambridge Companion to Rawls* (Cambridge: Cambridge University Press, 2003), esp. 249–56; S. Scheffler, 'What is Egalitarianism?', *Philosophy and Public Affairs* 31 (2003), 5–39, esp. 24–31. In my view Rawls' remarks are generally ambiguous. This is at least in part because he does not distinguish in the way that he should between what G. A Cohen calls fundamental principles of justice and principles of regulation (see G. A. Cohen, 'Facts and Principles', *Philosophy and Public Affairs* 31(2003), 241), so that even if the principles of justice he defends mitigate rather than neutralize the effects of differences in people's circumstances, this does not rule out the possibility that at the most fundamental theoretical level he is committed to neutralization. (In making this point I do not mean to endorse Cohen's claim that fundamental normative principles are necessarily fact insensitive.)

at all.[8]) The neutralization approach might nevertheless seem to be underpinned by a fundamental moral principle, namely, the principle that it is unfair if one person is worse off than another through no fault of his or her own. Any brute appeal to this principle in defence of that approach would be question-begging, however, for they are too closely entwined for one to provide independent support for the other. (It would be no different from appealing to the idea that it is unfair for one person to be too much worse off than another through no fault of his own in support of the mitigation approach.)

Critics of the neutralization approach sometimes think that a case against it can be constructed by appealing to feasibility constraints. The underlying argument here is that it is impracticable to neutralize fully the effects of differences in circumstances, so our commitment should be to mitigate these effects instead. A premise of this argument, often unstated, is the dictum that 'ought implies can'. Principles of justice can be expressed in terms of ought statements and, it is argued, a constraint on the acceptability of any ought statement, and by implication, any adequate principle of justice, is that it must be possible to fulfil its demands. The issues raised by this line of thought are complex but let me outline what I think is the right response to it.[9] There are different uses of the term 'ought'. When it is used to express general moral principles, it is used in a way that brackets at least some questions of feasibility. When we say that people ought to keep their promises, we do not imply that it is always possible for a person to do so; we simply mean that there is always a weighty moral reason for her to do so if it is possible. But would it make sense to say that people ought to do something if we knew that it was *never* possible for them to do so, given, say, the limits of human knowledge, or constraints on the design of institutions, or human nature? Does it make sense to suppose that a general moral principle might bracket issues of feasibility to this extent? I do not see why not. We can make sense of the idea that an adequate principle of justice might be expressed in terms of an ought statement the requirements of which it would never be possible to fulfil because we can make sense of the idea that if, contrary to

[8] See, e.g. J. Narveson, 'Egalitarianism: Partial, Counterproductive, and Baseless', in A. Mason (ed.), *Ideals of Equality* (Oxford: Blackwell, 1998), esp. 90.

[9] For further elaboration, see A. Mason, 'Just Constraints', *British Journal of Political Science* 34 (2004), esp. 256–8.

fact, it were possible to fulfil its requirements, there would be a weighty moral reason of justice to do so.[10] To put the same point in G. A. Cohen's terms, even if considerations of feasibility provide us with reasons to reject the neutralization approach when it is proffered as a principle of regulation, they do not provide us with reasons to reject it when it is conceived as a basic or fundamental principle of justice.[11]

I doubt whether there is any abstract argument of the sort that I have so far considered (i.e. one which either simply invokes a fundamental moral principle or appeals to feasibility constraints) which could show the superiority of the neutralization approach when compared to the mitigation approach, or vice versa. I propose to employ a less abstract line of argument in order to raise some worries about the neutralization approach and motivate further development of the mitigation approach. My argument focuses on the way in which egalitarian concerns should figure in the deliberations of parents when they are making decisions that significantly affect their children's future welfare.[12] My claim is that if the neutralization approach were the correct one, parents would have a reason of justice not to behave in any way whatsoever that advantages their child relative to others, yet this is highly implausible. Not even egalitarian parents believe there is such a reason. Because the neutralization approach in this respect is so at odds with our ordinary moral experience, there are grounds for rejecting it.

Parents make a variety of decisions that have a serious impact upon their children's access to advantage. Those who are committed to an egalitarian conception of justice do sometimes experience a tension between that commitment and their desire to do their best for their children, for example, in making decisions about whether to send their children to private schools. But egalitarian parents rarely think that the issue of how much personal attention they should give to their children (rather than, say, the children of others) itself raises concerns about justice. Yet according to the neutralization approach, they should be exercised by this issue, for this approach

[10] See Cohen, 'Facts and Principles', 230–1.

[11] See Cohen, 'Facts and Principles', 244.

[12] This argument is adapted and expanded from my 'Equality of Opportunity and Differences in Social Circumstances', *The Philosophical Quarterly* 54 (2004), S. I.

implies that there is an injustice whenever differences in children's social circumstances, such as differences between the practices of the families into which they are born, affect their relative access to advantage. And parents' decisions about how they should raise their children, such as those concerning the amount of time they spend with them and what they do with them, including the efforts they put into cultivating their children's talents, clearly have significant effects on their children's access to advantage relative to others.

Of course, it may be possible to reconcile the neutralization approach with the decisions that some parents make to devote considerably more time and energy than is the norm to developing their children's talents. For example, it might be argued that there is a moral prerogative which licenses parents to act partially towards their children.[13] But the neutralization approach will find it hard to avoid the conclusion that there is always a weighty *pro tanto* reason for parents to refrain from behaving in ways that advantage their children, even if, all things considered, they are permitted to do so, yet this conclusion is at odds with our ordinary moral experience. For when parents read their children stories, or teach them how to play a musical instrument, they experience no moral unease; they do not see themselves as exercising a moral prerogative that permits them to act against a reason of justice or fairness.[14] It is not enough to reply that there is such an overwhelming case for holding that parents should be permitted to act partially towards their children in these ways that it completely silences the reasons they may have for thinking that doing so creates unfair advantages. This is implausible

[13] See A. Swift, *How Not To Be a Hypocrite: Social Choice for the Perplexed Parent* (London: Routledge, 2003), ch. 1; A. Swift, 'Justice, Luck and the Family: Normative Aspects of the Intergenerational Transmission of Economic Status', in S. Bowles, H. Gintis, and M. A. Osborne (eds), *Unequal Chances: Family Background and Economic Success* (Princeton, NJ: Princeton University Press, 2005), 256–76.

[14] There are parallels here with the issue of whether someone committed to the neutralization approach should experience any moral unease if they demand a salary which in effect rewards their greater natural endowments. (For relevant discussion, see G. A. Cohen, *If You're an Egalitarian, How Come You're so Rich?* (Cambridge, MA: Harvard University Press, 2000), ch. 8) This issue is complex, but my claim would be that even if there is a moral prerogative that permits self-serving economic behaviour of this kind, those who exercise their prerogative despite genuinely endorsing the neutralization approach should experience some moral unease. See also D. Estlund, 'Liberty, Equality, and Fraternity in Cohen's Critique of Rawls', *Journal of Political Philosophy* 6 (1988), 99–112, esp. 111–2.

precisely because, from the perspective of the neutralization approach, these practices raise considerations of justice that should surely leave some residue. When one weighty value is sacrificed for another, we should experience some loss.

In defence of the idea that parents do have a reason of justice to refrain from behaving in ways that advantage their children, it might be argued that the general principle which underwrites this reason is in evidence when parents distribute benefits between their own children. In this context, we do seem to think that parents should distribute these benefits in a way that is responsive to the different needs of siblings but does not give any of them special favour. Considerations of fairness arise when parents distribute benefits amongst their children, but it seems to me that we misrepresent these considerations if we see them as expressing a general principle that requires us to neutralize the effects of differences in people's circumstances. Rather, parents are under a special obligation to treat their children in a way that involves comparative fairness.[15] Much the same point applies in the case of nurseries or orphanages: carers are expected to give equal consideration to the interests of their charges because they are under a special obligation to do so, unless arrangements are in place assigning particular carers special responsibility for particular children.

Might defenders of the neutralization approach hold that parents always have a *pro tanto* reason to refrain from advantaging their children but deny that this implies that they always have a *pro tanto* reason for, say, not reading to their children, or not passing on their talents and expertise to them? It might be argued that there is always a reason of the first kind but not necessarily one of the second kind, on the grounds that there is no necessary connection between parents attending to their children in these ways and their children gaining a comparative advantage as a result. In principle at least, parents might help their children to cultivate various talents and abilities whilst the state prevented them from benefiting in any extrinsic way from the exercise of these talents and abilities. But there is a distinction to be drawn here between ideal and non-ideal theory. At the level of ideal theory it might indeed be argued that

[15] How then is this special obligation to be justified? The point I am making does not require me to offer a justification for it, but note there is no need to suppose that it has to be justified from some impartial perspective.

it is possible to structure society so that (from the perspective of the neutralization approach) parents have no reason to refrain from passing on their skills and expertise to their children because there is a regime in place which ensures that behaving in this way does not give their children any overall comparative advantage.[16] The argument I am mounting against the neutralization approach is not defeated by this point, however. For that argument relies upon an intuition about what constitutes just behaviour even in an unjust society. If there is a *pro tanto* reason for parents to refrain from advantaging their children (using whatever measure of advantage is the appropriate one), then it is hard to block the inference that there is a *pro tanto* reason for parents to refrain from passing on their skills and expertise to them in any system which allows their offspring thereby to gain a comparative advantage. This conclusion is counterintuitive in a way that casts doubt on the premise.

An alternative way of arguing against the idea that the neutralization approach provides a weighty *pro tanto* reason to refrain from advantaging one's children would be to insist that, like all considerations of social justice, it applies to the basic structure of society and has no relevance to the behaviour of individuals within that structure. But as G. A. Cohen has argued in a related context, if the basic structure is to include those institutions which have profound effects on people's lives, since the practices of families and cultures do so as well, it is hard to resist the conclusion that, even if these practices are not formally part of the basic structure, they are nevertheless relevantly similar.[17] It follows that there is no good reason to deny that decisions of parents must be governed by principles of justice. And this conclusion does seem hard to deny. If, for example, fathers forbid their daughters from receiving a formal education, this surely violates principles of justice even if educational institutions in the wider society do not discriminate against girls.[18]

[16] This does depend to some extent on the currency we use to measure advantage. The point I am making is clearest when the currency is primary goods, for the distribution of wealth and income could be adjusted to ensure that people did not benefit, in terms of their overall quantity of primary goods, from differences in parental input of these kinds. The point is harder to make if the currency for measuring advantage is capabilities.

[17] See Cohen, *If You're an Egalitarian, How Come You're so Rich?*, 137–8.

[18] See Cohen, *If You're an Egalitarian, How Come You're so Rich?*, 138.

A defender of the neutralization approach might concede that principles of justice should govern practices within the family but argue that the principles which are appropriate in this context are different from those the state should employ. The goal of neutralizing the effects of differences in children's circumstances may be the correct principle for shaping state policy but not for governing the behaviour of parents. Why should this be so, however? The most obvious reason would be that individual parents do not have enough knowledge of the consequences of their own behaviour, and the behaviour of others and its consequences, to be able to judge whether their actions will promote or undermine the aim of neutralizing differences in circumstances. It is hard for individuals acting independently to promote the outcomes required by the neutralization approach, and this militates against the idea that each can be morally bound when acting alone to promote those outcomes. This collective action problem is exacerbated by the fact that the neutralization approach favours neutralizing the effects not only of differences in *social* circumstances but also the effects of differences in *natural* circumstances such as the different potentials with which people happen to have been born. This makes the epistemological problems much greater since a child might be favoured by their social circumstances but not their natural circumstances and it will be hard for parents to know whether trying to pass on their skills and expertise to their children will promote or undermine the overall goal of the neutralization approach. Although I concede that this raises a genuine difficulty for the argument that the neutralization approach must govern the decisions of parents, it would be rash to conclude that, say, parents can *never* know whether the time, energy, and resources they devote to their children's upbringing will advantage their children. It is hard to deny that the neutralization approach implies that people have a strong reason (though not necessarily a conclusive reason) for promoting the outcomes it demands *when they know they can do so*.

A different reason for denying that the neutralization approach should govern the choices of parents might emerge from reflecting on what constraints are imposed on principles of justice by the need for publicity. Andrew Williams argues that Rawls holds that any adequate principle of justice must be such that others can check the extent to which a person's behaviour conforms to it. In Williams' view this requirement means that rules must be capable of being formulated in ways that are not too vague or ambiguous, and that the information required in order to tell whether these rules have been obeyed should be available to others.[19] The neutralization approach would fail to meet such a condition when it operated as a guide to personal behaviour, but there is serious doubt about whether publicity, understood in this way, really is a constraint on an adequate principle of justice. There are many spheres of personal behaviour in which issues of justice arise where it seems impossible to formulate precise principles the application of which can be checked by others. For example, it is often thought that we have obligations of justice to future generations that require us to do our bit in preserving the environment, but it is hard to see how these principles could be formulated as precise guides to behaviour (e.g. concerning what size car we should drive, and whether and when we should shun aircraft travel in favour of some less-polluting alternative), the application of which might be publicly checkable.[20]

I have claimed that egalitarians do not experience the pull of the neutralization approach in their personal behaviour in the way that they should do if it were to be plausible as an expression of egalitarian justice. I do not deny that egalitarian parents are often troubled by whether their choices can be reconciled with their conception of justice: the issue of private schooling is an obvious case where these concerns arise. There is also a range of intermediate cases where concerns about justice arise in a forceful way, for example, whether to move house to fall within the catchment area of a school that may provide a better educational experience; whether to purchase private tuition as an addition to state provision; whether to buy expensive educational aids such as computers or encyclopaedias. We can make sense of these concerns from the perspective of either the mitigation approach or the neutralization approach; our ordinary moral experience in these cases does not provide any grounds for favouring one over the other. What I am claiming, however, is that the neutralization approach has implications that are at odds with our ordinary moral experience, and which therefore count against it,

[19] See A. Williams, 'Incentives, Inequality, and Publicity', *Philosophy and Public Affairs* 27 (1998), 225–47.

[20] G. A. Cohen addresses these issues in an unpublished manuscript, 'Rescuing Justice from Constructivism'.

for it implies that *any* variation in parenting practices that produces significant differences in children's relative access to advantage must raise concerns of justice. The neutralization approach does not allow us to make a distinction between ways in which parents may significantly advantage their children that are entirely innocent *from the point of view of justice* and those that are potentially problematic. It is this that is counter-intuitive. For it goes against the commonly held and plausible view that there is *no reason at all* for parents not to use their own particular skills and talents in ways that their children can learn from, for example, no reason for parents not to pass on their musical skills or their mathematical expertise, even if doing so has the effect of giving their children significant advantages over others.

Parents committed to egalitarian justice who enjoy reading to their children (and relating to them in other ways that are bound to give them significantly greater chances of obtaining qualifications) do not appear to experience any tension between their commitment to it and the energies they devote to passing on their skills and expertise to their children. The response those committed to the neutralization approach must make to this observation, namely, that parents should experience such a tension, and that there is a weighty *pro tanto* reason for them to refrain from passing on their own skills and expertise if that significantly advantages their children, serves to sharpen the perception that once the strict implications of the neutralization approach are made manifest, it should strike us as implausible.

The neutralization approach might allow that social circumstances can have an unequal impact without creating injustice so long as no one's condition is worsened. Parents may devote more time and energy to their offspring in the knowledge that doing so will significantly advantage their children relative to others, on the grounds that no one's *overall* condition will be worsened by their doing so. But the choice parents are making is not merely between, say, developing their children's skills and expertise or pursuing their own self-regarding projects, for there is also the possibility of giving this kind of attention to other children. Given that possibility, it is hard to believe that parents who spend time developing their already comparatively talented children's skills and expertise do not make the condition of others worse than it could otherwise be.

Is the difficulty I am raising for the neutralization approach simply a particular version of the general problem that partiality poses for any theory that is committed to impartiality? If the difficulty here is how to reconcile the moral permissibility, even desirability, of partiality with a commitment to impartiality, then it seems to me that the problem I have raised is different. I have accepted that there may be moral prerogatives that permit us to act partially and that reasons of justice may need to be balanced against other reasons we have for favouring our own interests or the interests of others to whom we are connected. My concern is rather with the kind of action-guiding reasons that are generated by impartial theories. In this context, compare the neutralization approach with act utilitarianism. Act utilitarianism is committed to the idea that we should maximize the good, impartially conceived. So it implies that parents always have a moral reason to maximize the good when making decisions about how to behave towards their children (including decisions about whether to pass on their skills and expertise to them), and that there is a moral reason for them not to benefit their children when they could produce larger benefits for others by behaving differently. This is implausible but not to quite the same extent as the idea that we have a reason of justice to refrain from acting in any way whatsoever that advantages our children relative to others, for act utilitarianism at least implies that there is no moral reason not to benefit our children unless we could otherwise provide larger benefits to others.

I have not said enough to refute the neutralization approach. Perhaps there is some way of avoiding what I have taken to be its unpalatable consequences, or perhaps they are not as unpalatable as I have claimed. Adam Swift, for example, is unperturbed by the idea that parents have a reason of fairness or justice (albeit one that is outweighed by other considerations) not to read to their children when this advantages them relative to others.[21] My argument would be strengthened by some account of why it is that these ways in which parents may advantage their children are unproblematic from the point of view of justice. Consider three possible explanations. First, these forms of parental behaviour do not generate significant advantage (or disadvantage). Second, the practices at issue play a

[21] See Swift, *How Not To Be a Hypocrite*, 17, 69; see also 29–30.

crucial role in forming the child's identity, and a person cannot be unjustly advantaged (or disadvantaged) by something that is part of his identity. Third, these practices are constitutive of the valuable relationship between parent and child, so there cannot be a reason of justice not to engage in them.

The first of these explanations relies upon empirical claims, for example, that a parent's passing on his or her skills and expertise to his child does not create significant forms of advantage, in the way that, say, the purchase of private education does. But that claim may be false. Parents who are able to help their children with their maths homework, or who are able to give their children piano lessons, may be providing them with considerable advantage, comparatively speaking.[22] (Of course, it might be replied that the intuitions I am drawing upon are nevertheless based on the assumption that these forms of parental behaviour do not create significant advantage, and that if this assumption turned out to be false, the intuitions would be undermined. It does not seem to me, however, that they do rely upon empirical assumptions of this kind.)

The second explanation is also problematic. Family relationships do contribute to the formation of the child's identity, parts of which he retains through adulthood; the talents, abilities, and values that a person acquires and develops during his upbringing may come to be part of who he is. But even if a person cannot be unjustly disadvantaged by aspects of his own identity, it does not follow that he cannot be unjustly disadvantaged by the processes or practices which contributed to the formation of that identity. So this explanation is at best incomplete because it does not rule out the possibility that parental behaviour which is implicated in forming a child's identity may be unjust when it fosters comparative advantage.

[22] There is no consensus in the literature on this empirical question. Some maintain that interaction between parents and children is crucial in creating inequalities of access to advantage, whilst others deny that it is, maintaining that peer groups and genes are much more important. For the former position, see B. Hart and T. Risley, *Meaningful Differences in the Everyday Experience of Young American Children* (Baltimore, MD: Brookes Publishing, 1995); A. Lareau, *Unequal Childhoods: Class, Race, and Family Life* (Berkeley and Los Angeles, CA: University of California Press, 2003). For the latter position, see J. R. Harris, *The Nurture Assumption: Why Children Turn Out the Way They Do* (New York: Free Press, 1998); D. C. Rowe, *The Limits of Family Influence: Genes, Experience and Behaviour* (New York: Guilford, 1994). For relevant discussion, see D. Miller, 'Equality of Opportunity and the Family'.

There are also difficulties with the key idea that a person cannot be unjustly disadvantaged or advantaged by aspects of his identity. Its plausibility will rest, at least in part, on what criteria we use for saying that something is part of a person's identity, and we need to be careful that our criteria do not make the argument question-begging. For example, Brian Barry writes: 'Natural strength and dexterity are, we might say, a part of someone's personality in a way in which a club foot or congenital heart disease is not. One is what we are, the other what befalls us'.[23] It is hard to believe that this thought does not involve some kind of circularity, however. Surely the reason why Barry wants to say that a person's club foot is not part of his identity is precisely because he thinks it would be unjust for someone to be significantly disadvantaged by such a disability. After all, this disability may be part of his identity in the ordinary sense that it is part of his self-conception, that is, an important part of how he regards himself.

The third explanation would involve distinguishing those forms of parental partiality that play a role in realizing the values that are central to the parent–child relationship (including passing on various skills and expertise) from those forms of parental partiality that do not play this sort of role but *merely* involve the transmission of advantage (e.g. the purchasing of private education with the aim of improving one's child's examination performance).[24] This distinction is important but why should we suppose that when a practice is partially constitutive of a valuable relationship, there can be no reason of justice not to engage in it?[25] One may care for one's needy but relatively well-off parent, child, spouse, or friend in ways that require resources which might otherwise be spent improving the condition of the worst off. If there is a reason of justice to give priority to the worst off, then it would seem to come into conflict with practices that are partially constitutive of valuable relationships. (Even if we were to ignore this worry, it is not clear how far this

[23] Barry, 'Equal Opportunity and Moral Arbitrariness', 43. For a development of this approach, see Miller, 'Equality of Opportunity and the Family'.

[24] Harry Brighouse and Adam Swift provide the materials for making this distinction in 'Parental Partiality: Legitimate and Excessive'.

[25] Brighouse and Swift in effect also reject that principle and hence are committed to rejecting the argument I am considering. According to their approach, legitimate forms of partiality may nevertheless involve a kind of unfairness. See Brighouse and Swift, 'Parental Partiality: Legitimate and Excessive'.

third approach could be extended. In this context, consider also the forms of comparative disadvantage that are created by differences in beauty, or in the ability to make friends, when these can be properly attributed to differences in people's natural endowments or social circumstances. These differences can profoundly affect relative access to advantage, yet we are not normally inclined to think that they have a bearing upon matters of justice.[26] Appeals to the value of the parent–child relationship have no relevance here, and it is hard to think of any plausible analogue to them.)

None of the explanations I have canvassed provides us with a convincing account of why it is entirely unproblematic from the point of view of justice for parents to pass on their skills and expertise to their children. It seems to me that the best overall strategy in response to those who demand such an explanation is simply to defend alternative principles for determining when the effects of differences in upbringing are just or unjust. Indeed, if the mitigation approach is to be persuasive, it needs to provide us with a set of principles for determining more generally when the effects of differences in people's circumstances are unjust.

IV. *Conclusion*

There is no easy way of demonstrating the superiority of the neutralization approach when compared with the mitigation approach (or vice versa) by appealing to the truth of some fundamental moral principle or by invoking feasibility constraints. If we are to find reason to favour one over the other, we need to explore the overall power of each of these approaches and consider their fit with our considered judgements. In this respect I have suggested that the neutralization approach has problems making sense of our reasoning in some cases where our decisions may significantly influence our children's relative access to advantage. For it implies that there is a reason of justice for parents not to use their own particular skills

[26] Of course those who defend the neutralization approach can simply grasp this nettle and insist that differences in people's circumstances of this kind do raise issues of justice (perhaps hiding behind the thought that since we can do little in practice to counteract the effects of these differences, they need not be of concern when it comes to the formation of public policy.) But in my view this is an unsatisfying response, for reasons similar to those I have considered.

and talents in ways that their children can learn from when this has the effect of giving their children advantages over others, yet this is counter-intuitive. I have struggled to find a convincing explanation for our intuitions here, and have suggested that the best way of proceeding is to defend an alternative set of principles for determining when the effects of differences in people's circumstances (including differences in their upbringing) are just or unjust.

In this context we need to distinguish once again between fundamental principles and principles that are derived (perhaps in conjunction with empirical premises) from these fundamental ones. It is also important to have some conception of what kind of fundamental principles might yield a plausible version of the mitigation approach, and what sort of grounding they might be given. The way that I have set up the distinction between the neutralization approach and the mitigation approach means that different versions of the latter are possible, with very different theoretical justifications. A theory which appeals to a pre-justicial notion of desert might be an example of the mitigation approach, for it can hold that we need to counteract the effects of differences in people's social circumstances before they can deserve the rewards they receive. (In other words, the idea would be that mitigation is a condition of rewarding people in accordance with desert.) So too a theory which appeals to the idea of citizenship, by arguing that we need to limit the effects of differences in people's circumstances to ensure equal access to the political process, might provide an example of the mitigation approach.[27] (The idea here would be that mitigation is a means to realize the value of citizenship.) These two versions specify what it is to prevent differences in people's circumstances from unduly affecting their relative access to advantage by appealing to independent considerations, in one case the importance of rewarding people in accordance with their deserts, and in the other case the value of citizenship. But other versions of the mitigation approach might simply appeal to the effects of differences in people's circumstances on how well off they are, without reference to any other considerations such as citizenship or desert. In doing so, they might draw upon some idea of sufficiency—that

[27] There are, however, limits on what kind of defences of inequality might count as manifestations of the mitigation approach. Robert Nozick's entitlement theory, for example, could not be an example of this approach, for it is not concerned with counteracting the effects of differences in people's circumstances.

the effects of differences in people's circumstances should never be such that some are left unable to lead a decent life—or draw upon some idea of giving priority to the worse off—that inequalities of access to advantage which are the result of differences in people's circumstances ought to be limited because the interests of the worse off should be given greater weight compared to those of the better off. Since this reflects the way in which I develop the mitigation approach, in the next chapter I propose to consider how the three-fold distinction between equality, priority, and sufficiency relates to the contrast between the mitigation approach and the neutralization approach, and explore the different forms that the mitigation approach might take in the context of this distinction.

CHAPTER 5

Equality, Priority, and Sufficiency

The neutralization approach might appear to be committed to equality, in the strict sense of that term, whereas the mitigation approach's concern to limit inequality might seem to be rooted in the idea that there is a duty of justice to ensure that everyone is in a position to lead a decent life, or in the idea that we have an obligation to give priority to the worse off.[1] I argue that this is too simplistic, however, not merely because there are versions of the mitigation approach that cannot be adequately captured in terms of the language of priority or sufficiency (such as those which are concerned with the way in which inequalities may impact upon other values such as that of citizenship). I claim that there is a version of the neutralization approach which is prioritarian in character, and that there are plausible versions of the mitigation approach which, even though they are not strictly egalitarian, involve principles that are essentially concerned with comparative advantage. I begin by explaining the differences between a commitment to equality, priority, or sufficiency more fully before identifying some of the strengths and weaknesses of these doctrines. I then suggest that there is no decisive reason for

[1] See D. Parfit, 'Equality or Priority?', in M. Clayton and A. Williams (eds), *The Ideal of Equality* (Basingstoke, UK: Macmillan, 2000); D. Parfit, 'Equality and Priority', in A. Mason (ed.) *Ideals of Equality* (Oxford: Blackwell, 1998). There is now a large literature on the distinction between equality and priority, much of it sparked by Parfit's discussion, see, for example, D. McKerlie, 'Equality and Priority', *Utilitas* 6 (1994), 25–42; J. Broome, 'Equality Versus Priority: A Useful Distinction', in D. Wickler and C. J. L. Murray (eds) *'Goodness' and 'Fairness': Ethical Issues in Health Resource Allocation* (World Health Organization, forthcoming); R. Crisp, 'Equality, Priority, and Compassion', *Ethics* 113 (2003), 745–63; L. Temkin, 'Equality, Priority or What?', *Economics and Philosophy*, 19 (2003), 61–87; N. Holtug, 'Prioritarianism', in N. Holtug and K. Lippert-Rasmussen (eds), *Egalitarianism: New Essays on the Nature and Value of Equality*. Oxford: Oxford University Press, (forthcoming in 2007).

favouring one of them in preference to the others. The kind of arguments commonly employed against rival doctrines appeal to intuitions that may not be shared and as a result have little force against opponents. My purpose is to arrive at a better understanding of the relationship between the neutralization approach and the mitigation approach, and at the same time develop a clearer picture of some of the different ways in which the mitigation approach might fruitfully be developed.

I. *Clarifying the Distinctions*

Egalitarianism, strictly understood, maintains that inequality is either bad or unjust, for non-instrumental reasons.[2] Responsibility-sensitive versions of strict egalitarianism maintain that inequality is bad or unjust unless it arises from the choices people make in a way that renders it fair to require them to bear some or all of the costs of those choices. Prioritarianism, in contrast, maintains that, when other things are equal (in particular, when benefits are of the same magnitude, and there is the same number of potential beneficiaries), benefiting the worse off always matters more than benefiting the better off, and benefiting the worse off matters more the less well off they are. It holds that in consequence there is a moral reason, perhaps a reason of justice, to give priority to benefiting the worse off, but it does not suppose that there is any non-instrumental reason for regarding *inequality* as bad or unjust.[3] It can be made sensitive

[2] See Parfit, 'Equality and Priority', esp. 5–7.

[3] See Parfit, 'Equality and Priority', 12–13. My formulation of the priority view is vague in various ways. Contrast the following two interpretations: (i) other things being equal, benefiting the worse off always matters more than benefiting the better off, and benefiting the worse off matters more the less well off they are in *absolute* terms; (ii) other things being equal, benefiting the worse off always matters more than benefiting the better off, and benefiting the worse off matters more the less well off they are in *relative* terms, that is, where they fall when ordered in terms of their level of 'well-offness'. So according to (ii) in deciding which individuals should receive benefits, we need to look at the relative position of individuals ordered in terms of how well off they are, whereas according to (i) we need to look at how well off they are in absolute terms. I classify these as different kinds of prioritarianism. Parfit has something like (i) in mind when he refers to the priority view, see, e.g., Parfit, 'Equality and Priority?', 13. Iwao Hirose regards (i) as prioritarianism proper and refers to (ii) as 'weighted egalitarianism'. He argues that weighted egalitarianism is superior to prioritarianism, so understood, partly

to considerations of personal responsibility, for example, by limiting its scope to differences in how people are faring that arise from their contrasting circumstances.[4]

Prioritarianism comes in moderate and extreme versions. Extreme prioritarianism maintains, in effect, that we should give absolute priority to benefiting the worse off rather than the better off, irrespective of the magnitude of potential benefits and irrespective of the number of potential beneficiaries. It holds that when we are faced with a choice between benefiting the worse off and the better off, we should always benefit the worse off, because benefiting the worse off matters more, even when we could provide only a very small benefit to the worse off and could otherwise provide a very large benefit to the better off, and even when we could provide the same size benefit to a much large number of the better off.[5] The moderate version maintains that when we are faced with a choice between benefiting the worse off and the better off, we are sometimes permitted to benefit the better off, because a sufficiently large benefit for a better off person may outweigh a sufficiently small benefit for a worse off one, and a benefit for each of a sufficiently large number of the better off may outweigh the same size benefit for each of a sufficiently small number of the worse off. In effect, the moderate version maintains that that there is a moral reason, perhaps a reason of justice, to maximize the sum of weighted individual benefits, where benefits are weighted such that they are assigned greater value

because he does not think we can make sense of the idea of an absolute scale of well-being. See I. Hirose, 'Equality, Priority, and Numbers', University of St Andrews Ph.D. Thesis, 2003, esp. ch. 5. I use 'prioritarianism' to cover both (i) and (ii), and I do not assess the relative strengths of each. There is a genuine theoretical issue here, but for my purposes it is not necessary to consider their merits.

[4] This is not the only way of making prioritarianism sensitive to considerations of personal responsibility, however. One might simply attach greater significance or value to benefiting those who are worse off through no fault of their own compared to those who are worse off through their own fault. See R. Arneson, 'Why Justice Requires Transfers to Offset Income and Wealth Inequalities', *Social Philosophy and Policy* 19 (2002), 177.

[5] The extreme version is, in effect, committed to 'leximin', that is, giving lexicographical priority to the worse off. The difference principle seems to be an extreme form of prioritarianism since it forbids benefiting the better off whenever that would make the worse off even worse off than they would otherwise be. Derek Parfit argues that the difference principle is not merely a form of prioritarianism, however. See Parfit, 'Equality or Priority?', 121.

the worse off the individual who accrues them. This covers a family of views, so I sometimes refer to it in the plural, for different weightings may be given to benefits to the worse off at different levels.

There is also another view which is formally distinct from the prioritarianism, at least as I have defined it, which we might term the sufficiency view. This view maintains that, other things being equal, benefiting people matters more the worse off they are in absolute terms, but *only* until a certain point has been reached, namely, when they are in a position to lead a decent or satisfactory life. After this point, benefiting them matters no more (or less) than benefiting the better off.[6] In consequence it maintains that there is a moral reason, perhaps a reason of justice, to give priority to those who are not in a position to lead a decent or satisfactory life. (It can be made sensitive to personal responsibility by limiting its scope to differences in how people are faring that stem from their contrasting circumstances, or by giving greater weight to benefiting those who are below the threshold through no fault of their own.)

There is a range of possible variants of the sufficiency view, which draw the line in different places above which benefiting the worse off ceases to matter any more than benefiting the better off. The sufficiency view proper (as I have defined it) maintains that this line is to be drawn where a person is in a position to lead a decent life, but these other variants might draw the line at a higher level. The notion of a decent life is flexible, however, and different versions of the sufficiency view might in any case be generated by different interpretations of it. Some, for example, might attempt to specify it by listing a number of 'functionings' the attainment of which is necessary and sufficient for a good enough quality of life;[7] others might specify it in terms of what is required for meaningful agency.

Different versions of the sufficiency view may also be generated from different accounts of how much priority we should give to benefiting those below the relevant threshold. What I call the

[6] My way of specifying the sufficiency view makes it rather different from what Frankfurt calls the doctrine of sufficiency, see H. Frankfurt, 'Equality as a Moral Idea', *Ethics* 98 (1987), 21–43.

[7] See M. Nussbaum, 'Human Functioning and Social Justice: In Defence of Aristotelian Essentialism', *Political Theory* 20 (1992), 202–46.

extreme version maintains that we should give absolute priority to those below this threshold. It holds that whenever we have a choice between benefiting someone above the relevant threshold and someone below it, we should benefit the latter, no matter how small the benefit would be to him nor how large the benefit would be to the person above the threshold, and no matter how many other people we could also benefit above the threshold. (The extreme version may also maintain that whenever we have a choice concerning whom to benefit below the threshold, we should benefit the person at the greatest distance below it, but this is not essential to the view as I understand it. Indeed, the extreme version might hold that when it is impossible for everyone to attain the threshold, we should distribute benefits so as to bring as many people up to it as possible.) The moderate version, in contrast, maintains that when we have a choice between benefiting someone above the relevant threshold and someone below it, we are sometimes justified in benefiting the former because sufficiently large benefits to those above that threshold outweigh sufficiently small benefits to those below it, and a benefit to each of a sufficiently large number of people above the threshold may outweigh the same size benefit to a sufficiently small number of people below the threshold. As such, it covers a multiplicity of different views that are distinguishable in terms of precisely how they trade off benefits to those below the threshold against benefits to those above it, and how they deal with conflicts that may arise concerning whom to benefit below this line.

II. *Egalitarianism and the Levelling Down Objection*

In my view, there is no general argument which provides an overwhelming case for preferring any one of the three positions I have distinguished—egalitarianism, prioritarianism, and the sufficiency view—to the other two. Different versions of these positions possess different strengths and weaknesses, however, which I propose to survey to prepare the way for developing a plausible version of the mitigation approach.

The levelling down objection is perhaps the most influential argument against egalitarianism. Strict egalitarians seem committed to the claim that society would be better, in one respect at least, if each person's condition were reduced to that of the worst off individual, yet this seems counter-intuitive. Is there any respect in which a society would be better if this sort of levelling down were to occur? (Unlike strict egalitarianism, prioritarian and sufficiency views do not seem to be vulnerable to this objection because they do not regard a state of affairs in which equality is produced through levelling down as an improvement in any respect.)

Egalitarians have responded to the levelling down objection in different ways. Some have tried to identify a principle on which it is based, and then show that this principle is implausible. Others have tried to develop a form of egalitarianism which is not committed to the claim that levelling down is in one respect an improvement. Consider the first strategy, which is employed by (among others) Larry Temkin. He argues that the appeal of the levelling down objection often derives from a principle that he refers to as the slogan, which holds that 'One situation *cannot* be worse (or better) than another *in any respect* if there is *no one* for whom it *is* worse or better *in any respect*'.[8] Temkin raises various objections against the slogan, for example, he argues that it is challenged by what Derek Parfit calls the non-identity problem.

The non-identity problem arises in deciding between two different policies that will have an impact on future generations. According to the 'live for today' policy, the current generation would have children immediately and deplete their natural resources, whereas according to the 'take care of tomorrow' policy, they would postpone having children for a few years and conserve their resources. The live for today policy would mean that the current generation would be better off but their children would be significantly less well off, whereas the take care of tomorrow policy would mean that they would fare slightly less well but their children would fare as well as they do. Many people favour the take care of tomorrow policy, but on plausible assumptions—namely, that the children involved under the two different policies would be different people, since they would be the product of different sperms and eggs, and that one does not harm a person by failing to conceive him—it is incompatible with the slogan.[9]

[8] L. Temkin, *Inequality* (New York: Oxford University Press, 1993), 256.

[9] See Temkin, *Inequality*, 255–6.

Critics of egalitarianism have sometimes responded to Temkin's argument by contending that the levelling down objection need not rest upon 'the slogan' but could rest upon some other more plausible idea, for example, the idea that if something matters morally its significance must be explicable in terms of the well-being of individuals.[10] Temkin seems to accept this point[11] but argues that this proposal is still too demanding because it rules out the possibility of non-instrumental impersonal ideals, that is, 'ideals whose non-instrumental value lies partly, or wholly, beyond any contributions they make, when realized, to individual well-being'.[12] Temkin thinks there are many potential examples of this kind, including what he calls 'proportional justice', which supposes that how well a person fares should be proportionate to how well they have led their lives.[13] In his view, we can understand the value of equality only if we regard it as an impersonal ideal, and if we do understand its value properly, we will be unimpressed by the levelling down objection, for that objection is motivated precisely by a rejection of the possibility of genuine ideals of this kind.

The other strategy that has been employed to defend egalitarianism against the levelling down objection is to identify a form of egalitarianism that avoids it. Derek Parfit, for example, distinguishes between deontic and telic egalitarianism. According to his formulation of this distinction, when deontic egalitarians object to inequality, they do so on the grounds that it is unjust or involves wrong-doing, whereas when telic egalitarians object to inequality they do so because they regard it as non-instrumentally bad.[14] The distinction that Parfit is drawing here is far from transparent, but he seems to think that the crucial point is that telic egalitarians are ultimately concerned with outcomes rather than actions or obligations: '[a]ccording to Telic Egalitarians, it is the state of affairs which is bad, or unjust; but Deontic Egalitarians are concerned only with what we

[10] See Crisp, 'Equality, Priority, and Compassion', 747; see also Holtug, 'Prioritarianism'.

[11] See L. Temkin, 'Egalitarianism Defended', *Ethics* 113 (2003), 777.

[12] Temkin, 'Egalitarianism Defended', 778.

[13] See Temkin, *Inequality*, 260.

[14] Parfit, 'Equality and Priority?', 7. In my 'Egalitarianism and the Levelling Down Objection', *Analysis* 61 (2001), 246–54, I suggest a different way in which egalitarians might avoid the levelling down objection, which involves developing a form of what I call conditional egalitarianism.

ought to do'.[15] Parfit believes that deontic egalitarianism can escape the levelling down objection altogether because it can maintain that 'we have a reason to remove inequality only *when*, and only *because*, our way of doing so benefits the people who are worse off'.[16]

It is not clear, however, that deontic egalitarianism can escape the levelling down objection quite as easily as Parfit seems to suggest. As Dennis McKerlie points out, deontic egalitarians cannot simply *stipulate* that we have a reason to remove inequality only when it benefits the worse off. They need to explain why this should be so, in a way that does not make their view indistinguishable from prioritarianism.[17] Deontic egalitarianism is concerned with fair and unfair treatment, and it is not clear why a form of treatment that generates an unequal outcome becomes fair merely because it benefits the worse off. Consider a simple illustration which raises such doubts. Suppose we are to divide a cake into portions for five children, and there is no special reason for favouring any of them with a larger slice. Suppose, further, that the only way we can divide the cake involves producing four equal sized slices and one smaller slice, and that the only alternative to this state of affairs would have involved baking a smaller cake such that, divided equally, everyone would have received a smaller slice. Why should we suppose that baking the larger cake, dividing it up in the specified way, and then distributing the different pieces by lot, would be fair, as opposed to unfair but nevertheless justified all things considered? Does the child who gets the smaller piece of cake really have no basis for complaint *at all*? Reflection upon examples such as these (and bracketing Nozickean worries about whether they throw any light at all on the activities of the state) suggests that defenders of deontic egalitarianism might be better advised to grasp the nettle and simply hold that it is precisely

[15] Parfit, 'Equality and Priority', 7, note 11. Kasper Lippert-Rasmussen attempts to clarify the precise nature of the distinction between telic and deontic egalitarianism in his 'The Insignificance of the Distinction between Telic and Deontic Egalitarianism', in N. Holtug and K. Lippert-Rasmussen (eds.), *Egalitarianism: New Essays on the Nature and Value of Equality*. Oxford: Oxford University Press (forthcoming in 2007). He argues that the distinction cannot be adequately understood as contrasting forms of egalitarianism that object to unequal outcomes and forms which object to the way in which inequalities are produced.

[16] Parfit, 'Equality and Priority?', 10.

[17] See McKerlie, 'Equality', 289. Lippert-Rasmussen also argues that deontic egalitarianism is vulnerable to a variant of the levelling down objection, see his 'The Insignificance of the Distinction between Telic and Deontic Egalitarianism'.

because we believe that the person who gets the smaller share has a justified complaint that egalitarian rather than prioritarian or sufficiency principles are the correct ones here.

Parfit believes that there may be a price to be paid for rejecting telic egalitarianism in favour of deontic. He argues that deontic egalitarianism may lack the resources to object to kinds of inequality which many egalitarians have found troubling, for example, inequalities that are not humanly produced, or inequalities that obtain between members of different communities which are not the product of wrong-doing of any kind. Some egalitarians have been especially disturbed by the vast inequalities that obtain across the globe, yet in Parfit's view deontic egalitarianism is hard pressed to explain what is objectionable about them. It is not clear that this problem is insuperable, however.

Global egalitarians are troubled by inequalities that emerge as a result of differences in people's circumstances, such as the political societies into which they are born. These inequalities are not deliberately produced, but it seems to me that a deontic egalitarian can still capture concerns about them. According to Parfit's formulation of the distinction, telic egalitarians are ultimately concerned with outcomes, whilst deontic egalitarians are ultimately concerned with actions or obligations. Deontic egalitarians have at least two strategies they might use in objecting to global inequalities. First, they might appeal to the idea that each person, across the globe, has a right to an equal share of some goods, such as natural resources, or a right not to be worse off than others through no fault of his own. Each has an obligation not to act in ways that violate this right and to act together to ensure that others receive what is due to them. Of course, ideas such as these would require support but they have been defended.[18] Second, they might appeal to the idea that even though global inequalities are not deliberately produced, at least some of them are the product of causal processes in which the advantaged are implicated. They might then argue that the advantaged have obligations to treat the disadvantaged as equals, with equal concern and respect, which they violate when they are involved in the generation

[18] Hillel Steiner, for example, argues that each person across the globe has a right to an equal share of natural resource values: see H. Steiner, *An Essay on Rights* (Oxford: Blackwell, 1994), 235–6, 262–5, 269–73.

of certain kinds of inequalities of outcome. This second strategy merits further elaboration.

Even though inequalities which result from differences in people's circumstances are not deliberately created, it would be incorrect to say that they are simply *permitted* to arise in such a way that the advantaged are not causally responsible for their creation.[19] When differences in circumstances generate inequalities of outcome, they do not do so on their own. They do so by combining with institutions that determine what property rights are to be enforced, including those rights that people are given over their own capacities and powers as well as those they are granted over external resources.[20] As a result, deontic egalitarians can legitimately regard the rules governing our social and economic structure as partially responsible for generating inequalities of outcome. To the extent that we are justified in supposing that there is a global social and economic structure, deontic egalitarians may be in a position to object to how it combines with differences in people's circumstances to generate inequalities of outcome in a way that is incompatible with treating people as equals.[21]

[19] For relevant discussion, see T. Nagel, *Equality and Partiality* (New York: Oxford University Press, 1991), 99–101. Although Nagel wants to deny that there is a morally fundamental distinction between what the state does and what it allows, he nevertheless seems to accept that it may be factually correct to say that the state merely allows differences in people's circumstances to generate inequalities of outcome, whereas I would hold that it is always causally implicated in this process.

[20] Lesley Jacobs argues that there is no such thing as natural inequality; all inequalities are socially produced (see L. Jacobs, *Pursuing Equal Opportunities: The Theory and Practice of Egalitarianism* (Cambridge: Cambridge University Press, 2004), ch. 3. My argument does not require this claim, but if the claim is correct, that argument would receive further support.

[21] For a sense of how the idea that the global social and economic order is causally implicated in the creation of inequalities might be developed, see T. Pogge, *World Poverty and Human Rights* (Cambridge: Polity, 2002). For a critique of Pogge's thesis that the global order harms the poor, see M. Risse, 'How Does the Global Order Harm the Poor?', *Philosophy and Public Affairs* 33, 2005, 349–76. Some would deny that being causally implicated in the production of inequality is enough to raise questions of distributive justice. It might be argued that what it is to treat people as equals depends, at least in part, on whether or not they are fellow citizens. Thomas Nagel, for example, maintains that the fact that citizens are both joint authors of a coercively imposed system and subject to its norms means that treating fellow citizens as equals imposes more demanding requirements of distributive justice, requirements that would not follow from merely being subject to the same global economic institutions. See T. Nagel, 'The Problem of Global Justice', *Philosophy and Public Affairs* 33 (2005), 113–47. For general scepticism

III. *Prioritarianism Versus the Sufficiency View*

As these reflections show, it is not easy to dispose of egalitarianism. But nor is it easy to refute prioritarianism or the sufficiency view. We can, however, make some progress here by identifying the strongest forms of each. For a start, moderate versions of prioritarianism (or some of them at least) are much more plausible than the extreme version: surely, for example, we should allow the possibility that sufficiently large benefits to the better off may outweigh sufficiently small benefits to the worse off.

It might seem that the extreme version of the sufficiency view suffers from a similar problem, giving us a reason to favour moderate versions of that view instead. It can, however, be interpreted in a way that makes it more plausible than the comparable version of the priority view. For if we suppose that benefiting those below the threshold is a matter of justice, we might think that this outweighs any other moral reason we have for benefiting those above this threshold. Despite its greater plausibility, and its resonance with Rawls' views on the primacy of justice, this position still seems much too uncompromising.[22] Surely benefits to those above the threshold can be sufficiently large to outweigh very small gains for those below it. A moderate version of the sufficiency view which acknowledged this point might preserve the idea that there is a reason of justice to benefit those below (but not those above) the threshold, but maintain that justice is not always of overriding importance.

So moderate versions of both the priority view and the sufficiency view are preferable to the extreme versions of those views. But is there any reason in general to favour moderate versions of the priority view over moderate versions of the sufficiency view, or vice versa? Richard Arneson rejects what he calls 'sufficientarianism', which (as he characterizes it) holds that the distribution of resources in a society is just if, and only if, everyone has enough, on the grounds that it cannot provide us with a non-arbitrary account of what constitutes 'having enough', and that even if it could do so, setting a threshold of this kind leads to implausible conclusions

about the possibility of this sort of manoeuvre, see S. Caney, *Justice Beyond Borders: A Global Political Theory* (Oxford: Oxford University Press, 2005), ch. 4.

[22] See Rawls, *A Theory of Justice*, 3–4. Rawls acknowledges that his remarks about the primacy of justice may be expressed too strongly.

in some cases where there are conflicts of interest. In particular, Arneson argues that sufficientarianism requires us to benefit those below the threshold even when we could do so only by a very small amount and could otherwise provide sizeable benefits to large numbers above the threshold; and that it requires us to bring a person up to the threshold when he is marginally below it even when we could provide much larger benefits to those further below the threshold but not bring them up to it.[23] The moderate form of the sufficiency view that I have distinguished does not suffer from these implausible consequences, however.[24] Nor is the problem of providing an account of what is to constitute 'having enough' quite so troubling for it. The sufficiency view defines having enough in terms of 'being in a position to lead a decent life'. There is a degree of arbitrariness involved in specifying what is to count as a decent life, but this does not create the same kind of difficulty for moderate versions of the sufficiency view because they do not suffer from the same kind of discontinuities. According to these versions, our reason to give priority to those below the threshold gradually diminishes as we approach it, so there is no radical break when the threshold is reached.

Indeed, *pace* Arneson, some have thought that there is good reason to favour the sufficiency view over the priority view. Roger Crisp, for example, argues that the priority view has two kinds of implausible consequence.[25] Consider the first of these. Suppose we have a choice between providing a very small benefit to those who are already very well off, or providing a very large benefit to someone who is very badly off. If the number of very well-off people is large enough, then whatever weighting is given to benefits to the worse off, the priority view will require us to benefit members of the very well off group rather than the very badly off individual.

[23] See Arneson, 'Why Justice Requires Transfers to Offset Income and Wealth Inequalities', esp. 187–9. See also R. Arneson, 'Equality', in R. Goodin and P. Pettit, *A Companion to Contemporary Political Philosophy* (Oxford: Blackwell, 1991), esp. 496–500.

[24] Nor is it vulnerable to the critique that Richard Arneson gives of what he calls the revised doctrine, which is equivalent to what I have called the extreme version of the sufficiency view. Arneson does not seem to acknowledge the possibility of the moderate versions I have distinguished, see Arneson, 'Why Justice Requires Transfers to Offset Income and Wealth Inequalities', 194–5.

[25] See Crisp, 'Equality, Priority, and Compassion'.

The second consequence that Crisp highlights stems from the prioritarian assumption that (other things being equal) benefiting the worse off always matters more than benefiting the better off, irrespective of how well off or badly off they are. If someone is very well off, but marginally worse off than another, the priority view must hold that there is nevertheless a reason to benefit him rather than the other person. This might seem implausible. The sufficiency view makes no such claim, for it maintains that benefiting the worse off matters more than benefiting the better off only up until the point at which the former are in a position to lead a decent life. Even if we suppose that the point at which people are in a position to lead a decent life is too low a level to set the threshold above which benefiting someone who is worse off matters no more than benefiting someone who is better off, we might think that there must be some such threshold, or we would be committed to the view that it is more morally important to provide the same size benefit to a person who is extremely well off as opposed to someone who is more than extremely well off.

These arguments are not decisive against the priority view, however. Even if the first argument has successfully identified a counterintuitive feature of the priority view, this feature cannot give us reason to reject it in favour of a moderate version of the sufficiency view, or at least not as I have characterized the latter, for they share the consequence that a small benefit to a sufficiently large number of very well off people will outweigh a large benefit to a very badly off person. In order to avoid the objection, we might retreat to the extreme version of the sufficiency view, which maintains that benefiting those below the threshold always takes priority over benefiting those above the threshold, irrespective of the size of benefits or the number of potential beneficiaries. But that has implausible consequences too, as I pointed out above. Alternatively, we might reformulate the sufficiency view so that it holds that we have a reason to give priority to benefiting the worse off until they are in a position to lead a decent life but no reason to benefit anyone who had already reached that position. But then it would face the kind of difficulties that Arneson raised and which I considered above, which exploit the discontinuity between benefiting those below the threshold and benefiting those above it. (Viewed in this light, the intuitions that Crisp is drawing upon might seem to favour some strict form of egalitarianism rather than the sufficiency view.)

The second argument is inconclusive because it appeals to an intuition that may not be shared by prioritarians. Indeed, Nils Holtug describes a case which might lead us to accept that we do indeed have a reason to benefit the very well off as opposed to benefiting the extremely well off when faced with that choice.[26] Imagine two groups containing equal numbers of people who are both above whatever threshold the sufficiency view adopts. But one group of people have access to a special fruit which contains vitamins that enable them to live much healthier and much longer lives than the other group. Let us suppose that we could divide out the fruits equally between members of the two groups, such that the gains in health and life expectancy experienced by the second group would be equivalent to the losses experienced by the first group. According to the sufficiency view, there is no reason to divide the fruit equally since (*ex hypothesi*) everyone is above the threshold, and when everyone is above the threshold there is no reason to give priority to benefiting the worse off. But surely there is a reason to do so, a reason whose force the priority view can explain.

Holtug's example is powerful but there is room for doubt about whether it really does favour a version of the priority view. For we might be able to explain the intuition that he is drawing upon equally well by combining the sufficiency view with what I call 'quasi-egalitarian principles'. Quasi-egalitarian principles object to inequality of a certain degree or kind as such. They differ from egalitarian principles because they do not object to inequality as such; they object to inequality when it is of a particular size or has a certain kind of character. Like egalitarian principles, however, they are essentially comparative, and this distinguishes them from both prioritarian and sufficiency principles. So, in relation to Holtug's example, one might think that the character and degree of the inequality—that the distribution of fruit means that some people are able to live only 100 years, say, whilst others are able to live for 200 years—is objectionable as such, not simply because it fails to give the appropriate kind of priority to the worse off. We might think that the effects of differences in people's social circumstances should never be such that some but not others have the resources to obtain a good that is important in

26 See Holtug, 'Prioritarianism'.

general for a person's access to overall advantage. And we might appeal to this as a fundamental principle.

More generally, quasi-egalitarian principles can limit inequalities in a way that moderate versions of the priority view or the sufficiency view cannot, and by doing so they may be in a position to accommodate the intuitions which Crisp draws upon in his first argument against the priority view. For moderate versions of both views seem to allow that a small benefit to a sufficiently large number of better-off people may outweigh a large benefit to a sufficiently small number of worse-off people, even when these worse-off people are below the threshold at which they can lead a decent life, yet that seems unjust. Quasi-egalitarian principles, because they are concerned to limit comparative advantage, may give us reason to resist some of these trade-offs, and hence may be able to accommodate the relevant intuitions.

IV. *Quasi-egalitarian Principles*

Quasi-egalitarian principles are not uncommon. It is not unusual, for example, to hear people defending the idea that income differences should never be such that those at the highest income level earn more than some particular multiple of the income earned by those at the lowest level. But these kinds of principles are not plausibly regarded as fundamental, for in the absence of some further principle from which they are derived, it is hard to see how we could justify commitment to a particular multiple here. The crucial issue, then, is whether there could be a quasi-egalitarian principle that was fundamental, in the sense of not derived from some other principle that was either egalitarian, prioritarian, or sufficientarian in character.

On what grounds might we object to the size or character of an inequality without appealing to some instrumental reason why it is objectionable? The idea that there might be fundamental principles which object to a particular degree of inequality (or its particular character) as such, without maintaining that whenever there is some degree of inequality, to whatever extent, it is objectionable, might seem strange. We can of course make sense of the idea that an inequality is too great because of its impact upon democratic citizenship, or because redistribution in the direction of greater equality would enable the worst off to live a decent life, but neither of these reasons is of the right sort. Neither objects to the inequality in access to advantage as such: the former is concerned with democratic citizenship, whereas the latter is concerned with being in a position to live a minimally decent life. There is a genuine alternative here, however. For it is possible to object to the degree or character of inequality *as such*, in much the way that it is possible for a strict egalitarian to object to an inequality as such. In making this sort of objection to the degree of inequality we might maintain that it is inconsistent with treating people as equals, or with them enjoying equal standing, without supposing that we are thereby appealing to some independent ideal. Consider, for example, a principle which holds that the effects of differences in people's circumstances should never be such that some can acquire the resources that are necessary in order to be able to lead a decent life whilst choosing not to work to earn an income when others are not able to do so. This principle might govern the effects of differences in natural endowments on income and wealth, and also the effects of differences in the inheritance of wealth to the extent that these can be attributed to differences in people's social circumstances. It would not insist that these effects should be neutralized but it would maintain that they need to be limited in order for people to enjoy equal standing or be treated as equals, thereby restricting the degree of comparative advantage that these differences may permissibly create.

I concede that there may be various worries about the defensibility of particular quasi-egalitarian principles such as this one, but for the moment my claim is simply that they are conceptually coherent. It becomes easier to detect the logical space for quasi-egalitarian principles if we introduce Parfit's distinction between telic and deontic egalitarianism, and ask whether the quasi-egalitarian principles that I have in mind are best understood as relatives of telic egalitarianism or as relatives of deontic egalitarianism. There are competing pressures here. These principles do not seem to be relatives of telic egalitarianism, for they do not suppose that inequality itself is non-instrumentally bad, and it would be odd to hold that some specific degree of inequality is non-instrumentally bad, or to maintain that some specific degree of equality is non-instrumentally valuable. On the other hand, unlike deontic egalitarianism, they do not seem to require objectionable inequalities to be the product of any wrong-doing, for these inequalities may simply be the result of allowing differences in circumstances unduly to influence distributive shares.[27] If deontic egalitarianism objects only to forms of unequal *treatment*, it would seem that it must lack any deep connection with principles that object to the inequalities which emerge as a result of allowing differences in people's circumstances to have too great an impact, or the wrong kind of impact, upon distributive shares.

It seems to me, however, that the quasi-egalitarian principles with which I am concerned are best seen as relatives of deontic egalitarianism. There are at least two strategies that deontic egalitarians might employ in objecting to inequalities of outcome that arise from differences in people's circumstances. First, they may argue that these inequalities violate the rights of the disadvantaged, for example, they might claim that each person has a right not to be worse off than others through no fault of his own. In much the same way, quasi-egalitarians might argue that each person has a right not to suffer inequalities of a particular degree or kind through no fault of his own. Second, deontic egalitarians may argue that even when inequalities of outcome arise from differences in people's circumstances, the advantaged may nevertheless be causally involved in the production of these inequalities. Even though inequalities which result from differences in people's circumstances are not deliberately produced, they may nevertheless be, in part, the product of social and economic institutions. As a result, deontic egalitarians can legitimately argue that the rules governing our social and economic structure do not treat those subject to them as equals when these rules combine with differences in, say, natural endowments to generate inequalities of outcome.[28] In much the same way, defenders of quasi-egalitarian principles can hold that these rules do not treat those subject to them as equals when they combine with differences in people's circumstances to generate inequalities of outcome that are too great or of an inappropriate kind.

It might be thought that incorporating quasi-egalitarian principles, whatever their specific content, would create problems for the

[27] See D. McKerlie, 'Equality', *Ethics* 106 (1996), 281–2.

[28] Even if the advantaged are not causally responsible in any way for the plight of the seriously disadvantaged, it might still be possible to argue that the former do not treat the latter as equals unless they come to their aid.

mitigation approach, since it then becomes vulnerable to a variant of the levelling down objection. Quasi-egalitarians seem to be vulnerable here, for they seem committed to the claim that when an inequality exceeds a particular degree, in one respect it would be better to reduce that inequality even if that would make everyone worse off, or some worse off and no one better off. So, for example, the principle that the effects of differences in people's circumstances should never be such that some can acquire the resources that are necessary in order to be able to lead a decent life whilst choosing not to work to earn an income, whereas others are unable to do so, is a quasi-egalitarian principle that is essentially concerned with comparative advantage, and as such seems to be vulnerable to the variant of the levelling down objection that I have identified.

But I have already given reasons for doubting the force of the levelling down objection. We might think that, for example, the effects of differences in people's circumstances should never be such that some have the choice of leading a life of leisure whilst others do not, and that in a society where this state of affairs obtained, those without this choice have a justified complaint. And we might think that it would be better in one respect to redistribute resources so that no one has this choice as a result of their fortunate circumstances than to allow some to have it whilst others do not. It may even be easier to see why someone might have non-instrumental reasons for wanting to *limit* inequality in relation to particular goods, where it would be implausible to suppose that there is a non-instrumental reason for favouring strict equality in relation to those goods.

V. *Mapping the Distinctions*

With the distinctions between egalitarian, quasi-egalitarian, prioritarian, and sufficiency principles in place, we are in a position to reflect further on the character of versions of both the neutralization approach and the mitigation approach. The neutralization approach might seem to be egalitarian in the strict sense because it maintains that inequalities that are generated by differences in people's circumstances are unjust (except perhaps when these inequalities do not worsen any one's position), whereas the most plausible versions of the mitigation approach might seem to express either a priority or a sufficiency view because they aim to limit the effects of differences in people's circumstances in the light of a properly weighted concern for the interests of the worse off or the interests of those who lie below a certain minimum level. If we probe more deeply, however, it becomes apparent that the neutralization approach may involve prioritarian or egalitarian principles, or both, whilst the mitigation approach may involve quasi-egalitarian, prioritarian, or sufficiency principles, or even some combination of these, perhaps with different kinds of principles governing different goods or different aspects of people's circumstances.

Versions of the neutralization approach which permit inequalities of access to advantage that result from differences in people's circumstances when no one's condition is worsened by them can be construed in prioritarian or egalitarian terms, or both, depending on the precise reasons for regarding these inequalities as just.[29] If the reason is that we should give lexical priority to benefiting the worse off, so inequalities are justified only when no one's condition is worsened by them, then this position is in effect an extreme form of prioritarianism. On the other hand, if the reason for regarding these inequalities as just is that when some benefit from them and no one is made worse off by them, these benefits outweigh the non-instrumental value of equality, then this position is combining an egalitarian principle with some other principle.[30] This further principle might be utilitarian in character, with it being maintained that the loss of equality is outweighed by the benefits to others when no one's condition is worsened by that loss,[31] or the further principle might be prioritarian in character, with it being maintained that the loss of equality under these conditions is outweighed by the benefits, suitably weighted, to others.

[29] Note, however, that the aim of neutralizing the effects of differences in people's circumstances, as I have specified it, could not play a role in justifying either strict equality or prioritarianism. It simply presupposes one or the other. Cf. S. Hurley, *Justice, Luck, and Knowledge* (Cambridge, MA: Harvard University Press, 2003), ch. 6, esp. 156–7.

[30] It would also involve an egalitarian principle if the idea is that equality is non-instrumentally valuable on condition that no one's plight is worsened by it. According to this sort of view equality is non-instrumentally, but not intrinsically, valuable. See Mason, 'Egalitarianism and the Levelling Down Objection', 246–54.

[31] This would be an example of what Parfit calls moderate egalitarianism: see Parfit, 'Equality and Priority', 17–18.

It is natural to think that in so far as the mitigation approach can be located in terms of the distinctions between equality, priority, and sufficiency, it must consist of either a prioritarian principle or a sufficiency principle, but, again, the situation is more complex. In order to show this, consider some of the reasons that a version of this approach might give for regarding inequalities in access to advantage as unjust. First, it might object to the way in which differences in people's circumstances adversely affect the level of access to advantage enjoyed by the worse off. This reason seems to express a prioritarian view (or perhaps a sufficiency view), for it is concerned with benefiting the worse off. Second, it might object to the way in which the effects of differences in people's circumstances are such that some are left unable to lead a decent life. This reason is best understood in terms of the sufficiency view. There is no essential concern with relative differences in access to advantage; from this perspective, what matters is the absolute condition of the worst off group and whether it meets some minimum standard. Third, it might regard an inequality of access to advantage that is due to differences in people's circumstances as unjust simply because of its size or character, independently of its causal effects. This reason seems quasi-egalitarian, even if it is not strictly egalitarian, for it is essentially concerned with relative differences in access to advantage.

So the mitigation approach might express a priority view, or a sufficiency view, or a quasi-egalitarian principle. But it would also be possible for a version of it to combine egalitarian, quasi-egalitarian, prioritarian, and sufficiency principles (or some subset of these). For example, a version of the mitigation approach might adopt a sufficiency view but combine this with egalitarian or quasi-egalitarian principles for governing specific goods, such as health care or education, thereby limiting inequalities of access to these goods which would otherwise be permitted by the sufficiency view on its own.

VI. *Conclusion*

The distinction between egalitarian, quasi-egalitarian, prioritarian, and sufficiency principles is important in helping us to understand the structure and character of different versions of the neutralization and the mitigation approach. I have argued that there is no general case that is overwhelming for preferring one kind of principle to the other three, and indeed that it may be possible to combine different kinds of principles within a version of either the neutralization or the mitigation approach.

My aim in the next chapter is to develop a plausible version of the mitigation approach. It seems to me that the correct way of working here is to construct the theory from the bottom-up, to try to find principles for governing different goods or different aspects of people's circumstances, and then ask whether they should be seen as derived from more abstract principles. We are much more confident of our intuitions when we focus on specific goods, such as education or health care, and consider specific aspects of the circumstances in which people find themselves. It may turn out that the specific principles we arrive at by reflecting in this way are best understood as derived from a single fundamental principle, or from a small set of such principles, perhaps in conjunction with empirical premises. But we should not start with the assumption that this must be the case. Even when we arrive at a set of specific principles that display a degree of fit with a more abstract principle, it does not follow that they are derived from it or justified by it. And even when we do think that this fit is of the right kind for there to be a logical relationship between an abstract principle and a set of specific principles, we should consider the possibility that the specific principles, or at least, judgements about the weight to be given to them, might be best understood as grounded in the abstract one in such a way that they express what it requires in a specific context, so giving partial content to it rather than being derived from it. The method I have in mind aims at a kind of reflective equilibrium but not one in which fully determinate abstract principles are tested against prior intuitions, rather the process of reflection on intuitions yields specific principles, and judgements about the weight to be accorded to these specific principles, which may then enable us to make the abstract principles more determinate.

This method is especially appropriate when developing a moderate version of either the sufficiency view or the priority view, for our intuitions about when to trade off benefits to the worse off in favour of benefits to the better off seem much less clear when these choices are presented abstractly. Developing specific principles to govern particular goods or particular aspects of people's circumstances, and then reflecting upon the weight to be accorded to them may, therefore, be a way of giving content to a moderate version of the sufficiency view or the priority view. In the next chapter I use this method to identify some of the principles that might plausibly be regarded as constitutive of the best version of the mitigation approach, having in view the distinctions I have drawn in this chapter between egalitarian, quasi-egalitarian, prioritarian and sufficiency principles.

CHAPTER 6

Mitigating Principles

In order to defend a version of the mitigation approach as opposed to the neutralization approach, at the very least we need to identify a plausible set of principles that might constitute it. My strategy here is to work from the bottom up: to seek defensible principles to govern specific goods or specific aspects of people's circumstances, and then to see whether they can be grounded in more abstract principles. I focus on three areas: first, access to qualifications, second, the giving of gifts and bequests; third, the effects of differences in natural talents and abilities. The principles that emerge should be thought of as working together to spell out what kind of impact differences in social circumstances and natural endowments may justly have upon access to advantage. I also try to locate the principles I defend in the logical space of the distinctions drawn in the previous chapter between quasi-egalitarian, prioritarian, and sufficiency views. I suggest that these different principles have different characters: some are best understood as quasi-egalitarian, whilst others are grounded in a moderate version of the sufficiency view.

I. *Access to Qualifications*

Since my interest in the mitigation approach was fuelled by the difficulties the neutralization approach encounters in giving a plausible view of what considerations of justice bear upon the decisions of parents, this is a good place to begin. The neutralization approach ran into trouble for it seemed to imply that a parent has a *pro tanto* reason of justice to refrain from acting *in any way whatsoever* that advantages his children relative to others, including, for example, refraining from passing on his skills and expertise to them when that would give them a comparative advantage. What principles, then, should the mitigation approach adopt in this context?

The mitigation approach might start from the principles of justice it thinks should govern access to qualifications, deriving principles to govern the behaviour of parents towards their children from these. A plausible candidate for one of these principles is what I call the basic skills principle: each child should be provided with an education, both formal and informal, that enables him to acquire a set of general and particular skills which will allow him to have an adequate range of options, irrespective of his level of natural endowment, so long as that level permits him to acquire these skills. Whatever employment and leisure possibilities exist within a society, they could not be real options for a member of it unless he possesses a range of such skills. It is highly unlikely that someone who lacks the general ability to read and write, or who lacks basic numerical skills, could have an adequate range of options when the possibilities on offer in his society are, for the most part, options only for those who are literate or numerate. In a society with a variety of social forms and practices, just as no individual option is necessary in order to have an adequate range of options,[1] no particular individual skill is required, but a person will need a range of such skills, provided in large part through the educational system.[2]

The basic skills principle imposes some constraints on how parents raise their children, for parental neglect of various kinds may stand in the way of children acquiring the skills they need in order to possess an adequate range of options. But this principle will permit differences in family structure and in parental attitudes towards their role in developing their children's abilities. It is vague in various respects, however, and what it demands from both parents and the state will depend on how it is interpreted. Consider a set of hard cases. Given their level of natural endowment, some children will find it difficult to acquire both the general and the particular skills

[1] J. Raz, *The Morality of Freedom* (Oxford: Oxford University Press, 1986), 410–1.

[2] By specific skills, I have in mind the following sorts of thing: the ability to work cooperatively with others; extract the main points from a report; organize tasks so as to meet deadlines; understand diagrams or pictorial representations; dexterity in confined spaces.

needed for them to possess an adequate range of options. A small proportion of them will face learning difficulties which mean they have trouble acquiring basic literacy and numeracy. Does this imply that a society truly committed to the basic skills principle should make available unlimited economic resources in order to enable these children to acquire the necessary skills, to whatever degree they are capable? And does it imply that parents have an unlimited obligation to help in any way they can? That would be a highly demanding view. It would favour directing any available educational (or indeed other) resources towards children who have learning difficulties, even when those resources could be used to provide much greater benefits to others. For example, when faced with a choice between enabling a child who is experiencing severe difficulties in learning to read and write to make some small progress towards that goal, and enabling the others to make great advances in their education beyond the acquisition of the minimum level of skills, this version of the mitigation approach would always favour the former.

The issue of how demanding the principle is can be recast in terms of its relationship to the sufficiency view. We might suppose, for example, that the basic skills principle is grounded in another one which requires us to provide the conditions necessary for each person to lead a decent life, regardless of their natural endowments and social circumstances, in so far as this is possible. This more abstract principle could then be understood as derived from a version of the sufficiency view (perhaps weighted to take account of personal responsibility when that is relevant). The idea would be that, other things being equal, benefiting people matters more the worse off they are, until they reach the point at which they are in a position to lead a decent life, after which benefiting the worse off matters no more (or less) than benefiting the better off. This formulation is indeterminate in crucial ways, however, for it does not distinguish between the moderate and extreme versions of the sufficiency view that I identified earlier.[3] As a result, it does not provide us with any indication of how much weight should be given to benefiting the worse off when they are below the relevant threshold compared to benefiting those above this level. Given the case against the extreme version, we should resist interpreting the principle in these terms,

[3] See Ch. 5, S. I.

and instead formulate it in terms of the moderate version. In the context of access to qualifications, the idea would be that schools and parents should give greater weight to the interests of those who experience difficulty in acquiring the skills they need to be able to lead a decent life, but that those interests must be balanced against the sizeable benefits that can be secured for other children (whether siblings or classmates) by employing those resources differently. Bringing a child up to the level at which they acquire the skills needed for them to be in a position to lead a decent life matters more than providing the same size benefit to someone who is already in that position. However, when a given unit of resource would provide very large benefits to a number of people who already possess such skills, but would enable someone who lacks them to make only very limited progress towards acquiring them, then the former may take precedence.

I am not claiming that the weight we should give to the basic skills principle can straightforwardly be derived from some moderate version of the sufficiency view. My proposal is rather that by reflecting upon the issue of what constitutes fair access to qualifications, we can arrive at the basic skills principle, which can then be seen as grounded in a moderate version of the sufficiency view. This does not enable us to determine how much weight should be given to satisfying the basic skills principle as opposed to benefiting those who have already acquired a set of the relevant skills, but that issue can be addressed by considering what we should say about specific cases, and these judgements can then enable us to give more content to a particular version of the sufficiency view. (Grounding the basic skills principle in a sufficiency view also allows us to raise the question of whether resources would be better spent subsidizing forms of work that do not even require basic literacy or numeracy to increase the opportunities for those who lack these basic skills, rather than investing in trying to cultivate these skills more widely amongst those with severe learning difficulties when the progress to be expected would be small.)

It would be implausible to maintain that the principles I have identified provide an exhaustive account of what variations in social circumstances are compatible with justice in the context of access to qualifications, and no plausible version of the mitigation approach could hold that these principles do so. For if these principles were regarded as exhaustive, they would allow the different economic resources available to different families to have too deep an impact upon their children's access to qualifications for us to say that the effects of differences in people's social circumstances have been limited in the way that justice requires. Suppose that two children receive a secondary education that enables them to acquire equivalent qualifications, but one child has available to him the economic resources to go on to a higher education, which would then permit him to train to become a doctor, whereas the other does not. The principles that I have so far defended would seem to leave open the possibility that this state of affairs might be permissible. If the effects of differences in social circumstances and natural endowments on access to qualifications are to be mitigated in the way that justice requires, then surely this possibility must be excluded. So there is a strong case for adding a further principle.

It might be thought that the principle I defended in Chapter 2, namely, that the best-qualified candidates should be appointed to advantaged social positions, which I grounded in the idea of respect for persons, is all that is needed here.[4] But that principle is not obviously incompatible with a policy of offering places in higher education to the best-qualified candidates while requiring them to finance their studies themselves, with no help forthcoming to those who are unable to do so. Yet that would seem unjust. We need a principle which regulates access to higher education in a way that is not merely formal. My proposal is that any plausible version of the mitigation approach must hold that the effects of differences in social circumstances should never be such that some people can enjoy a level and quality of education which others with equivalent qualifications are denied, or which they could enjoy only if they or others made sacrifices that it would be unreasonable to expect. Let us call this the educational access principle.

This principle would place constraints on what effect differences in people's social circumstances can legitimately have on their access to higher education. For it could not be reconciled with a state of affairs in which some, as a result of their fortunate social circumstances, possessed the resources necessary to go on to higher education whilst others with equivalent qualifications, but less fortunate

[4] See Ch. 2, S. IV.

social circumstances, did not possess the necessary resources to do so and could not reasonably be expected to acquire them (e.g. they could not acquire them except by taking out a loan the repayment schedule for which would place massive burdens on them, or without making unreasonable demands on family members, such as asking their parents to cash in their pension funds). It would also have implications for primary and secondary education. Private schools at these levels are compatible with it only if there is state provision of comparable quality, or the fees they charge are within the means of each family. (In an educational system where there is state provision of comparable quality, parents might still choose private schools if, for example, these schools offered boarding facilities or after hours childcare that parents, given their career choices, needed.)

Some will argue that the educational access principle allows inequalities of access to education that are too great, others may maintain that it should permit inequalities that are even more pronounced. It would not entail the idea that there should be equal access to higher education in the sense that equally qualified individuals should face precisely the same-sized obstacles to entering it. (Nor would it entail the more radical idea that anyone who can benefit from higher education should have access to it, or that any particular percentage of the population should go on to higher education.) In support of the idea that the principle is sufficiently demanding, however, I would point out that a commitment to equal access to education is hard to defend without incurring a more general commitment to the neutralization approach, and I have already raised some worries about that approach. In response to those who say that the principle is too demanding, I would argue that if we are concerned at all about the impact of differences in people's social circumstances on their access to education, as defenders of the mitigation approach must be, it is hard to see how we could fail to be concerned about a state of affairs in which these differences meant that some could enjoy access to a level or quality of education which others are denied. Indeed, it is hard to see how citizens could possess equal standing in society unless the educational access principle is satisfied.

In the context of higher education, the resources necessary to secure compliance with the educational access principle might be provided in a number of different ways and from different sources.

Some will argue that these resources should be provided from public funds, raised through taxation and given in the form of state grants; others may argue in favour of repayable loans, perhaps at preferential rates of interest. Another possibility that has been discussed in the literature is that each person, upon reaching adulthood, might receive a capital grant from the state, the use of which might be restricted to various purposes that are perhaps linked to productive contribution to the community.[5] Like the neutralization approach, however, the mitigation approach is a form of responsibility-sensitive egalitarianism; as such, it operates with a presumption that people should bear the costs of their choices. This in turn creates a presumption that parents (rather than the state or other citizens) should bear the costs of having children, that is, of providing them with the food, shelter, nurturing, and education that they need to become well-adjusted adults. Now it is true that this does not have a direct implication for the funding of higher education, since this is something that people embark upon when they have reached adulthood. But it may nevertheless still have an indirect bearing upon the availability of resources to fund higher education. Let me explain.

Eric Rakowski, who defends the neutralization approach, supposes that if we are to neutralize the effects of differences in circumstances, 'everyone born into a society is entitled, at a minimum, to the same quantity of resources that all who participated in the original division of the community's goods and land received',[6] where the original division was one of equal shares. He then argues that the obligation to provide this quantity of resources falls 'wholly or almost entirely on those responsible for his existence', which in most cases means the child's natural parents.[7] It is therefore open to him to argue that parents, rather than the state, owe their children a capital grant, unless the parents have already discharged their obligation to provide the required quantity of resources in the process of bringing up their children. This capital grant might then be used by its recipients to fund their higher education, wholly or in part. Defenders of the mitigation approach may take a less demanding

[5] See S. White, *The Civic Minimum: On the Rights and Obligations of Economic Citizenship* (Oxford: Oxford University Press, 2003), 189.

[6] E. Rakowski, *Equal Justice* (Oxford: Oxford University Press, 1993), 150.

[7] See Rakowski, *Equal Justice*, 153.

view than Rakowski of the quantity of resources that parents owe their children. For this reason it may be easier for them to argue that parents' obligations towards their children are discharged simply in the process of bringing them up, and do not extend to providing them with a capital grant which might then be used to fund their higher education. If this argument can be sustained, then the principle I have described will need to be met in some other way in relation to access to higher education, and that might be done through some system of state grants, or by loans from public or private sources, or by some combination of the two.

Should we regard the educational access principle as derived or as fundamental, however? The reason we care about access to educational qualifications is that we know these strongly influence the chances of occupying advantaged social positions (at least when appointments are made on the basis of qualifications, a practice I defended earlier[8]). Given the intrinsic and extrinsic rewards connected to these positions, a person's access to them has a strong influence on his access to overall advantage. Once this line of reasoning is made explicit, however, it becomes implausible to suppose that the educational access principle is fundamental. But what then is the fundamental principle at work here?

One possibility would be a principle which holds that the effects of differences in people's social circumstances should not be such that some possess, or can reasonably be expected to acquire, the resources (or other means) necessary to obtain a good that is important in general for a person's access to overall advantage whilst others do not possess these resources and cannot reasonably be expected to acquire them. (It might cover some goods which have little or no positional character as well as others the relevance of which for the principle derives mainly from the fact that they are positional goods. So, for example, we might suppose that this principle governs goods such as health care as well as educational qualifications.) This principle would not require equality of access to these goods, that is, it would not require that each person face obstacles to these goods that are of equivalent size (so, for example, differences in economic resources that are due to differences in social circumstances might be allowed to create some inequalities of access to them), but it would

[8] See Ch. 2, S. IV.

place limits on the degree of inequality of access that is permissible—limits that it might claim are necessary for individuals to enjoy equal standing. But is even this principle fundamental? Should we understand it as grounded in a version of the priority view? (That might also give us reason to question whether the basic skills principle which I defended earlier is best understood as grounded in a version of the sufficiency view as opposed to a version of the priority view.)

The priority view goes well beyond the principle I am defending. If it were to be grounded in a version of the priority view, its defence would have to appeal to various empirical conjectures concerning the best means of benefiting the worse off. But it seems to me that we are less confident of these empirical conjectures than the principle itself. Indeed, if it turned out that these empirical conjectures were false—that satisfying the principle did not benefit the worse off in the way required—it seems to me that our confidence in it would not be undermined. I favour an alternative way of understanding this principle, which sees it as a fundamental, but independent of, the priority view, with an irreducibly quasi-egalitarian character. It is partly a pressure towards reduction, motivated by a desire to reduce the number of fundamental principles that we need to invoke, which inclines us towards the idea that this principle is grounded in the priority view. We should resist that pressure. (Of course, a theory with more fundamental principles is faced with more potential conflicts between them, but my concern is to identify the correct set of such principles, an issue that is independent of what scope there is for conflict between them.)

If this principle does have an irreducibly quasi-egalitarian character, it is essentially concerned with comparative disadvantage independently of its causal effects, and places limits on the degree of inequality of access to goods such as education that can be reconciled with justice (albeit in a context where further principles govern other goods or other aspects of people's circumstances). Someone who endorses the principle can consistently allow some departures from it, for example, when departing from it would improve everyone's absolute level of access to these goods. They might nevertheless insist, in the face of a variant of the levelling down objection, that in one respect it would be better for everyone to be denied access to these goods than for some but not others to have access to them simply as a result of material advantages that they owe to their fortuitous social circumstances.[9]

By combining this principle with a moderate version of the sufficiency view, it is also possible to block some trade-offs that might otherwise be permitted by the latter on its own. In Chapter 5, I pointed out that moderate sufficiency views might be regarded as counter-intuitive because they allow that in principle a small benefit for a sufficiently large number of well-off people could outweigh a large benefit to a sufficiently small number of badly-off people who are below the threshold at which they would be able to lead a decent life.[10] As a result, I suggested that moderate sufficiency views might be more appealing when combined with quasi-egalitarian principles, for these principles may prevent the interests of the worst off being sacrificed in favour of the interests of the better off in at least some of these cases. The educational access principle (and the deeper principle which grounds it) can play such a role, for it would prohibit educational benefits from being provided to those above the relevant threshold when those below it are denied access to these benefits simply because of their less fortunate social circumstances.

If we go down the path I am proposing, then it leads to a version of the mitigation approach that invokes two principles in the context of access to qualifications. First, the basic skills principle, which holds that each child should be provided with an education that enables him to acquire a set of skills which will allow him to have an adequate range of options. (This principle can be seen as grounded in a moderate version of the sufficiency view. It governs the effects of differences in both social circumstances and natural endowments.) Second, the educational access principle, which holds that differences in people's social circumstances should never be such that some people can enjoy a level and quality of education that others with equivalent qualifications are denied, or could enjoy only if they or others made sacrifices that it would be unreasonable to expect. (This principle is quasi-egalitarian in character and can be seen as grounded in a deeper one which maintains that the effects of differences in people's social circumstances should not be such that some possess, or can reasonably be expected to acquire, the resources or other means necessary to obtain a good that is important in general

[9] Cf. Ch. 5, S. IV. [10] See Ch. 5, S. III.

for a person's access to overall advantage whilst others do not possess these resources and cannot reasonably be expected to acquire them.)

Does this version of mitigation approach avoid the problems faced by the neutralization approach in governing access to qualifications? It promises to do so. Unlike the neutralization approach, the principles I have described do not imply that there is always a reason to refrain from behaving in any way that advantages one's children, nor do they entail that we should systematically prevent differences in social circumstances from having an effect on people's chances of occupying advantaged social positions. These principles will undoubtedly place constraints on how parents raise their children, and on the educational system in a society. Parental neglect of various kinds may stand in the way of children acquiring the skills they need in order to possess an adequate range of options; and in cases where children are in danger of failing to acquire these skills, parents and the state have a demanding obligation to help. When parents can, by turning their attention away from their own children, help other children who are struggling to acquire the skills they need to be able to lead a decent life, or provide larger benefits to other children who have already reached that position than they can to their own children, then they have a moral reason to do so that will need to be weighed against any special obligations they have to their own children.[11] But according to the account I am defending, mitigating the effects of differences in social circumstances in terms of access to qualifications will nevertheless permit differences in family structure and the kind of support and attention parents provide, and differences in the quality and quantity of education children receive. Within limits, different families might have different economic resources available to them, enabling the wealthier to purchase extra tuition, books, and computers, and making it easier for them to provide quiet spaces in which their children can study. In terms of higher education, wealthier parents may smooth their children's passage through higher education by providing them with extra funding. Disputes are possible about what particular policies, practices, and institutions are needed to satisfy these principles, but it is clear that they could be met even though different

[11] Note, however, that the moral reason we may have to provide benefits to other children who are already in a position to lead a decent life might be construed as a reason of justice: see the discussion of moderate and extreme versions of the sufficiency view in Ch. 5, S. III.

individuals have different chances in life because of their different social circumstances.

It would be question-begging at this point simply to assert that there cannot be fair access to qualifications unless there is equal access to them. The mitigation approach provides an interpretation of fair access to qualifications, but it simply denies that *fair* access must mean *equal* access. My suspicion is that liberal egalitarians are drawn to the idea that 'fair access' must mean 'equal access' because they are in the grip of the neutralization approach. In response it might be said that even if fair access does not mean equal access, to the extent that we are concerned with creating a level playing field, it must place serious limits on inequalities of access to qualifications that are created by differences in social circumstances (and indeed differences in natural potential), more serious limits than those implicit in the view that I am advancing. But the account of fair access I am defending is part of an approach that aims to mitigate other effects of differences in social circumstances, such as those created by gifts and bequests, and to mitigate other effects of differences in natural endowment. We can see this broader account as a vision of what it means to level the playing field, one which allows some inequalities of access to qualifications, for example, some that are the result of different parental choices.

In so far as the mitigation approach has implications for access to qualifications, we can think of the principles that it involves in this area as an account of what has been traditionally understood as equality of opportunity. In other words, we can think of those principles which explain what it is to mitigate the effects of differences in social circumstances and levels of natural endowment on access to qualifications as principles of equality of opportunity. In the next two sections I turn to some other principles that it seems to me should be partially constitutive of the best version of the mitigation approach, and which further explain what it is to level the playing field in the way that justice requires, including principles that govern other potential effects of differences in natural endowments, and principles that govern gifts and bequests.[12]

[12] Why should we suppose that these principles spell out what it is to level the playing field rather than merely explain what justice requires in response to the effects of differences in people's circumstances? These principles govern people's relative access to advantage, which makes it appropriate to regard them as partially determining what it is to level the playing field in the way that justice requires.

II. *Gifts and Bequests*

Gifts and bequests can create serious inequalities by themselves, or be part of a process that does. (Here we must distinguish gifts and bequests from transfers of resources which might be regarded as the fulfilment of parents' obligations to their children to provide them with a fair share of initial resources.) It might seem that the neutralization approach would be disposed to regard the receipt of gifts and bequests as a matter of good brute luck and hence to insist that we should use taxation to neutralize the differential effects of gift-giving and the making of bequests. But, as defenders of the neutralization approach have recognized, things are not that simple for a number of reasons. First, if the neutralization approach is to incorporate a genuine commitment to respecting the choices of individuals, it would seem that it must permit them to make gifts, just as we should allow them to make other choices about what to do with their resources.[13] Furthermore, if the differential effects of gift-giving or the making of bequests were to be neutralized, these practices would lose their point, and the scope for the exercise of various virtues such as kindness, gratitude, and generosity, and the context in which they flourish, would be severely diminished.[14] Second, if the effects of these practices were to be neutralized, then this would remove various incentives that would otherwise exist for people to use their talents to good effect. If people were no longer able to pass on the fruits of their work to those they care about, they would lose one of their reasons for exercising their productive capacities.[15] Third, it might be argued that not all gifts and bequests are a matter of good brute luck for their recipients.[16] Some are the result of choices made by the recipient, for example, those that express the gratitude of the gift-giver for something the recipient has done or for the friendship they have enjoyed together.

[13] See Rakowski, *Equal Justice*, 158; R. Dworkin, 'Sovereign Virtue Revisited', *Ethics* 113 (2002), 125.

[14] See White, *The Civic Minimum*, 181–3.

[15] See White, *The Civic Minimum*, 183.

[16] See Rakowski, *Equal Justice*, 158–62. See also P. Vallentyne, 'Self-Ownership and Equality: Brute Luck, Gifts, Universal Dominance and Leximin', *Ethics* 107 (1997), 333.

Some of these observations may require a modification of the neutralization approach; others it may be possible to accommodate within it.[17] But what matters for my purposes is how these issues bear upon the way in which the mitigation approach should deal with gifts and bequests. Since the mitigation approach can allow gifts and bequests to have some differential effect on people's access to advantage, the various worries that arise in relation to the neutralization approach need not trouble the mitigation approach to the same extent. For it can maintain that gifts and bequests are legitimately subject to taxation, but that recipients should be allowed to retain at least some of their value. This restricts the freedom of gift-givers—they will not always be free to make a gift the whole value of which is retained by the recipient—but does not destroy the freedom to give gifts. It will also preserve incentives for those who are motivated to work by the prospect of being able to benefit others through giving or bequeathing the rewards they receive as a result of doing so. And even if the receipt of gifts and bequests is not always wholly a matter of brute luck, to the extent that it is, its effect will fall within the purview of the mitigation approach; there may be a presumption that when parents make gifts or bequests to their children, their receipt is largely a matter of brute luck, but a presumption in the opposite direction when gifts or bequests are received from a spouse or friend.

This does not settle the more difficult question, however. What principles should be used to determine the rate at which gifts and bequests should be taxed? One plausible principle that would have an impact here is that the effects of differences in people's circumstances should never be such that some can (substantially before the average retirement age) acquire the resources that are necessary in order to be able to lead a decent life whilst choosing not to work to earn an income, whereas others cannot. Let us call this the accumulation of wealth principle. This principle seems to be quasi-egalitarian in character, for it seems to be essentially concerned with comparative advantage. In defence of the principle, it might be said that unless it is satisfied, citizens cannot enjoy equal standing. A society which allows some as a result of their advantaged circumstances to have the

[17] For relevant discussion, see M. Otsuka, 'Luck, Insurance, and Equality', *Ethics* 113 (2002), 51–4; Dworkin, 'Sovereign Virtue Revisited', 125.

option of enjoying a life of leisure, whilst others have no choice but to work to earn an income, does not treat its citizens as equals.[18]

But might the accumulation of wealth principle be grounded in a moderate version of the priority view? Again, it is hard to see why we must suppose that it should be understood in these terms unless we bow to the pressure of reductionism. We should see it instead as a fundamental principle with a quasi-egalitarian character. That is perfectly consistent with allowing departures from it when these would benefit everyone (or when some would benefit from them and no one's position would be worsened), and with insisting in the face of a variant of the levelling down objection that, in one respect at least, a society would be better if no one had the possibility of leading a decent life whilst choosing not to work to earn an income as a result of their fortunate circumstances than if some had that possibility but not others.

An alternative candidate for grounding the accumulation of wealth principle would be a principle which appeals to the contribution an individual makes to society, for example, that people should be rewarded in proportion to their productive contribution to it. But this contribution principle is much more demanding than the accumulation of wealth principle I am proposing and there is no strong reason to think that my principle is grounded in it. It is true that when some, as a result of their circumstances, choose not to work and are still able to lead a decent life, whilst others do not have this option, the former are being rewarded without making a contribution, but the idea that rewards should be proportionate to contribution goes far beyond the accumulation of wealth principle that I am advancing.

A more plausible candidate for grounding the accumulation of wealth principle is one which holds that those who receive a high share of resources have an obligation of justice to make a decent productive contribution, proportionate to their abilities, to the community in return.[19] Still, however, the accumulation of wealth principle is rather different from this reciprocity principle. It is possible

[18] Note that this principle does not exclude the possibility that through modest effort-making some might acquire the resources necessary to lead a comfortable life of leisure. But the principle would be consistent with this state of affairs only if others could also gain access to those resources through modest effort-making.

[19] See White, *The Civic Minimum*, 49.

that someone who, as a result of their circumstances, has enough resources to be able to lead a decent life without working will nevertheless choose to work and make an important contribution to the community by doing so. According to the accumulation of wealth principle, the unfairness would still be there, however: as a result of differences in their circumstances, he or she is in a position to choose not to work to earn an income and yet still lead a decent life whilst others are not. (I am not denying, however, that the reciprocity principle might be defended as an independent principle of justice.)

Nor is it the case that some, as a result of their circumstances, are being denied access to leisure activities, a good which is arguably of great importance in general for people's access to overall advantage, thereby violating the principle I advocated in the previous section, that the effects of differences in people's social circumstances should not be such that only some possess (or can reasonably be expected to acquire) the resources necessary to obtain a good that is important in general for a person's access to overall advantage. Those who have to work for a living may still have access to leisure, even though they do not have equal access to it. Might, therefore, the relevant grounding principle be that everyone should have equal access to leisure? No, that would be going too far: in contrast, the principle I am defending aims to place limits on inequalities of access to leisure, but does not require equal access. Some might think that this principle nevertheless permits inequalities of access to leisure that are too great. For it would allow some to be in a position, as a result of their circumstances, to choose to work only a very small number of hours per week, or only a few hours over the course of a year, and thereby earn enough to lead a decent life, whilst others have to work much longer hours. The principle might be modified, however, to avoid the most extreme of these cases without embracing the idea, which in my view goes too far, that fairness requires equal access to leisure. We might, for example, substitute 'whilst choosing not to spend much time working to earn an income' for 'whilst choosing not to work to earn an income' in the accumulation of wealth principle as it is formulated above (though we would then need to clarify what is to count as not having to spend much time earning an income).

We should also remember that the accumulation of wealth principle operates in conjunction with other principles governing access to fundamental goods (such as education and health care) and the effects of differences in natural endowments. It implies that gifts and bequests should be taxed at the rate that is required to prevent differences in people's circumstances from generating a state of affairs in which some but not all are in a position to choose to lead a life of leisure, but we might also suppose that gifts and bequests should be taxed at a rate that is high enough to ensure that the educational access principle can be satisfied, by providing grants to those who would otherwise not have the reasonable access to higher education that is enjoyed by others with equivalent qualifications but more fortunate circumstances. This illustrates the way in which the various principles I am defending are intended to work together to mitigate the effects of differences in people's circumstances.

III. *The Effects of Differences in Natural Circumstances*

In order for the mitigation approach to provide a genuine account of what it is to level the playing field, it must also provide principles which govern the effects of differences in natural endowments on access to both the intrinsic and extrinsic rewards of advantaged social positions. How are these differential effects to be mitigated? Some of the principles I have already defended have implications for this question, in particular the accumulation of wealth principle and the basic skills principle. But these principles could hardly be regarded as exhaustive.

Consider Ronald Dworkin's hypothetical insurance model as a way of addressing this issue. According to this model, compensation for those with bad genetic luck should be set in the light of what protection against various risks, such as the risk of having low earning power, or of being unemployed or unhealthy, 'average people of normal prudence … would likely have purchased if they had had the opportunity to do so on equal terms, given the premiums that insurers in a competitive insurance market would have charged for such insurance'.[20] (In the case of disabilities people would be on equal terms if we assume that they have the same initial resources available to them but are unaware of what, if any,

[20] Dworkin, 'Sovereign Virtue Revisited', 108.

disabilities they suffer from, whereas in the case of differences in earning power people are on equal terms if they have the same initial resources available to them and are aware of their talents and powers, but ignorant of what return these are likely to command in the market.)

But can the hypothetical insurance model be adopted by a defender of the mitigation approach or is it essentially part of the neutralization approach? According to Dworkin's theory of equality of resources, justice permits people to enjoy (or suffer) the consequences of option luck, but not of brute luck. Seen in this light, Dworkin might appear to be defending the neutralization approach. If we reflect upon the hypothetical insurance model, however, it becomes apparent that this model is better suited to a mitigation approach, for it would have to be judged inadequate from the perspective of the neutralization approach. If individuals who are subject to bad brute luck are compensated in a way that reflects the level of insurance they would have bought against the occurrence of that bad luck if they had had the opportunity to do so on equal terms, they may still be considerably worse off than they would have been had they not been subject to it. As Michael Otsuka points out, there is a range of cases where the cost of insurance which would fully compensate a person against the occurrence of an event would be prohibitively expensive. In cases such as these, it would be implausible to suppose that if that event does occur, compensating a person in a way that reflects the level of insurance they would have bought, neutralizes the effects of differences in his circumstances compared to those of others.[21]

The interpretation of the envy test which Dworkin employs to govern the effects of differences in natural endowment gives further reason to doubt that he is committed to the neutralization approach in this context. According to the original form of that test, two people are equal in terms of their impersonal resources when neither prefers the other's bundle. But Dworkin rejects the idea that we should extend this test to cover personal resources (such as natural endowments) by maintaining that two people are equal in terms of their total shares of personal and impersonal resources when neither prefers the other's bundle. Yet if we were to take seriously the idea

[21] See Otsuka, 'Luck, Insurance, and Equality', 44.

that we should neutralize the effects of differences in natural endowments, it is hard to see how this interpretation of the envy test could be resisted. So it seems to me that Dworkin's device of the hypothetical insurance market is best understood as a way of interpreting the principle that people should not be unduly disadvantaged relative to others by their level of natural endowment, for it does not provide a way of construing the envy test that is consistent with the aim of neutralizing the effects of differences in natural endowments. He is in effect providing us with a quasi-egalitarian principle for limiting these effects: they are just only if they are mitigated in the way that the hypothetical insurance model requires.

I do not intend to give a full evaluation of Dworkin's hypothetical insurance model. In my view it is an attractive device, but it has some problematic features, and it does not tell the whole story. Consider, for example, its treatment of disability. The model aims to compensate for disabilities by giving private resources to those who suffer from them. Yet it may be the case that sometimes what is needed to compensate adequately for a person's disability is the public provision of a social environment which is better adapted from the point of view of enabling him to lead a good life.[22] Building regulations that require new or existing spaces, especially in work environments, to be adapted to ensure that they can be accessed by those in wheelchairs or by those who are blind, are surely one important way in which justice requires us to mitigate the effects of disabilities. For justice requires us to counteract the effects of disabilities by combating the marginalization from which disabled people suffer when the social environment is constructed in such a way that it restricts their access to jobs and various other social activities.

IV. *The Mitigation Approach and the Meritocratic Conception*

The mitigation approach incorporates principles that govern access to qualifications and which determine what is to count as fair access. It can, therefore, provide us with one of the elements of a meritocratic conception of fair equality of opportunity. Does it also have

[22] See C. Macleod, *Liberalism, Justice, and Markets: A Critique of Liberal Equality* (Oxford: Oxford University Press, 1998), 106–9.

a role for the idea that selection procedures should be designed to identify the best-qualified applicants, which is the other element that is partially constitutive of a meritocratic conception? If so, it would in effect be permitting inequalities of access to the goods that are supplied by advantaged social positions (whether they are intrinsic or extrinsic to these positions) to arise in part from differences in natural ability.

I see no reason why the mitigation approach cannot defend the principle that the best-qualified candidates should be appointed to advantaged social positions by employing the argument which I developed in Chapter 2, which appeals to the idea of respect for persons. This principle would in effect circumscribe ways in which differences in social circumstances may unduly affect access to advantage (ruling out various forms of discrimination), and also specify a way in which differences in natural endowments may fairly influence access to advantage, at least when other principles are in place, such as those defended in the earlier sections of this chapter.

In one respect at least, the mitigation approach seems better able to incorporate a robust commitment to appointing the best-qualified candidates than does a pure version of the neutralization approach. In so far as the neutralization approach itself has a commitment to such a practice it will have to rest upon the argument that it is part of the best means of neutralizing the effects of differences in social circumstances. But to the extent that advantaged social positions carry with them rewards (whether these rewards are intrinsic or extrinsic to these positions) it would seem that appointing the best-qualified candidates to them would pull in the opposite direction to that required by the neutralization approach. Such a policy would involve rewarding people for their qualifications and to some degree at least these will be due to their fortunate level of natural endowment, whereas the neutralization approach requires us to prevent differences in these levels from influencing distributive shares.

In reply it might be pointed out that the neutralization approach can permit the inequalities of access to advantaged social positions which are created by a practice of selecting the best-qualified candidates so long as there is compensation for those who are less well-qualified as a result of their level of natural endowment. Of course, only if a person has access to advantaged social positions can she have available to her the rewards that are intrinsic to those positions.[23] But under the regime that the neutralization approach envisages, the extrinsic rewards that are contingently attached to these positions, such as the salaries they command, could be adjusted to neutralize the effects of distributing internal rewards to those who are better qualified in part because of their higher level of natural endowment. The question, however, is not whether the neutralization approach permits the selection of the best-qualified candidates, but whether in ordinary circumstances it requires it. It is hard to see why it does.

This problem with the neutralization approach is brought into sharp relief by considering what account it can offer of the wrongness of racial or sexual discrimination. The neutralization approach has trouble explaining what is wrong with discrimination, for, in principle at least, discounting black applicants or women applicants in the process of filling a particular set of prestigious advantaged social positions might be fully compensated by adjusting the overall distribution of benefits and burdens, through some system of redistributive taxation. But surely even if the effects of selecting in this way are neutralized, there is something objectionable about such a practice. We need some explanation of why this should be.

It might be argued that the neutralization approach will in practice condemn selecting on the basis of race or sex in this way. For if it is to be plausible, the neutralization approach must allow us to depart from practices if by doing so we can make some better off and no one worse off. When a Paretian proviso of this sort is incorporated, there will always be an objection to selecting on the basis of race or sex. Even if the effects of such a practice are neutralized through some redistributive scheme, it would be bound to lead to outcomes that were not Pareto optimal. Yet, this does not seem a satisfactory response. For a start, to be an effective answer to the problem, it would have to be assumed that Pareto optimal departures from a distribution that nevertheless neutralizes the effects of selecting on the basis of race or sex are not merely permissible but required by justice. Even that would seem insufficient to explain the injustice of selection practices of this sort, for surely their injustice does not

[23] Note, however, that these intrinsic rewards may be available only to those with specific natural abilities, so giving a person access to an advantaged social position will not mean she is automatically in a position to obtain these rewards.

rest upon the fact that they are not Pareto efficient. At root, our objection to them is that it is unjust in some other, more immediate way.

In my view, the problem that the neutralization approach faces in giving an adequate account of the injustice of selecting on the basis of race or sex is part of the more general difficulty it encounters in providing a satisfactory justification of the principle that we should (in general at least) appoint the best-qualified candidates. Even if by making various empirical assumptions we can derive such a principle from it, we would still seem unable to account for the significance of this principle. The point here is not that we have an unconditional commitment to such a principle which the neutralization approach, considered in isolation, cannot justify; the point is rather that this principle has a status and significance for which this approach cannot account. If the neutralization approach is all that we have available to us, the defence of the principle that the best-qualified candidates should be appointed has to rest squarely on the fact that everyone gains from its being implemented (or at least that some gain and no one loses). Yet this principle seems more deeply rooted in our thought about justice and injustice than this. Of course, this is not a conclusive argument against attempting to justify the principle from within the neutralization approach. It may be that the widely held intuitions upon which I am drawing simply reflect the misconception that a practice of appointing the best-qualified candidates can be given an independent moral justification. If this were so, we would have to accept that the nature of our commitment to the idea that selection procedures should be designed to identify the best-qualified candidate was suspect. But we should not draw this conclusion if there is an alternative way of grounding the principle that the best-qualified candidate should be appointed. I have argued that there is a way of doing so that draws upon the idea of respect for persons and I have suggested that this argument can be readily incorporated into the mitigation approach. I do not deny that it could be combined with the neutralization approach as well, but in that case it would have the role of an independent commitment.[24] We have a reason to favour the mitigation approach over any 'pure' version of the neutralization approach.

[24] See my 'Equality of Opportunity, Old and New' 774–5.

V. *Conclusion*

The version of the mitigation approach I have defended is undoubtedly messy. It does not provide any single fundamental principle governing access to advantage (in the way that the neutralization approach does) that could be employed to determine which principles should govern specific contexts and which would enable us to resolve conflicts between these more specific principles. This is not to say that it must regard different goods as incommensurable, or that it must deny the possibility of some overall measure of advantage, or that it must maintain that there is no rational way of resolving conflicts between different fundamental principles when they arise. My claim is merely that there is no single fundamental principle that determines or provides guidance on what justice requires in relation to the distribution of access to overall advantage. The version of the mitigation approach that I have defended maintains that a range of principles, some highly abstract, others more specific, work together to limit the effects of differences in people's circumstances on their access to advantage, and that determine what it would mean for these differences to have an undue effect on that access.

Is the theoretical messiness of the mitigation approach a reason to reject it? I think not. Although at the level of fundamental principle, the neutralization approach is very tidy, it will also be messy when it comes to determining what principles should govern different goods or different aspects of people's circumstances and how conflicts between them are to be adjudicated. For in this context it will need to make empirical claims, and the guidance it gives is bound to leave considerable scope for reasonable disagreement and a correspondingly large role for judgement.

It would also be a mistake to think that the version of the mitigation approach I am defending must suppose that we can fully assess each of the various fundamental principles it endorses individually and singly, with no account being taken of the others, and without considering the specific principles that are grounded in them. Rather, in order to assess them we need to look at the kind of distribution of advantage that these principles, both fundamental and derived, would justify when combined together and ask whether it is too great. In order to answer this question, we have no further principle to appeal to; we have to fall back on the exercise of judgement. If we judge that the overall inequalities of access to advantage are too great, then we will need to adjust one or more of the specific principles to reduce it.

In this chapter, I have explored how the best version of the mitigation approach would deal with the effects of differences in people's circumstances. But the mitigation approach is a form of responsibility-sensitive egalitarianism, so it must also take a view of what justice requires in relation to differences in choice, and indeed operates with a presumption that it is just to require individuals to bear the costs of their behaviour. It can thereby provide an answer to the charge that egalitarianism fails to respect the autonomy of individuals by ignoring, or giving insufficient weight to, the way in which an individual's choices affect how well his or her life goes. But should it hold that it is *always* just to require people to bear the costs of their choices? This is the issue addressed in the next chapter.

CHAPTER 7

A Responsible Egalitarianism

All forms of responsibility-sensitive egalitarianism, including both the neutralization approach and the mitigation approach, make some normatively relevant distinction between choice and circumstance.[1] They argue that justice requires us to counteract the effects of differences in people's circumstances, but at the same time they give a central role to the idea of personal responsibility, insisting that individuals should be held appropriately accountable for the choices they make. In effect they maintain that inequalities may emerge as a result of different choices in a way that is consistent with levelling the playing field as justice demands. In earlier chapters I have focused on differences in people's circumstances, exploring in what way justice requires us to counteract the effects of those differences. This chapter, in contrast, is primarily concerned with people's choices, in particular the issue of when it would be just to require a person to bear the costs of his choices.

I use the term 'costs' broadly, to capture any consequence of a person's actions which counts as a burden for others (or for him) because it adversely affects their (or his) access to advantage, by making that access worse in at least one respect than it would otherwise have been. So, in principle at least, the costs of a person's behaviour may include the damage he causes to another's reputation, either by speaking the truth or by libelling him, the physical injuries caused to himself or to others by his negligent actions, as well as the scarce resources that are consumed in pursuit of his goals. I do not assume

[1] I use the expression 'responsibility-sensitive egalitarianism' to cover responsibility sensitive forms of both the priority and sufficiency view, as well as egalitarianism strictly conceived.

that all costs are fully commensurable, nor that full compensation is always possible for a cost imposed on others: it may be, for example, that we cannot compare the damage to a person's reputation with a physical injury in a way that would enable us to determine what, if anything, would constitute adequate compensation for each. This raises difficult practical issues for answers to the question of when it is fair to require a person to bear the costs of his behaviour, since even if we reach the conclusion that in principle the agent should bear those costs, in practice that may be impossible.

The category of choice is also a broad one. In Chapter 4, I stipulated that a person's choices are that part of his condition which lies within the space of his rational agency, that is, any aspect of his condition, including his beliefs and many of his desires, which it is intelligible to ask him to justify or evaluate in terms of his reasons (whereas a person's circumstances are that part of his condition that lies outside of this space). According to this way of drawing the distinction, 'choice' covers a wide range of phenomena. An outcome falls within this category if it is one that an agent exerted some influence over, no matter how small. So it covers an outcome where the agent gambled successfully despite knowing that he had a very low probability of securing it, as well as an outcome which the agent brought about knowing in advance that he had a very high probability of success. It also includes an outcome which the agent could have prevented only at a great cost to himself as well as one he could have prevented at a very little cost to himself. In addressing the issue of when it is fair to require people to bear the costs of their choices, any defensible form of responsibility-sensitive egalitarianism must acknowledge the moral relevance of differences in the context of choice and differences in the risks involved in making choices.

It is often clear where justice requires or allows the costs of choices to fall. A person is entitled to refuse to accept a marriage proposal and impose the full costs of this rejection on his or her suitor. Likewise, under ordinary circumstances a person is entitled to turn down another's request to help mend his car, or to lend him a book that he wants to borrow, without being required to bear any of the direct costs involved in doing so. At the other end of the spectrum, a person might make choices which violate the rights or entitlements of others (for example, when he commits an assault or breaks a contract), creating costs that it is clear he is not entitled simply to externalize. In between these two sets of cases, which I put to one side, there are occasions when a person acts in a way that is morally permissible, that is, involves no wrong doing, but which nevertheless creates costs, and where it is not clear how these costs should be distributed. For example, people may permissibly make decisions about what way of life or conception of the good to pursue. These choices have costs, if only because they have resource implications. It would be unjust to expect others to bear these costs in full, yet at the same time it is not obvious that it would always be just to require the agent to do so. So how does justice require these costs to be apportioned?

In addressing this issue, we should bear in mind that the outcome of one person's choices, or indeed the outcome (intended or not) of a plurality of other people's choices, may constitute part of another person's circumstances. In the context of a market economy this is significant, for part of a person's circumstances will be constituted by the preferences of others and the effect these have on the cost of the resources that he needs to satisfy his own preferences. For the costs of satisfying his preferences will be affected by the supply of, and demand for, the resources that he needs to do so, which in turn will be determined in part by the number of others who share these preferences. This unavoidably raises the question of whether it is fair to require a person to bear the full costs of his choices when these costs are due, wholly or in part, to his circumstances, even if (as I claim) everyone, in the relevant respects, faces the same circumstances. Some will argue that if the agent formed a conception of the good knowing that it would be expensive to pursue, then it is fair to require him to bear those costs. Indeed, defenders of this view will point out that the alternative would be to require other people to subsidize his pursuit of that conception of the good. Other theorists will maintain that when a person's preferences are the product of his conception of the good, that is, some relatively worked out vision of what is valuable or important which he cannot simply opt to abandon, the preferences of others should not be allowed to determine how costly it will be to him to pursue that conception of the good.[2]

[2] This issue is part of what divides Ronald Dworkin and G. A. Cohen in a recent exchange: see G. A. Cohen, 'Expensive Taste Rides Again', in J. Burley (ed.), *Dworkin and his Critics* (Oxford: Blackwell, 2004). R. Dworkin, 'Replies to Critics', in J. Burley (ed.), *Dworkin and his Critics* (Oxford: Blackwell, 2004), 339–50.

This chapter considers various ways in which the issue of when it is just to require a person to bear the costs (full or partial) of his choices can be addressed, focusing to begin with on two different conceptions, which I call the control conception and the responsiveness to reason conception. Each conception takes into account the way in which the cost of a person's choices may be deeply affected by the choices of others, and the way in which choices may be more or less constrained, allowing agents different degrees and kinds of influence over outcomes. Although in the end I reject both, I adopt elements of the responsiveness to reason conception, including its account of the conditions under which moral appraisal is intelligible.

The framework I develop is intended to supplement the mitigation approach I defended in the previous chapter. The issue of when it is fair to hold people responsible for their choices by requiring them to bear the costs of these choices cannot be treated as entirely independent of whether the effects of differences in people's circumstances have been counteracted in the way that justice demands: it would be unfair, for example, to require a person to bear the costs of his choices if his options, unlike those of others, have been severely curtailed as a result of differences in their circumstances. In reflecting upon the issue of when it is fair to require people to bear the costs of their behaviour, I simply assume that the effects of differences in people's circumstances have been mitigated in accordance with the kind of principles I defended in Chapter 6. This means that my reflections do not have straightforward application to real world practices where these differences have been allowed an unconstrained impact.

The account I provide is also removed from these practices in another way: I do not consider the costs of *implementing* an account which holds people responsible for their choices when it is fair to do so. These costs may go beyond the funding of a bureaucracy tasked with collecting the information required, for it may be that implementing my account would require intrusive surveillance of people's lives or state officials to show disrespect to citizens.[3] If so, these costs, which register on the scale of injustice, will need to be

[3] For relevant discussion, see E. Anderson, 'What is the Point of Equality?', *Ethics* 109 (1999), 287–337; J. Wolff, 'Fairness, Respect, and the Egalitarian Ethos', *Philosophy and Public Affairs* 27 (1998), 97–122.

weighed against any unfairness that would be involved in requiring some to subsidize the choices of others.

I. *Control, Moral Responsibility, and Responsiveness to Reason*

Let me distinguish two views of when it is fair to require a person to bear the costs of his behaviour which presuppose different accounts of moral responsibility, that is, different accounts of the conditions under which moral appraisal (such as that involved in praising or blaming) is appropriate.[4] Although these conceptions diverge in terms of their accounts of moral responsibility, they each hold that it is fair to require a person to bear the full costs of his behaviour only if he is morally responsible for it, and both deny that moral responsibility on its own is sufficient to justify doing so. The two conceptions often reach the same conclusions concerning when it is fair to require a person to bear the costs of his behaviour, but their different accounts of moral responsibility sometimes lead to divergent judgements on this matter. Although it would be a mistake to read too much into the labels, I call these conceptions 'the control conception' and the 'responsiveness to reason conception'.[5]

The control conception holds that it is fair to require a person to bear the costs of his behaviour or his preferences, tastes or desires, only if it is appropriate to subject them to moral appraisal. This conception then maintains that moral appraisal of a person's behaviour is appropriate only if he could have acted otherwise, whilst moral appraisal of a person's tastes, desires, preferences, or feelings is appropriate only if he cultivated them or is now able to influence them. Being able to act otherwise requires the ability to identify

[4] In Scanlon's terms I am using 'moral responsibility' in the sense of responsibility as attributability. The question which motivates the current chapter, viz., 'when is it fair to require a person to bear the costs of their behaviour?', addresses what Scanlon calls 'substantive responsibility', see Scanlon, *What We Owe to Each Other*, 248. As Scanlon points out, moral appraisal of a person's behaviour may be appropriate even when there is reason not to *express* that appraisal (e.g. because of the effects this would have on the agent).

[5] The labels I am using—'control' and 'responsiveness to reason'—can be misleading. The responsiveness to reason conception does not deny the importance of control for the issue of when it is fair to require a person to bear the costs of his choices, and the control conception does not deny the importance of responsiveness to reason for that issue. Nor is the name of the control conception meant to suggest that it is a purely causal account: see over on pp. 163–4.

alternative courses of action and decide amongst them, as well as the presence of at least one other possible course of action (which might simply be the option of refusing to act). Even if a person did not cultivate a desire or taste, he may be able to change it, or be able to take steps to change it; in so far as he can, the control conception maintains that his failure to change it, or his reluctance to take the steps necessary to do so, may appropriately be subject to moral appraisal.

Bracketing those cases where an agent is entitled to impose the full costs of his behaviour on others, the control conception then maintains that whether it is fair to require an agent to bear some or all of the costs of his behaviour or its consequences, or of some aspect of his own condition including his preferences, depends on the presence or absence of a number of potential excusing conditions.[6] First, the agent may be deprived of the knowledge or understanding required to judge well. He may be subject to manipulation, or simply not be in full possession of the facts, through no fault of his own. Second, the agent may be subject to coercion or natural forces that leave him with no reasonable alternative (for example, he may be unable to fulfil some agreement because he is stuck in an unexpected traffic jam), or he may have been subject to social forces which mean that he did not have an adequate opportunity to behave otherwise, even though he wishes he had had other options (for example, peer pressure as an adolescent may have been such that it would have been extremely costly for him to refrain from smoking cigarettes when he was growing up). Third, the agent may have done all that could reasonably be expected of him to ensure that harm did not befall others as a result of his behaviour, but that harm still occurs. For example, before putting out to sea, a ship's captain may ensure that all necessary checks have been made on his vessel's seaworthiness, but these checks may be incapable of identifying a serious problem with it, as a result of which it sinks.

The control conception is not simply a causal account of when it is fair to require a person to bear the costs of his behaviour, for it

[6] G. A. Cohen's position as expressed in 'On the Currency of Egalitarian Justice', *Ethics* 99 (1989), 906–44, may be an example of the control conception (though there is room for doubt here, see note 23 below). However, his position has been revised and refined in various ways which mean that it can no longer be understood in these terms, see his 'Expensive Taste Rides Again'.

invokes normative considerations.[7] For example, it maintains that in determining whether an agent should bear the costs of his behaviour, we need to assess whether he has done all that could reasonably be expected of him. If a person is the occupant of a social role with special duties attached to it, then what counts as 'all that could reasonably be expected of him', as opposed to, say, negligence or excessive vigilance, will be determined in part by those duties; in other cases it may be determined by general duties of care that we owe to others.

The second conception of when it is fair to require people to bear the costs of their behaviour, or of their tastes, preferences and desires, which I call the responsiveness to reason conception, is influenced by the work of T. M. Scanlon and others on responsibility, and by Ronald Dworkin's account of egalitarian justice.[8] Like the control conception, the responsiveness to reason conception maintains that it is fair to require a person to bear the costs of her behaviour, or her preferences and desires, only when it is appropriate to subject these to moral appraisal. It then holds that this is appropriate only to the extent that she is self-governing, where '[a] person governs herself in the sense required if she is sensitive to the force of reasons and to the distinctions and relations between them and if her response to these reasons generally determines her subsequent attitudes and actions'.[9] In contrast to the control conception, the responsiveness to reason conception does not suppose that the agent's inability to bring about a different outcome, or change his preferences, necessarily makes

[7] For reasons that Arthur Ripstein gives, no purely causal conception could provide us with an adequate answer to the question of when it is fair to require a person to bear the costs of his behaviour, see A. Ripstein, 'Equality, Luck, and Responsibility', *Philosophy and Public Affairs* 23 (1994), 6–10; A. Ripstein, *Equality, Responsibility, and the Law* (Cambridge: Cambridge University Press, 1999), esp. 291–4.

[8] When I say it is influenced by these writers, I do not mean to imply that it would be accepted by them. In Scanlon's case especially, it is not clear whether he would endorse the responsiveness to reason conception or prefer what I later call the pluralist conception, see M. Matravers, 'Responsibility and Choice', in M. Matravers (ed.), *Scanlon and Contractualism* (London: Frank Cass, 2003), 86, for relevant comment. It would also be mistaken to suppose that the control conception incorporates what Scanlon calls 'The Forfeiture View' of substantive responsibility, see Scanlon, *What We Owe to Each Other*, ch. 6, Ss 2–3.

[9] Scanlon, *What We Owe To Each Other*, 281.

it inappropriate to subject his behaviour or preferences to moral appraisal.

The responsiveness to reason conception acknowledges a number of different respects in which a person may fail to be self-governing in the way that is necessary for moral appraisal of his behaviour to be appropriate (and hence necessary for it to be fair to require him to bear its costs). The link between the agent's behaviour and his judgement may be severed so that his behaviour is no longer responsive in the right way to his reason or rational capacities, and his behaviour cannot be regarded as the product of his own judgement or reasoning.[10] Scanlon's examples are when a person's behaviour is the result of stimulating his brain with electrodes, or occurs whilst sleepwalking, or is the product of post-hypnotic suggestion, or induced by drugs or by sudden episodes of mental illness.[11] As Scanlon argues, in these cases moral appraisal of the agent's behaviour, such as that involved in praising or blaming him for what he did, would be inappropriate. (In a real sense, there was nothing that *he* did. His bodily movements lie outside 'the space of his rational agency', making them part of his circumstances according to the way in which I have drawn the distinction between choice and circumstance.)

A person may also lack full self-government in relation to his desires (or tastes or preferences). For he may be the victim of desires that he would rather not have (which may be due to his physical make-up, or the social environment he happens or happened to inhabit), which are not responsive to his reason in the sense that, despite regretting that he has them, he is unable to bring about a change in them. The responsiveness to reason conception maintains that it is not appropriate to praise or blame the agent for having these desires, and hence allows that any burdens that may be imposed on the agent by them are such that it would be unfair to require him to bear the full costs. (Even though it would be inappropriate to praise

[10] This idea that a person's behaviour must be responsive to their reason in the right way needs much more development. The literature on moral responsibility offers a number of possible ways of unpacking what it is for that to be the case which I do not consider here. See, for example, J. M. Fischer, *The Metaphysics of Freewill: An Essay on Control* (Oxford: Blackwell, 1994); J. M. Fischer and M. Ravizza, *Responsibility and Control: A Theory of Moral Responsibility* (Cambridge: Cambridge University Press, 1998); Hurley, *Justice, Luck, and Knowledge*, esp. 32–61.

[11] Scanlon, *What We Owe To Each Other*, 277–8.

or blame the agent for having these desires, they nevertheless lie on the choice side of the choice/circumstance distinction provided that it is intelligible to ask him to evaluate them in terms of his reasons.)

A person may also lack the general capacities required for moral agency, including not just the ability to use his reason to affect his desires, preferences, and actions, but also the ability to understand and assess his reasons.[12] For example, someone whose mental capacities are severely impaired may be unable to understand the risks involved in jumping from a bridge into shallow water. In cases of this kind, the responsiveness to reason conception maintains that moral appraisal is inappropriate. There are other cases, however, where the agent possesses the relevant capacities to some degree but not fully, or where he possesses the relevant capacities in general but not in relation to some particular class of reasons, for example, a person who has been subject to religious indoctrination might be unable to subject the reasons that bear upon his religious faith to critical scrutiny in any full-blooded way.[13] Here the responsiveness to reason conception might judge that when a person's behaviour reflects this inability, praising or blaming him for that behaviour is appropriate in principle but that it would be unfair to require him to bear all of its costs, or indeed anything more than an equal share of these costs.

The responsiveness to reason conception holds that when the conditions for moral appraisal are satisfied, unless the agent is entitled to impose the full costs of his behaviour on others, there is a presumption that it is fair to require him to bear them (and indeed to bear the

[12] See Scanlon, *What We Owe To Each Other*, 280.

[13] The extension of this idea to various cases can be tricky, however. Is the psychopath morally responsible for his behaviour in the relevant sense? Suppose, for the sake of argument, that the psychopath is unable to understand the force of moral reasons. Then it is tempting to conclude that he cannot be morally responsible for his behaviour because he is not self-governing in the required way. This does not seem to be Scanlon's conclusion, however. In discussing a related example, he says: 'Consider ... a hardened criminal who commits terrible crimes. The fact that ... he is someone who is unable to see the force of morally relevant reasons does not seem ... to block moral criticism. If he commits these crimes because he does not place any value on other people's lives or interests, what clearer grounds could one have for saying that he is a bad person and behaves wrongly' (Scanlon, *What We Owe to Each Other*, 284). As Matt Matravers points out, however, if the psychopath is unable to see the force of moral reasons, it is hard to understand how he can be self-governing in the way required for him to be morally responsible for his behaviour: see Matravers, 'Responsibility and Choice', 84–5.

costs of any aspect of his condition, such as some of his preferences, that are burdensome to him). But it acknowledges a number of ways in which that presumption may be defeated to justify sharing the costs. For the responsiveness to reason conception, like the control conception, maintains that the context in which the agent acts may be such as to excuse him from bearing the full costs of his behaviour, and the kinds of excusing conditions that it acknowledges are much the same as those recognized by the control conception. Where one or more of these excusing conditions applies, the connection between the agent's behaviour and his judgement or reasoning nevertheless remains intact, and moral appraisal of his behaviour is in place. Consider, for example, a case in which a shop assistant is forced to hand over the day's takings under threat. As Scanlon emphasizes, the assistant is still in a straightforward sense morally responsible for what he did.[14] Indeed, we might even praise the shop assistant for his coolness and for the way in which he did not unnecessarily endanger the lives of his customers.

The distinction between the control conception and the responsiveness to reason conception is largely metaphysical in character, though this metaphysical difference has normative consequences. These conceptions agree that it is fair to require a person to bear the costs of his behaviour only when he is morally responsible for it, that is, only when the conditions for moral appraisal to be appropriate are satisfied, but they diverge in their accounts of these conditions. The difference between the two conceptions can be illuminated by a distinction between actual sequence and alternate sequence requirements of moral responsibility, which identifies two different kinds of accounts of the conditions that need to be met before moral appraisal is appropriate. An account of moral responsibility which requires the simple ability to act (or desire) otherwise imposes an alternate sequence requirement, for it requires 'the outright possibility of an alternate sequence of events',[15] whereas an account of moral responsibility which merely requires that the way in which the agent acts (or desires) be responsive to reasons imposes an actual sequence requirement since it places a constraint on the way events must unfold for the agent to be morally responsible. We might say

[14] Scanlon, *What We Owe to Each Other*, 279.
[15] Hurley, *Justice, Luck, and Knowledge*, 17.

that the control conception imposes an alternate sequence requirement, for it holds that moral appraisal is out of place when a person could not have acted otherwise or had different preferences, whereas the responsiveness to reason conception imposes an actual sequence requirement, for it allows that moral appraisal may be appropriate when his behaviour or preferences are properly responsive to his reasons even if he could not have acted otherwise or had different preferences.

Following Scanlon, defenders of the responsiveness to reason conception would argue that the truth or otherwise of determinism is irrelevant to whether people can legitimately be required to bear the costs of their behaviour or aspects of their condition.[16] Instead what matters is whether a person's actions or condition are responsive to his reasoning in the right way, so that his behaviour or desires can properly be regarded as the product of his own judgement. When external events act 'through a person' in a way that does not threaten the connection between his judgement and his preferences or behaviour, they need not affect the fairness of requiring him to bear the costs of his behaviour or his preferences; but when external events act 'on a person' in a way that does threaten or undermine that connection, then the fairness of doing so is brought into question.

Any adequate approach to the issue of when it is fair to require a person to bear the costs of his choices must confront the complexities involved in the formation of people's characters, desires, preferences, and beliefs, especially the undeniably profound effect of social forces that constitute part of their circumstances. In doing so it should not treat people's choices, let alone the costs of those choices, as if they were wholly independent of their circumstances; it must give due weight to 'the facts of socialization', for example, the gender identities and the cultural identities that people acquire as a result of growing up in a particular social context. The responsiveness to reason conception and versions of the control conception converge in many respects in their approach to the effects of socialization. If an agent's socialization means that he lacks the knowledge and understanding necessary to identify different courses of action and assess their risks, the responsiveness to reason conception, like the control conception, would accept that this gives us reason to judge it

[16] Scanlon, *What We Owe To Each Other*, 250.

unfair to require him to bear the full costs of his behaviour because a relevant excusing condition is present. But the control conception and the responsiveness to reason conception diverge in important respects. The responsiveness to reason conception holds that provided the causal influences to which a person is subject are not such that they undermine the general capacities he needs to be an agent (including the responsiveness of his behaviour to his reasoning), or such that they result in a discrepancy between his judgement and the desires, preferences or tastes to which he is subject (such that he regrets those desires, preferences, and tastes but this makes no difference to the hold they have over him), no further question about whether he had the personal capacity to choose otherwise or to have different tastes is relevant to the issue of whether he can legitimately be required to bear the costs of his behaviour or these aspects of his condition.

This divergence between the control conception and the responsiveness to reason conception is sometimes significant. Consider cases of expensive tastes that are familiar from the literature on egalitarian justice. A person grows up within a family in which he learns to love fine food and wine. Unlike others with modest tastes, he finds eating bland food deeply unsatisfying, and his palate rebels against anything other than the best wines. Can it be fair to require such a person (call him the gourmand) to bear the costs of having his expensive tastes?

In answering this question, the control conception will focus on whether the gourmand has cultivated these tastes and whether he could change them given their expensiveness. If these tastes were not deliberately cultivated and he could not change them, then the control conception will maintain that it is unfair to require him to bear the costs of having them, whereas if they were deliberately cultivated, or he could change them, then this conception will maintain that it is fair to require him to bear those costs. The responsiveness to reason conception will focus instead on whether the gourmand's preferences and behaviour are subject to his reason in the appropriate way and whether any excusing conditions are present. If, for example, he is able to subject his preferences and behaviour to critical scrutiny, he accepts or reflectively endorses these preferences, and he has not been indoctrinated or manipulated, then it would seem that, according to this conception, the issue of whether they are under his control in any further or deeper sense is irrelevant.[17] If these conditions are met and the gourmand accepts or reflectively endorses his tastes, for example, values his powers of culinary discrimination and his inability to tolerate bland food or inferior wines, then it would seem that the responsiveness to reason conception must regard it as fair to require him to bear the costs of having those tastes, even if he could not abandon them and made no choice to develop them, and even though the expensiveness of his tastes is due to factors beyond his control, such as the costs of producing the food he enjoys or the culinary preferences of others.

So the control conception and the responsiveness to reason conception are likely to judge cases of expensive tastes the same when these tastes are accepted or reflectively endorsed and under the agent's control, but judge them differently when the tastes are accepted or reflectively endorsed but outside the agent's control. What about cases where the agent does not accept or endorse his tastes and has no control over them? Suppose that the gourmand regrets the having of his expensive tastes (rather than, say, regrets the fact that they are expensive). If his behaviour is compulsive—he cannot help acting upon his 'tastes'—then both the control conception and the responsiveness to reason conception will converge in holding that it would be unfair to require him to bear its costs. If he cannot change his tastes, but *can* refrain from acting on them, then the responsiveness to reason conception, like the control conception, may hold that he should still not be required to bear the full costs of being burdened by these cravings. So in cases where the agent positively dislikes having his expensive tastes (rather than merely the fact that they are expensive) and these are beyond his control, the control conception and the responsiveness to reason conception are likely to reach the same normative conclusions.

II. *The Control Conception Versus the Responsiveness to Reason Conception*

Which conception of when it is fair to require people to bear the costs of their choices should we adopt? Are there any general reasons

[17] A person accepts a preference or taste if they do not mind having it, whilst they reflectively endorse a preference or taste if they judge it to be valuable.

for favouring the control conception over the responsiveness to reason conception, or vice versa? In order to address these questions, we need to examine the different accounts of moral responsibility that lie at the heart of the two conceptions and explore the problems that they encounter.

Employing the control conception unavoidably requires us to make a judgement about whether the agent could have acted otherwise, and whether he had the personal capacity to cultivate different tastes, for the control conception maintains that only then is moral appraisal in place, and that it is unfair to require him to bear the costs of his behaviour or his tastes when he lacks this ability or personal capacity. This might be regarded as a disadvantage. If what Scanlon refers to as the Causal Thesis is right, that all our actions have antecedent causes to which they are linked by causal laws of the kind that govern other events in the universe, then this immediately raises the question of whether anyone could have acted other than they did or could have had different preferences. If no one could have acted otherwise, or have had different preferences, then the control conception is forced to the conclusion that it is never fair to require a person to bear the costs of his behaviour or his preferences. (I do not deny, however, that defenders of the control conception can live with this implication; they may argue that it does not diminish the appeal of that conception at the most fundamental theoretical level.)

The responsiveness to reason conception, in contrast, does not require that the agent always possess the ability to act otherwise or to have different preferences in order for moral appraisal to be in place, and for it to be fair to require him to bear the costs of his behaviour or his preferences (although, of course, lack of a reasonable alternative or of an adequate opportunity to behave otherwise often serves as an excusing condition). This is not to say that this approach can sidestep all the various philosophical difficulties that arise in relation to the existence of freewill and moral responsibility. Like the control conception, it offers an account of moral responsibility, that is, an account of the conditions under which moral appraisal is appropriate, and it will be vulnerable to any argument which can show that these conditions are impossible to satisfy. The most obvious difficulty here concerns whether the responsiveness to reason conception can meet what Susan Hurley calls 'the regression requirement', which maintains that 'to be responsible for *X* you must also be responsible for its causes'.[18] But Hurley considers various ways in which that requirement might be met, any of which might be adopted by the responsiveness to reason conception.[19]

The most common strategy in arguing for the account of moral responsibility presupposed by the responsiveness to reason conception is to maintain that our ordinary practices of excusing, and of praising and blaming, can be fully understood without supposing that a person's behaviour is open to moral appraisal only if he possesses the personal capacity to act otherwise. In cases where we blame a person (or hold that it is fair to require him to bear the costs of his behaviour or preferences), we do so because we think his behaviour and preferences are appropriately connected to his reason and no excusing conditions apply. This strategy need not be uncritical of our ordinary practices—it allows that they may rest upon some misconceptions—though it does assume that they are not wholly misguided.[20] It seems to me to be largely successful, and the resources for it are to be found in a number of different writings on moral responsibility.[21] Since it would involve a large detour, I do not propose to defend it in any depth against critics, though I give some indication of how it might be developed.

In order for the strategy to be persuasive, we need clear examples where we think it is appropriate to appraise a person's behaviour because it is properly connected to his judgement and responsive to his reason, even though he did not have the personal capacity to act otherwise. Harry Frankfurt has presented a number of cases which

[18] Hurley, *Justice, Luck, and Knowledge*, 20. See G. Strawson, 'The Impossibility of Moral Responsibility', *Philosophical Studies*, 75 (1994), 5–24, for an argument that moral responsibility is impossible since this requirement cannot be met.

[19] See Hurley, *Justice, Luck, and Knowledge*, esp. 24–8, 46–53.

[20] So this strategy does not make the mistake that Matt Matravers identifies, of giving undue weight to the convictions of ordinary people (see M. Matravers, 'Responsibility, Luck, and the "Equality of What?" Debate', *Political Studies* 60 (2002), 563). Rather, the aim is 'to appeal to the best sense we can make of our ethical practices in general, and our practices of holding responsible, and of excusing responsibility, in particular' (Matravers, 'Luck, Responsibility, and "The Jumble of Lotteries that Constitutes Human Life"', 40).

[21] See, for example, Fischer and Ravizza, *Responsibility and Control: A Theory of Moral Responsibility*; J. R. Wallace, *Responsibility and the Moral Sentiments* (Cambridge, MA: Harvard University Press, 1994); T. M. Scanlon, 'The Significance of Choice', in S. Darwall (ed.), *Equal Freedom: Selected Tanner Lectures on Human Values* (Ann Arbor, MI: University of Michigan Press, 1995).

appear to be of the right kind, and these have been developed by others, including John Fischer. In one of Fischer's examples, Jones is in a voting booth deliberating about whether to vote for Gore or Bush and after serious reflection opts for Gore and marks his ballot in the appropriate way. Unknown to him, a neurosurgeon has implanted a device in Jones's brain which monitors his brain activity. If he chooses to vote Democrat, the device remains dormant, but if he chooses to vote Republican it produces an electronic stimulation sufficient to produce a vote for Gore, the Democrat. Fisher maintains that since the device plays no role in Jones's deliberations and act of voting, he is morally responsible for voting for Gore even though, given the device, he did not possess the personal capacity to act otherwise (even though he believed he did).[22]

Cases of this sort seem to me to be persuasive.[23] Discussion of them has been extensive, however, and I do not intend to survey the various arguments and counter-arguments that have been brought into play. Instead of considering in more depth the different conceptions of moral responsibility that are presupposed by the control conception and the responsiveness to reason conception, let me consider a different argument which purports to show that responsibility-sensitive egalitarianism is committed to the account of moral responsibility which the control conception involves, and hence that defenders of this form of egalitarianism must prefer the control conception to the responsiveness to reason conception.

[22] See J. Fischer, 'Recent Work on Moral Responsibility', *Ethics* 110 (1999), 109–10.

[23] These sorts of cases are crucial in determining whether a person subscribes to the control conception or the responsiveness to reason conception. Whether G. A. Cohen's position in 'On the Currency of Egalitarian Justice' is best seen as expressing the control conception depends, in part, on how we should understand his claim that it would be unfair to require those who could not help forming their expensive tastes, and could not now get rid of them, to bear the costs of those tastes (see ibid., 923). What would Cohen (*c.* 1989) say of a case where the agent has a non-voluntarily acquired expensive taste for plovers' eggs, and makes no attempt to rid himself of it even when offered appropriate therapy (see ibid., 927), *but* if he had tried, then he would have found that he was unable to do so, perhaps even because an electronic component had been inserted in his brain that would prevent him from succeeding? If Cohen says that the agent should not be required to bear the costs of that taste because it is not properly under his control, then he is aligning himself with the control conception, whereas if he maintains that the agent's taste is appropriately responsive to his reason, and that the agent should therefore bear its costs, he is aligning himself with the responsiveness to reason conception.

This argument maintains that if we think justice demands that we counteract the effects of differences in people's circumstances, and therefore not require people to bear the full costs of differences in their circumstances, our reason must be that their circumstances are beyond their control. If this is our reason, then surely consistency requires us to maintain that it would be unjust to require a person to bear the full costs of his behaviour when he lacks control over it because he could not have behaved otherwise, but this is at odds with the responsiveness to reason conception.

This argument is flawed, however. Responsibility-sensitive egalitarianism does maintain that justice requires us to counteract the effects of differences in people's circumstances, but a person's circumstances are constituted by what lies outside the sphere of his rational agency, that is, what is beyond his control *and* does not lie within the space of his reasons. Responsibility-sensitive egalitarianism can maintain that it would be unjust to require a person to bear the full costs of his relatively disadvantaged circumstances precisely because they meet both of these conditions, that is, they are beyond his control and outside the space of his reasons. When a person's preferences lie within the space of his reasons, that is, when they are such that it is intelligible to ask him to justify them or evaluate them on the basis of his reasons, responsibility-sensitive egalitarianism can consistently hold that it may be just to require him to bear the full costs of these preferences even when he cannot influence them. This is what a defender of the responsiveness to reason conception would contend—with the support, he would claim, of our ordinary moral practices of praising, blaming, and excusing.

I have not attempted to demonstrate the superiority of the responsiveness to reason conception over the control conception, but I hope I have provided some basis for favouring it, partly by drawing upon an extensive literature, which, although it has not gone unchallenged, makes a case for the superiority of the view of moral responsibility that lies at its heart. In the next two sections I propose to examine the responsiveness to reason conception in more depth, by exploring its implications for a number of difficult cases where an agent's fundamental commitments or some aspect of their identity (cultural or gender) is at stake, which in my view raise difficulties for it.

III. *Moral Commitments, Cultural Identity*

Consider a deeply committed pacifist who lives in a region where most of the available employment is in the weapons industry. Although he is qualified for the jobs that are available, he believes he should not take them because of his moral commitments. Is it legitimate to require him to bear the costs of his refusal? For example, would it be legitimate to disallow him from receiving unemployment benefit? It might seem that defenders of the responsiveness to reason conception must argue that provided he is self-governing in the relevant way, and no excusing conditions apply, it is fair to require him to bear the full costs of his refusal. He is self-governing in this way, provided that his commitments are appropriately responsive to his reason, which requires that he be able to understand and assess the different considerations that bear upon them. He must not, for example, have been the victim of any indoctrination which has rendered him unable to explore the consistency of these commitments with other beliefs, or which has meant that he is blinded to evidence that would undermine them. If the pacifist is able to subject his beliefs to critical scrutiny in this way, then it might seem that the responsiveness to reason approach implies that he can legitimately be required to bear the costs of behaviour which flow from them (unless some excusing condition applies, for example, he has been deprived of information relevant to assessing these beliefs), and this may appear unduly harsh.

The choice facing the pacifist is relevantly similar to a range of cases that arise in discussions of the political significance of cultural diversity.[24] Suppose that a significant proportion of the jobs in some region are in the construction industry, and require workers to wear hard hats for safety reasons. Sikhs are unwilling to take these jobs because this would require them to refrain from wearing their turbans at work, thereby violating what they regard as one of their religious commitments. As a result, it is more difficult for Sikhs to find employment, and a high proportion of them in this region become unemployed. This raises the question of whether it would be legitimate to hold them responsible for their refusal to

[24] For relevant discussion of these cases, see S. Mendus, 'Choice, Chance and Multiculturalism', in P. Kelly (ed.), *Multiculturalism Reconsidered* (Cambridge: Polity, 2002).

take these jobs, for example, by regarding them as unwilling to take suitable work when determining the allocation of welfare benefits. In relevant respects this case is similar to the one of the pacifist (though the story to be told about how Sikhs acquire their religious or cultural identity may be considerably different from the one concerning how pacifists acquire their moral identity), so the responsiveness to reason conception must treat it in the same way, and as a result might again seem to have consequences that are unduly harsh.

Is the defender of the responsiveness to reason conception that I am envisaging in effect mistakenly treating the pacifist and the Sikh as if they were no different from someone who refuses to work in the construction industry because he hates the protective clothing he would have to wear, and has an expensive taste for wearing fashionable clothes? In response to this charge it might be said that the responsiveness to reason conception has the resources to treat these cases differently, and should utilize those resources. For it can maintain that, given their commitments, both the pacifist and the Sikh have no reasonable alternative but to refuse the jobs on offer, or no adequate opportunity to behave otherwise. An excusing condition is therefore present which means that it is illegitimate to require them to bear the full costs of their refusal to accept employment.

The notion of what constitutes an adequate opportunity is flexible, and different interpretations of it will generate different variants of the responsiveness to reason conception. The idea that the Sikh and the pacifist lack a reasonable alternative is plausible,[25] and certainly does not seem to involve stretching the notion beyond its legitimate limits. But it might be argued that, in principle, at least the same move can be made on behalf of the person with an expensive taste for fashion, forcing us to revisit the issue of what the responsiveness to reason conception implies in relation to expensive tastes, an issue I discussed in Section I of this chapter. For why cannot a person have the kind of commitment to fashion that would make it unreasonable for him to accept work when that would require him to dress in a way that is at odds with this commitment? Given his tastes and his conception of how to live, he may have no reasonable

[25] Note that even if a person does not have a reasonable alternative to performing some action, it may nevertheless be *possible* for him not to perform it, and indeed he may decide not to perform it.

alternative but to refuse work, and no adequate opportunity to behave otherwise.

It would seem that these kinds of cases can be kept apart in a principled way only if we employ a conception of what it is to have a reasonable alternative or adequate opportunity that is influenced by our assessment of the reasonableness of the agent's commitments and his conception of the good; one which allows us to declare, in the light of an assessment of his conception of the good, that the person with the expensive taste for fashion does have a reasonable alternative to unemployment—namely, to work in unfashionable clothing—whereas the Sikh or the pacifist does not. But this runs the risk of disturbing a hornet's nest of difficulties. For it would require us to distinguish those commitments that are objectively fair or reasonable from those that are not, and it is hard to see how this could be done without appealing to considerations which are deeply controversial. Except in extreme cases, such as those which involve counting blades of grass in a field or pebbles on a beach, or cases in which people's commitments are of a kind that explicitly or implicitly denies people's equal status as citizens, there is no widely shared basis for making such a distinction.

In practice, however, there are likely to be differences between the predicament of the pacifist or the Sikh and the person with a taste for fashion that would allow the responsiveness to reason conception to treat these cases differently even if it does take for granted the agent's commitments in determining whether he possesses a reasonable alternative. It is likely to be the case that the commitments of the person with a taste for fashion are such that he does have reasonable alternatives available to him that he declines to take, ranging from wearing designer clothes outside the workplace to wearing designer protective gear inside it. Although it is not inconceivable that the person's taste for fashion, and his conception of how to live, really are such that it would be unreasonable for him to work in the construction industry, in practice this must be judged unlikely. (Indeed, when we are devising practical schemes for allocating costs, it might be argued that we should ignore this possibility since it is so unlikely and will be so hard to determine whether a given case meets the criteria.) In relation to the pacifist or the Sikh, however, we do not need to make outlandish assumptions to conclude that, given their commitments, they have no reasonable alternative but to refuse to take the jobs that are available.

The way in which the responsiveness to reason conception maintains that people should bear the costs of the expensive tastes they accept or reflectively endorse, unless they have been indoctrinated or some excusing condition is present, and the implications this has for cases in which people's fundamental moral commitments or cultural identity is at stake, may nevertheless make one doubt whether it gets these cases right. The problem here need not be that it treats those who face costs as a result of having or acting on their fundamental moral commitments or cultural identity as relevantly similar to those burdened by expensive tastes, but rather its central claim that people should bear the costs of choices they reflectively endorse provided no indoctrination has taken place and no excusing conditions apply. G. A. Cohen in effect distances himself from both the responsiveness to reason conception and the control conception by arguing that when people identify with an expensive taste that they have chosen to develop, or could rid themselves of, it does not follow that they should bear the costs of this taste, adding that it 'is *precisely* because they *did* and *do* identify with it, and therefore cannot reasonably be expected to have not developed it or to rid themselves of it' that they should not be required to do so. Rejecting Dworkin's position on this issue, he maintains that

> what Dworkin gives as a reason for *withholding* compensation—the subjects' approving identification with their expensive tastes—is something that I regard as a reason for offering it, since, where identification is present, it is, standardly, the agents' very bad luck that a preference with which they strongly identify happens to be expensive, and to expect them to forgo or to restrict satisfaction of that preference (because it is expensive) is, therefore, to ask them to accept an alienation from what is deep in them.[26]

There is considerable force to Cohen's argument. For the ability of someone to pursue his conception of the good, if market forces are allowed to prevail, is deeply affected by the preferences of others and the availability of the resources required to pursue it. When a person reflectively endorses (or even merely accepts) an expensive taste, so that, in effect, it forms part of his conception of the good, this provides good reason to hold that he should not bear the full

[26] Cohen, 'Expensive Taste Rides Again', 7, emphasis in original.

costs of it, given that the cost of having and satisfying this taste is due in large part to the circumstances in which he happens to find himself.

Note that this is not because we should 'extinguish the influence of brute luck on distribution'.[27] Even if the neutralization approach were the correct one, it is not well expressed by this idea. The neutralization approach does not object to the influence of brute luck as such. It is bad brute luck for each of us that we cannot jump twenty feet in the air unaided, or work out the value of *pi* to one hundred decimal places in our heads, but defenders of the neutralization approach are rightly untroubled by this fact. They are concerned about the effects of *differences* in bad brute luck, or differences in people's circumstances, on their relative access to advantage. Although the expensiveness of a person's tastes may be a result of bad brute luck, or a consequence of the circumstances he faces, this does not generate a case for compensation from the perspective of the neutralization approach (or indeed the mitigation approach), for everyone faces the same circumstances in the relevant sense: what is expensive for one person, as a result of the availability of resources and the demand for them, is also expensive for another person as well.[28] It will not do to reply to this by arguing that they do face a difference in their circumstances because those with expensive tastes find it costly to pursue their conception of the good unlike those with cheap tastes. According to my way of drawing the distinction between choice and circumstances, this is a difference in choice, for it is a difference that arises within the space of reasons. My claim, however, following Cohen, is that even though it reflects a difference in choice, the expensiveness of a person's tastes may merit compensation when the costs of satisfying them are particularly high, given that these costs are a function of their circumstances.

Cohen can of course maintain that there are cases when people should bear the full costs of their choices or enjoy the full benefits of them. He can insist that when people choose to put in differential effort in their productive activities, justice allows, or even requires,

[27] Cohen, 'On the Currency of Egalitarian Justice', 931.

[28] Here I am in disagreement with Terry Price, who in my view misunderstands the neutralization approach (or what has become known as luck egalitarianism) on this point, see T. Price, 'Egalitarian Justice, Luck, and the Costs of Chosen Ends', *American Philosophical Quarterly* 36 (1999), 267–78.

us to reward those whose exertions are greater. He also can and does maintain that the decisions people take when they develop expensive tastes, may make a difference to whether justice requires us to compensate them for having those tastes. According to his account what matters here are the *reasons* they have for cultivating these tastes. If people cultivate expensive tastes for snobbish reasons, or if they have 'brute' tastes they chose to develop or which they could change, or if they gambled on getting more welfare from developing a taste in the knowledge that this might mean that they would be able to obtain less welfare in the future, then it is plausible to suppose as Cohen does that justice does not require others to subsidize their choices. (Cohen acknowledges that our practical schemes for allocating costs and benefits may be unable to track the reasons people have for cultivating these tastes; his point is that this is what justice requires at the level of fundamental principle.)

Precisely how justice requires us to distribute the costs of having and satisfying expensive tastes is a complex issue, and in my view it is unlikely that anyone could come up with an abstract formula for determining what it requires. The fact that someone developed a conception of the good knowing that it would be expensive to pursue provides a strong reason for not requiring others to bear equal proportions of the cost of doing so, and for requiring him to bear a considerably larger than equal proportion of that cost. But so too the fact that someone has developed a conception of the good by reflecting on what is valuable or important to him, which is expensive to pursue because of what the preferences of others happen to be and the availability of resources, provides a reason for not requiring him to bear the full costs of pursuing it, a reason that will gain in strength the more difficult it becomes to pursue in the absence of a subsidy.

These conclusions clearly have relevance for the cases I have discussed. Even if the pacifist's (or the Sikh's) commitments can legitimately be regarded as in relevant respects similar to expensive tastes, and even if there are no excusing conditions that might militate against requiring him bear the full costs of those commitments, there is still scope to argue that it would be unjust to require him to do so. For the expensiveness of his commitments is, in part, a product of his circumstances, that is, the availability of resources, and the preferences and beliefs of those who reject pacifism (or Sikhism), which determine the demand for those resources.

Cohen's argument also has implications for the predicament faced by members of minority cultures who are confronted with the demise of their own culture, not merely with hard choices about the extent to which they can grasp opportunities available in the wider society to which they belong.[29] In an influential body of work, Will Kymlicka has argued that when a culture disintegrates, its remaining members face disadvantages through no fault of their own. He maintains that these disadvantages are, in effect, a product of the different circumstances they confront compared to those who belong to the dominant culture, whose cultural membership is secure, and that justice requires us to counteract the effects of these differences.[30] In making this case, he argues that cultures, or more specifically 'societal cultures', provide individuals with a context of choice. When an individual's culture disintegrates, that context of choice disappears, and she may be unable to lead a life she can find meaningful outside of it.[31] It is not clear, however, that this provides us with an adequate basis for arguing that the disadvantages experienced by members of a minority cultural community who are faced with the prospect of its disintegration arise from their specific circumstances, whereas the disadvantages experienced by those with expensive tastes, such as the gourmand, arise from their choices. The distinction that Kymlicka draws between a context of choice and the choices made within that context cannot justify the conclusion that there is a fundamental normative difference between the two cases, for the gourmand too may be unable to lead a life he can find meaningful if he cannot satisfy his tastes

[29] See G. A. Cohen, 'Expensive Tastes and Multiculturalism', in R. Bhargava, A. Bagchi, and R. Sudarshan (eds), *Multiculturalism, Liberalism and Democracy* (New Delhi: Oxford University Press, 1999).

[30] See W. Kymlicka, *Liberalism, Community, and Culture* (Oxford: Oxford University Press, 1991), esp. chs 8–9; W. Kymlicka, *Multicultural Citizenship: A Liberal Theory of Minority Rights* (Oxford: Oxford University Press, 1995), esp. chs 5–6.

[31] Note that this is different from the case in which members of a minority culture become assimilated because their beliefs and evaluative commitments change as a result of exposure to the beliefs and commitments of people in the wider society. The case we are envisaging in one in which members of a minority culture retain their beliefs and evaluative commitments but the disintegration of that culture makes unavailable the practices required to lead what from the perspective of those beliefs and commitments counts as a meaningful life.

through no fault of his own, just like the person faced with a disintegrating culture.[32] Again, there seems no difference in principle, even if in practice it may be hard to find gourmands who fit this description.[33] Once we accept, however, that it may be unjust to require people to bear the costs of their commitments when those costs are large and due in significant part to the choices of others, we have reason for seeking to prevent the demise of a cultural community when this would make it difficult or even impossible for its members (or some of them) to lead a life they can find meaningful, even if we do not suppose that they face different circumstances in the relevant sense.

IV. *Gender Identity*

In the previous section I explored the implications of the responsiveness to reason conception for cases in which people's moral commitments or cultural identities are at stake and argued that there is a wider range of possible reasons than it recognizes that may make it unfair to require a person to bear the costs of his choices. In this section, I try to reinforce this conclusion through a discussion of a case which I refer to as 'the career sacrificing mother'.[34]

Like cultural identity, gender identity poses a challenge. The effects of gender socialization and gender-differentiated norms are profound but how do they bear upon the issue of whether, and

[32] See A. Patten, 'Liberal Egalitarianism and National Cultures', *The Monist* 82 (1999), 400–3; Cohen, 'Expensive Tastes and Multiculturalism', esp. 91–9.

[33] We are imagining a person faced with the demise of his culture who is unable to lead a meaningful life outside of it. Now we can conceive of someone with a set of expensive tastes for a way of life that involves a large estate in the country, a house in the city (with the servants to run them both), and extravagant entertaining, who is genuinely unable to lead a life he can find meaningful without the resources to sustain this lifestyle. This case is surely fanciful, however. As Alan Patten points out, the inability of a person faced with the disintegration of his culture to lead a life he can find meaningful may rest upon his inability to master the language of the wider society to which he belongs, or to master the conceptual framework which shapes its practices (see Patten, 'Liberal Egalitarianism and National Cultures', 403–7). In this way the wider society may offer him no possibilities that he can understand and appreciate. It is hard to think of a realistic analogue to this in the case of the gourmand.

[34] Much of my discussion of this case is taken from an earlier article, 'Equality, Personal Responsibility, and Gender Socialisation', *Proceedings of the Aristotelian Society* 100 (2000), 227–46.

when, it is fair to require men and women to bear the costs of their behaviour? I propose to explore this question through a set of cases that bring into focus some of the difficulties that arise more generally. The cases I have in mind are when women are denied jobs or promotions, or do not apply for them in the first place, either because their childcare commitments mean that they have devoted less time to acquiring the necessary skills and experience, or because they would be expected to work long hours or extra hours at short notice. These women have had the opportunity to develop the relevant career-related skills and experience without their children being neglected, or could work long hours or extra hours at short notice. (Perhaps they have partners who are willing and able to look after their children, or perhaps they can earn enough money to be able to employ others to do so instead.) But they were unwilling to take advantage of that opportunity: they may believe that they, as mothers, have a responsibility to look after their children personally, or they may simply want to devote themselves to the care of their own children, or both. Would it be just to require the career sacrificing mother that I have described to bear the full costs of her behaviour, including, for example, any shortfall in her pension when she reaches retirement age? Before that question can be answered adequately, the case needs to be specified in greater detail. Consider three possible ways of expanding upon it.

According to the first elaboration, the woman involved accepts the conventions of her society, with minimal critical reflection upon them. Her behaviour in some sense involves the exercise of her rational capacities, but not in a way which leads her to reflect upon the norms that govern child-rearing practices. She unreflectively accepts the idea that mothers have the primary responsibility for providing childcare, including looking after their children personally, and organizes the way in which she and her partner raise their children in the light of it.

According to the second elaboration, the woman's decision is in part the outcome of critical reflection upon the norms which govern child-rearing practices—she denies that women have primary responsibility for childcare—but also reflects her deep desire to devote herself to her children. However, she does not fully appreciate the way in which the socialization she has experienced has exerted, and continues to exert a profound influence upon her behaviour. (Even when people gain a critical distance on the cultural images and social norms they have imbibed, these images and norms may continue to affect their behaviour. For example, men and women may deny that mothers have primary responsibility for looking after their children, but find that this idea continues to shape their behaviour. Women may continue, in subterranean ways, to feel that childcare is primarily their responsibility and their male partners, in a similar fashion, continue to believe at some level that it is not primarily their responsibility.)

According to the third elaboration, the woman involved possesses reasons for acting as she does, and she is fully and vividly aware of the way in which her desires and dispositions have been influenced by processes of socialization. She rejects the idea that women are primarily responsible for childcare, but she has a deep desire to devote herself exclusively to raising her children. She acknowledges that socialization has shaped her very identity, including her deepest needs and desires, to the point of conceding that she might not have had these desires but for her socialization. But she still reflectively endorses those needs and desires as her own.

Each of these ways of developing the abstractly specified case seems coherent, and may indeed provide the basis for a true account of some cases that actually occur. In relation to each, the responsiveness to reason approach is likely to support the conclusion that the career-sacrificing mother can legitimately be required to bear the full costs of her decision. Although there is some scope for argument about whether according to the first two elaborations her decision really is responsive to her reason in the way this approach requires in order for it to be legitimate to insist that she bears its costs, that conclusion is consistent with the description given. (To maintain that she has been indoctrinated or manipulated would be to go beyond the description of the case.) Furthermore, it is built into this description that she has a reasonable alternative or an adequate opportunity to avoid the sacrifice of her career.[35] But to

[35] Might it be argued that she does not have a reasonable alternative because she cannot take a costless career break? The notion of a reasonable alternative, and what is required for there to be one, is amenable to different interpretations, but to insist that she does not have a reasonable alternative unless the state or her employer makes available a costless career break seems to me to stretch this notion beyond its legitimate bounds.

the extent that the responsiveness to reason account does entail that the career sacrificing mother should bear the costs of the behaviour, I think this should raise doubts about its adequacy, for reasons I explain.

Women make the choice to sacrifice their careers against a background in which the norm that mothers should look after their children personally is widely accepted and transmitted in a variety of different ways through a complex process of gender socialization. Given this background, it seems to me that it may be unjust to require them to bear the full costs of their decision to look after their children personally (with the consequence that they do not acquire the skills and experience necessary for success in the job market, and perhaps do not contribute to occupational pension schemes that would provide them with a higher income at retirement), even if their decision is fully autonomous. In other words, the extensive socialization which is shaped by (and fosters behaviour which accords with) the norm that mothers should look after their children personally may mean that it is unfair to require them to bear the full costs of the consequences of acting in a way which accords with that norm, even when they reject the norm.

In response it might be objected that the presence of socialization alone cannot account for the apparent unfairness of requiring the career sacrificing mother to bear the costs of her decision, and that any adequate explanation of this apparent unfairness must cite the content of the norm itself. To see the potential force of this objection, consider a different case where socialization also has a profound effect but the norms which shape it, and are transmitted through it, are not sexist. Imagine a society which in various ways fosters a desire (uniformly amongst those of both sexes) to raise children, and there is a widely accepted principle that fertile couples should have children. Those who do not do so are regarded as selfish, perhaps as failing in their religious duty, and in various ways are subject to informal criticism and sanctions. From an early age children are raised with the expectation that they too will become parents, and are taught that there is something wrong with childlessness. Intuitions about this case may vary, but it is less clear that there would be anything unjust about requiring parents to bear the costs of having children, even when a sizeable minority rebel and refuse to abide by the social norm.

This suggests that the main worry about how the responsiveness to reason conception deals with the case of the career sacrificing mother must rest, at least in part, upon something other than the profound way in which gender socialization moulds desires and aspirations. The most obvious proposal is that the sexism of the norms which shape this process makes a significant difference. The norm that mothers rather than fathers should take primary responsibility for childcare is prima facie unjust, in a way that has no analogue in the other case described where the relevant norm is not even gender-differentiated. In other words, it is partly the injustice of this norm (not *merely* the process of gender socialization that is shaped by it and fosters behaviour that is in accordance with it) which explains why it would be unjust to require the career-sacrificing mother to bear the costs of her decision to act in a way that is consistent with the norm, even when she rejects it.

This proposal receives further support if we imagine a relevantly similar case. Suppose that as a result of being subject to socialization involving racist norms, members of a particular racial minority develop a slave mentality. Some internalize the idea that they have a special obligation to reduce work burdens on members of the dominant group, to work harder than them for no recompense. Others develop a strong desire to do so even when they reject the idea that they are under such an obligation. Even if their decision to act in a way that is consistent with this supposed obligation meets the relevant conditions laid down by the responsiveness to reason conception, it would seem unjust to require them to bear any of the costs (extrinsic, at least) of that decision, for example, any medical costs that arise from overwork.

At this juncture it might be argued that defenders of the responsiveness to reason conception have the resources to explain why it may be unfair to require the career-sacrificing mother to bear the full costs of her choice in at least some cases. Ronald Dworkin's version of something akin to the responsiveness to reason conception incorporates a principle of independence which entails that it is unfair to require a person to bear the costs of her choices when her preferences are (partly or wholly) a product of prejudice against a group to which she belongs. If the career-sacrificing mother's preference to look after her children is in part a product of the influence of sexist norms, then it would follow that it may be unfair to require her to bear the costs of her choice.[36]

While it is true that such an account can deal with the career-sacrificing mother in this way, this shows how far removed it is from any simple version of the responsiveness to reason conception. We are allowing that the career-sacrificing mother has adequate opportunity to behave otherwise, that her decision is a product of the exercise of her rational capacities, and that she was not subject to manipulation or indoctrination. She need not accept the norm that mothers should take primary responsibility for childcare; indeed, she may vehemently oppose that idea. Her preferences have been affected by a process of socialization, such that we might truthfully say that she would not have made this choice had she been socialized differently, but in this respect her position is no different from anyone else's. It will generally be possible to say of a person: he would not have had that ambition (or preference or desire) if he had not been subject to some particular set of influences. So by incorporating the independence condition, we are sanctioning a very different class of exceptions to the principle that people should bear the costs of their choices and, in my terms, moving beyond the responsiveness to reason conception. Indeed, this class of exceptions is potentially very large, for there may be many preferences that women have which they would not have had but for the impact of sexist norms concerning how women should behave, what careers they should pursue, and the like.

My proposal might even go one step further by maintaining that even if the mother's preferences have not been shaped by sexist norms—if somehow or other her preferences escaped the impact of such norms—it would nevertheless be unfair to require her to bear the full costs of her choice because that choice is made against a background of social expectations which have been influenced by these norms. Where these norms continue to be widely accepted and promulgated, even those women whose preferences have not been shaped by them should not be required to bear the full costs of acting in a way that accords with them. There is something hypocritical, and also unfair, about a society where a norm that mothers should

[36] See Dworkin, 'Sovereign Virtue Revisited', 136–7.

take primary responsibility for childcare influences social expectations but which requires mothers to bear the costs of behaviour that accords with it, and this is true irrespective of whether they are acting from that norm or even whether that norm has causally influenced their preferences. This position also has a practical advantage over Dworkin's: there is no need to engage in the complex sociological and psychological investigation that would be required to determine whether a person's preferences were, wholly or in part, the product of prejudice against a group to which they belong.

V. *A Pluralist Conception*

Rather than defending the responsiveness to reason conception against the threat posed to it by the case of the career sacrificing mother by wheeling in a separate principle to qualify it—namely, the principle of independence—my suggestion is that we think beyond that conception, and recognize a plurality of reasons, relevant in different kinds of cases, for why it may be unfair to require a person to bear the costs of his behaviour. The responsiveness to reason conception acknowledges a particular set of reasons for not requiring a person to bear the full costs of his behaviour, but we should not regard them as exhaustive. When people are subject to a process of socialization which is shaped by an unjust norm which it also imparts, it would be unfair to require them to bear the full costs of acting in accordance with that norm when these costs are large. In section III, I also argued that there are reasons for thinking that it would be unjust to require a person to bear the full costs of his choices when the expensiveness of those choices places a large burden on him and is due in significant part to some feature of his circumstances, such as the preferences of others.[37]

[37] Seana Shiffrin presents a case for 'accommodation' (that is, for not always requiring people to bear the costs of their choices) which appeals to the importance of meaningful freedom and which would provide further support for a pluralist conception of the kind I am advocating. See S. Shiffrin, 'Egalitarianism, Choice-Sensitivity, and Accommodation', in R. J. Wallace, P. Pettit, S. Scheffler, and M. Smith (eds), *Reason and Value: Themes from the Moral Philosophy of Joseph Raz* (Oxford: Oxford University Press, 2004; 294). For reasons I do not need to go into here, I am unpersuaded by her general argument despite sharing many of the conclusions she reaches in relation to particular cases of accommodation.

In support of a pluralist account, I also want to draw attention to another kind of case where we might think it unfair to require a person to bear the full costs of his behaviour, for example, we might want to say that it would be unfair to require a person to bear these costs if he could not reasonably be expected to behave otherwise, given, for example, the socialization that has shaped his character and dispositions. For example, it might be claimed, albeit controversially, that a person subject to violent abuse as a child could not reasonably be expected to refrain from using violence against others when he felt threatened in later life, even if it was within his power to do so.

It might be thought that cases of this last kind, when they are properly understood, can be accommodated by the responsiveness to reason conception. We might suppose, for example, that they illustrate the way in which a person may lack a reasonable alternative or an adequate opportunity to avoid developing the kind of character which his actions express, and hence they invoke an excusing condition. Scanlon discusses a relevantly similar case in which a person is horribly treated as a child and is subjected to the kind of upbringing which results in him becoming undisciplined and unreliable. Scanlon concludes that if he becomes unemployable, it would be unfair to deny him welfare support because he has not had an adequate opportunity to avoid being subject to these traits.[38] If this is so, it would appear that it can be accommodated by defenders of the responsiveness to reason conception, since it falls within a class of cases where they acknowledge it would be unfair to require the agent to bear the full costs of his behaviour. But we are not forced to understand these cases in this way. We might say that such a person did have adequate opportunity to avoid these traits, and indeed support this conclusion by drawing attention to others who had experienced a similar kind of upbringing but managed not to develop the traits (or not act upon them), but insist that we cannot reasonably expect him not to have done so given how few people who have experienced this kind of upbringing have succeeded in avoiding doing so.

In spelling out this idea we might turn to the kind of account that John Roemer gives (although he favours the neutralization approach

[38] See Scanlon, *What We Owe To Each Other*, 292.

rather than a mitigation approach).[39] In order to determine the extent to which a person is accountable for his behaviour in the light of the social forces to which he has been subject, Roemer argues that all the factors which played a causal role in generating his actions need to be identified. Consider one of his examples, namely, lung cancer suffered as a result of smoking. He maintains that in order to determine how much control a person had over his habit of smoking, we need to identify all those factors beyond his control which had a causal impact on his decision to smoke and continue doing so. Suppose, for example, that his economic class, his ethnicity, whether his parents smoked, and his level of education, constitute a complete list. Roemer would then maintain that in determining comparable degrees of accountability, we need to divide people into types, the members of which have equivalent circumstances, that is, belong to the same economic class, the same ethnic group, have the same level of education, and whose parents share the same smoking (or non-smoking) habit.[40] Roemer argues that those of the same type can be said to possess the same degree of control over whether or not to smoke, and that those who belong to the same type who have smoked the same amount for the same number of years can be said to share the same degree of accountability. People of different types whose behaviour lies at the same percentile in their respective types for the number of years and amount they have smoked can also be said to possess a comparable degree of accountability.

The allocation of individuals to types, and the claim that those whose behaviour falls in the same percentile within their type share the same degree of accountability, does not give an answer to the question of whether, or when, it is fair to require a person to bear

[39] See J. Roemer, *Equality of Opportunity* (Cambridge, MA: Harvard University Press, 1998).

[40] Roemer then maintains that the identification of these causal influences, and hence the individuation of types, should be left to the political process (with citizens and politicians having access to evidence from relevant disciplines such as sociology), together with judgements about when individuals within types should be held accountable to some degree for the adverse consequences of their behaviour. In the face of disagreement over what is the correct list of causal factors that influence a pattern of behaviour, it may be appropriate to use the political process to select a particular list, but we should recognize that the list which is arrived at in this way may be incorrect. This criticism, however, does not undermine the point I am making using Roemer's work.

the costs of his behaviour.[41] Roemer's account does, however, place limits on what could be an adequate answer to this question. He argues that if no one in a given type has managed to avoid some particular pattern of behaviour that has adverse consequences, then no one in that type should be required to bear the costs of it, for it would be unreasonable to expect members of that type to have avoided that pattern of behaviour (even though it might be appropriate to criticize them or blame them for it).[42] Roemer also distinguishes between what we can reasonably expect of a person and what is 'physically possible' for her.[43] Even if a person could have acted otherwise, it is not necessarily fair to require her to bear its costs, for it may be unreasonable to expect her to behave any better than she did. In maintaining this position, Roemer apparently rejects the idea inherent in the control conception, namely, the idea that it is fair to require a person to bear the full costs of his behaviour if he could have behaved otherwise, and none of the standard excusing conditions apply. He maintains instead that we need to decide what can reasonably be expected of persons of a given type, which he regards as partly independent of what lies within their control. If we decide that only those whose behaviour is worse than the median within their type should bear the costs of their behaviour, then we should maintain the equivalent in relation to the behaviour of those who belong to other types.

Even those who are sceptical about the details of Roemer's approach can take on board what I think is the insight contained in it, namely, that whether it is fair to require a person to bear the costs of his behaviour depends on whether he could reasonably be expected to behave otherwise given his upbringing and his social circumstances, rather than in some straightforward way on whether he could have made the choice to act otherwise and the presence or absence of items from some standard list of excusing conditions (including the presence of, or lack of, an adequate opportunity to

[41] Roemer's theory is in effect merely a set of conditionals. It says, for example, that *if* a person is required to bear the costs of the adverse consequences of his behaviour and his behaviour is at the median for his type, *then* others whose behaviour is at the median for their type should also be required to bear the costs of the adverse consequences of their actions.

[42] Roemer, *Equality of Opportunity*, 13–5.

[43] Roemer, *Equality of Opportunity*, 14.

behave otherwise). There are a variety of different circumstances and background conditions the presence of which may make it unreasonable, to some degree at least, to require the agent to bear the full costs of her choices.

VI. *Conclusion*

There are a number of reasons for wanting what happens to people to depend on the choices they make. These reasons create a presumption that people should bear the costs of their choices but do not justify the conclusion that a person should incur these costs whenever his choices are freely endorsed and no excusing conditions apply. Those who have thought that there is some simple connection between the issue of when it is fair to require people to bear the costs of their choices, and whether those choices are under their control (with no excusing conditions present), or whether they are properly responsive to their reason (with the agent having adequate opportunity to behave otherwise), have, I suggest, been nourished by a one-sided diet of examples.[44] They have been impressed by cases where inequalities emerge as a result of the different values of individuals, or the different kinds of effort people consciously decide to put in, such as in Kymlicka's homespun example of the leisure-seeking tennis player and the profit-seeking gardener.[45] They have then generalized from these cases to reach the conclusion that it is fair to require people to bear the costs of their choices when these are under their control, or freely endorsed, with no excusing conditions. My argument, in contrast, has been that there is a variety of different reasons we might have for supposing that it would be unjust to require people to bear the costs of their choices, regardless of whether their choices are under their control or freely endorsed, and even in the absence of any excusing conditions.

Because they generalize from a one-sided diet of examples, both the control conception and the responsiveness to reason conception are implausible in other ways. For their underlying logic leads them to endorse extremely harsh conclusions concerning the entitlements of individuals who become needy as a result of their imprudent

44 Cf. Wittgenstein, *Philosophical Investigations*, S. 593.
45 Kymlicka, *Contemporary Political Philosophy*, 72–3.

but fully autonomous choices. Suppose, for example, that a person participates in a dangerous sport such as rock climbing, knowing the risks attached but without taking out adequate insurance. Both the control conception and the responsiveness to reason conception will be inclined to maintain that the rock-climber can legitimately be required to bear the cost of treating any injury that results from his decision to engage in this sport. The pluralist conception, however, allows space for the idea that it would not be legitimate to require the rock climber to bear the full costs of an accident that has happened to him, on the grounds that this would leave him destitute. I pursue this proposal further in the next chapter, in the context of considering a forceful criticism of the neutralization approach, which may also apply to the mitigation approach, namely, that it is objectionably individualistic, reflected for example in the way that it allocates the costs of caring for those in need.

CHAPTER 8

Individualism and Personal Responsibility

Critics of what I call responsibility-sensitive egalitarianism have often claimed that it is individualistic in an objectionable way. Do these criticisms have any force? 'Individualism' is a slippery term that is employed in many different senses. My purpose in this chapter is to distinguish some of these different senses, to explore the extent to which responsibility-sensitive egalitarianism counts as individualist in each of them, and to determine what problems it may face as a result. Given the role it accords the idea of personal responsibility, there is an obvious sense in which any form of responsibility-sensitive egalitarianism must be individualistic, and self-consciously so. But if the accusation of individualism is made to rest simply on the fact that it holds people accountable for their choices, then defenders of it should not feel threatened. If the charge is to possess any critical bite, it must be shown that responsibility-sensitive egalitarianism, or some versions of it at least, give the wrong kind of role to personal responsibility, or that they are individualist in some other way that is problematic.

There are at least four potential criticisms that merit scrutiny in this context. The first is that the role responsibility-sensitive egalitarianism gives to personal responsibility makes an individual's entitlements depend on facts about him or her in a way that is at least sometimes independent of the overall distribution of economic benefits and burdens across society, whereas the justice of any allocation of economic benefits to a particular individual must always depend on that distribution. Let us characterize this as the charge that responsibility-sensitive egalitarianism is *distributionally individualistic* in a problematic way. The second potential criticism is that this form of egalitarianism is committed to *ontological individualism*, that is, it denies the reality of groups and collectives, and for this reason is unable to acknowledge genuine cases of collective responsibility. The third criticism is that it is committed to *methodological individualism*, that is, it supposes that any explanation of behaviour, whether individual or collective, has to be reducible in principle to explanations which mention only properties of individuals, such as their beliefs and desires, and relations between individuals, and that this makes it unable to understand the way injustice may be caused by, or attach to, social structures. The fourth charge is that this form of egalitarianism embodies *atomistic egoism*, that is, it fails to provide appropriate support for the social relations that sustain individuals, or it distributes the costs of caring for others inappropriately or unjustly. Is responsibility-sensitive egalitarianism committed to any of these forms of individualism, and if so, does this show that it is defective?

I. *Distributive Individualism*

The charge that responsibility-sensitive egalitarianism makes an individual's entitlements depend on facts about him in a way that is at least sometimes independent of the overall distribution of economic benefits and burdens across society, whereas the just allocation of economic benefits to particular individuals must always depend on that distribution, might appear as a simple refusal to take account of facts about personal responsibility that are clearly relevant to the justice of a distribution. This is a misperception, however, for this line of criticism has a deeper basis in the case for an holistic conception of distributive justice. In Samuel Scheffler's view, the argument for such a conception is partly moral and partly empirical in character, appealing to 'a strong sense of the equal worth of persons and ... a firm conviction that in a just society all citizens must enjoy equal standing', and to a conviction that 'citizens' material prospects are profoundly interconnected through their shared and effectively unavoidable participation in a set of fundamental practices and institutions ... that establish and reinforce the ground rules of social cooperation'. The holist draws the conclusion that 'it makes no normative sense to suppose that there could be, at the level of fundamental principle, a standard for assigning such benefits that appealed solely to characteristics of or facts about the proposed beneficiaries'.[1]

In Scheffler's view, the clearest example of a conception of distributive justice that is distributionally individualistic in a problematic way is one that appeals to a pre-justicial notion of desert. (Recall from Chapter 2 that a notion of desert is pre-justicial if it is conceived as prior to and independent of principles of justice.) He argues that in making desert claims, these notions appeal solely to facts about the subject of the claim (including relational facts, for example, that she has performed better than others in some competition). This stands opposed to holistic conceptions of distributive justice which maintain that 'the justice of any particular assignment of benefits always depends—directly or indirectly—on the justice of the larger distribution of benefits and burdens in society'.[2] Note, however, that responsibility-sensitive egalitarianism need not involve a pre-justicial notion of desert. If it employs a notion of desert at all, it can characterise desert by reference to independent principles of justice, by maintaining that individuals deserve what they receive from a just scheme that counteracts the effects of differences in people's circumstances and allocates benefits and burdens in a way that is sensitive to facts about the choices individuals make.[3]

Indeed responsibility-sensitive egalitarianism is a holistic conception even though it supposes that the just allocation of benefits and burdens must take into account facts about the choices of individuals. First, it maintains that there can be a just allocation of benefits and burdens to individuals only if there is a general scheme in place that counteracts the effects of differences in people's circumstances on their access to advantage. Second, facts about the choices an individual makes are relevant to determining the allocation of the costs (and benefits) of his actions, but even at this level what constitutes a just allocation may be determined in part by a judgement about what proportion of those costs it would be just to require others to bear. For example, the particular version of responsibility-sensitive egalitarianism that I have defended holds that it may be just

1 Scheffler, *Boundaries and Allegiances*, 191.

2 Scheffler, *Boundaries and Allegiances*, 166.

3 See the Conclusion of Ch. 2.

to require others to subsidize a person's expensive taste where its expensiveness is due in large part to their preferences, in particular, the way in which their preferences influence the supply and demand of the resources he needs to satisfy that taste.

II. *Ontological Individualism and Collective Responsibility*

Ontological individualism is the thesis that there are no groups or collectives, only individuals. It would seem that if responsibility-sensitive egalitarianism subscribes to this thesis, it will be unable to make sense of the idea of collective responsibility, for if there are no genuine groups or collectives it is hard to see how there could be genuine collective responsibility.

Ontological individualism is implausible, independently of whether it rules out the possibility of genuine collective responsibility. For there seem to be a number of actions regularly performed that it is hard to attribute to anything other than a collective. To take a mundane example, when a number of individuals together lift a heavy object, there seems to be an action performed that can be correctly described as 'the lifting of the heavy object'. That action can only be attributed to the group constituted by those individuals, for there is no individual member of it who does the lifting.

The members of a group may also share goals or purposes the specification of which makes an ineliminable reference to the group; each individual may want it to be the case that the group lifts the heavy object, and each may see himself as contributing to the realization of this goal by cooperating with the others. (There are also cases where a group performs an action which could not even in principle be performed by an individual. Consider the way in which a group of jazz musicians might have a musical conversation, where the conversation itself was a constitutive part of the piece of music that they played.[4])

Some genuine cases of a collective's acting presuppose a matrix of practices and institutions, such as when a jury finds in favour of a defendant. Juries are part of a legal system which defines the

[4] See D. Brudney, 'Community and Completion', in A. Reath, B. Herman, and C. Korsgaard (eds), *Reclaiming the History of Ethics: Essays for John Rawls* (Cambridge: Cambridge University Press, 1997; 397).

rules under which they operate. Under those rules the action of finding in favour of a defendant could not properly be attributed to all or even some of the jurors considered simply as individuals. This can be seen most clearly in cases where the decision of a jury is not based on a unanimous vote: in such cases it is the jury which finds the defendant innocent, not some subset of them such as those who voted in favour of acquittal, and if we focus on the individual jurors alone, the action of finding in favour of the defendant will be unattributable. We might express some of these points in the way that Keith Graham does, by maintaining that genuine collectives are such that

> although they consist of nothing over and above individuals in certain relations, it is not *as* individuals but only as members of the collective in question that those individuals have any role in the process which constitutes that collective's deliberating and acting.[5]

Forced into a corner, ontological individualists must either deny that there is any such action as the jury's finding the defendant guilty and the group's lifting the heavy object, or they must allow for the existence of actions that no agent has performed. Both are unattractive positions. In any case it is hard to see why there should be any theoretical pressure to deny the reality of collectives. Acknowledging their existence is metaphysically unproblematic. Just as a physicist may accept the reality of tables and chairs whilst maintaining that they are made up of atoms and molecules, so too social theorists can accept that groups and collectives are real, whilst maintaining that they are made up of individuals.

Ontological individualism is implausible. But this does not undermine responsibility-sensitive egalitarianism, for there is no reason to suppose that this form of egalitarianism is committed to it. Responsibility-sensitive egalitarianism does not have to deny the existence of groups or collectives. It is true, however, that it gives no account of how the costs and benefits of actions performed by groups should be distributed, and it might still be thought that the way in which it focuses on the individual makes it hard for it to accommodate a robust account of collective responsibility.

[5] K. Graham, *The Battle of Democracy* (Brighton, UK: Wheatsheaf, 1986; 103).

How might responsibility-sensitive egalitarianism go about constructing an account of collective responsibility? The simplest proposal would involve drawing a direct parallel between groups and individuals: just as there are circumstances in which it is legitimate to hold an individual responsible for his behaviour and require him to bear its costs, so too there are circumstances in which it is legitimate to hold a group responsible and require it to bear the costs of its behaviour. There is an obvious added level of complexity in the case of groups, however, because in most cases making a group bear the cost of its behaviour will require making some or all of its individual members share those costs. This raises the moral issue of when it is legitimate to require a member of a group to bear all or part of the costs of the actions it performs.[6] Is the mere fact that someone is a member of the group sufficient to justify the conclusion that it is legitimate to require him to bear some of the costs of its actions? What if he was unable to leave the group, expressed his disapproval of the relevant actions, and distanced himself from the group in every way that was available to him? What if the group caused the harm prior to him becoming a member?

These are difficult questions. It might seem that responsibility-sensitive egalitarianism can address issues of collective responsibility simply by providing an account of when an individual should be held responsible for his behaviour as a member of a collective by being required to bear some of the costs of its behaviour. But can it incorporate any such account or does the way in which it focuses on individual responsibility place constraints on what kind of account could be acceptable, perhaps ruling out some that are plausible from the standpoint of ideas of collective responsibility? Consider the proposal that merely through being a member of a collective, a person could legitimately be required to bear some of the costs of its behaviour, irrespective of what measures he had taken to oppose that behaviour, and irrespective of whether he had participated in the practices which generated those costs. Could responsibility-sensitive egalitarianism tolerate this idea, for under these conditions it would seem to be impossible to identify any action that he performed as a

[6] See D. Miller, 'Holding Nations Responsible', *Ethics* 114 (2004), 240–68, for further discussion of this issue.

member of the collective that we could regard as contributing to, or supporting, its behaviour?

It might seem that the proper response here is to deny that an account of collective responsibility which had these implications could be defensible, but it is not as implausible as it might seem at first glance. Consider, for example, the demand that a political community should bear some or all of the costs of an atrocity it committed in the past, even though there are very few members of that community who were alive at the time it occurred. If the demand for reparation is to be met, then this would involve even those members who were not alive at the time contributing to these reparations, perhaps through some general taxation scheme. The case here might not even rest upon the claim that all members of the community have benefited from the atrocity; perhaps none of them did, and in extreme cases the atrocity might have been part of a series of actions that adversely affected the group. At the very least, this case shows that it is not easy to reformulate issues about collective responsibility in terms of the individual's responsibility for his behaviour as a member of a collective.

I am not inclined to think that arguments such as these undermine responsibility-sensitive egalitarianism, however. They show that it requires some account of when individuals as members of a collective may legitimately be required to bear some or all of the costs of its behaviour—an account which may have the implication that a member of a collective can, under some circumstances, legitimately be required to bear some of the costs of its behaviour even if he did nothing to support it, or contribute to it. An account of this sort needs to focus not just upon collective acts, but also upon collective omissions (that is, the decisions groups make not to intervene) and collective inaction (that is, the failure of individuals to organize collectively in order to bring about an outcome, where no decision was made not to intervene collectively but collective action would have been possible).[7] Any plausible account will surely have to allow that collective omissions and collective inaction may have costs which members of the relevant collectives can at least sometimes legitimately be required to share.[8] If, for example, a group of individuals

[7] See L. May, *Sharing Responsibility* (Chicago, IL: University of Chicago Press, 1992), 107.

[8] See May, *Sharing Responsibility*, ch. 6.

fail to organize collectively to prevent a famine, which is the product of weather patterns which they are partially responsible for creating, when it was within their power to do so, it is fair to require them to bear at least some of the costs of providing famine relief.

Any account of collective responsibility is bound to have implications for international distributive justice. If a political community is (wholly or in part) causally responsible for its own ills, it may be legitimate to require it, and hence its individual members, to bear all or most of the costs of those ills. It is here that the most difficult questions will arise. Given that political communities are temporally extended, and that the individual members of such a community at time T_1 may be totally different from its members at time T_2, we need some account of under what circumstances its members at T_2 may legitimately be required to bear the costs of its actions at T_1. (Its actions at T_1 may to a significant extent be responsible for their predicament at T_2, for example, a famine they are facing.) Given that some members of a political community may disapprove of, and actively oppose, its actions, we need an account of when those who disapprove of its actions but do not actively oppose them, as well as those who actively oppose them, can legitimately be required to bear the costs of these actions (which, again, may be a cause of hardships they are experiencing).

In addressing these issues, the internal structure of a community, in particular, its political organization, must surely be relevant.[9] When a political community is undemocratic and allows most of its members few ways, if any, of influencing its behaviour, it would surely be unjust in many cases to require these members to bear the costs of its behaviour.[10] Considerations of this sort may lead us to think that imposing sanctions on a political community is often unjust if those who bear the brunt of these sanctions lie outside the governing elite with no influence on its policy. There are exceptions here, especially when the powerless support the actions of their political community even though they could not influence them.[11] But the case against imposing sanctions will be especially strong when the powerless would resent the sanctions, and there is evidence

[9] See Miller, 'Holding Nations Responsible', 260–5.

[10] For reservations about requiring members of a state to bear the costs of its behaviour under these circumstances, see Caney, *Justice Beyond Borders*, 130.

[11] For relevant discussion, see May, *Sharing Responsibility*, ch. 2.

to think that they would have opposed their political community's actions if they could have done so without considerable risk to their own security and well-being. (Indeed this is the argument that some critics levelled against continuing the sanctions that were imposed on Iraq at the end of the first Gulf War.)

When a political community is democratic (or allows its members significant ways of influencing its behaviour) the situation is different. There is a strong case for saying that in a democracy those who disapprove of their political community's actions but do not oppose them may legitimately be required to bear some of the costs of these actions. It might also be reasonable to maintain that in a democratic political community those who actively oppose the community's actions may nevertheless legitimately be required to bear some of the costs of those actions on the grounds that they participated in cooperative practices which led to them.[12] But even in a democratic political community there is at least one set of individuals whom it would be unjust to require to bear the costs of its behaviour, namely, children whose level of maturity is such that they cannot understand those actions or their significance. In practice, it will often be impossible to benefit children (or prevent them from suffering hardships) without benefiting their parents, so there will be limits to how far it is possible to require people to bear the costs of acts performed by the political community to which they belong without committing injustices against children.

The question of when it is fair to require a member of a collective to bear some of the costs of its actions, omissions or inaction is not the only responsibility-related issue that arises in relation to group action and inaction, especially in the context of concerns about global justice. Iris Young distinguishes between a liability model of responsibility and a model of political responsibility (or what she also calls a social connection model of responsibility).[13] The liability model is in large part an answer to the question of when an individual (or a collective) should be praised or blamed for, or be required to bear the costs of his (or its) behaviour, whereas the model of political responsibility is forward-looking in the sense that

[12] See Miller, 'Holding Nations Responsible', 264.

[13] See I. Young, 'Responsibility and Global Labor Justice', *Journal of Political Philosophy* 12 (2004), 365–88; I. Young, 'Responsibility and Global Justice', *Social Philosophy and Policy*, 23 (2006), 102–30.

it addresses the issue of how individuals and groups should respond to forms of structural injustice in which they are implicated.[14] To illustrate this issue, Young focuses on sweatshops in less developed countries that manufacture footwear and clothing in appalling conditions for consumption in North America and Europe. She argues that large numbers of people who live in different states are implicated in the processes that sustain and create structural injustice of this kind, perhaps as employees for retailers who sell the goods that are produced in this way or as consumers who buy them. Structural processes of this kind cannot be transformed by individuals acting alone but only by working together, and individuals who are implicated in them have a responsibility to participate in forms of collective action directed at changing these processes, for example, by becoming involved in the boycotting of goods, or by taking part in rallies.

Responsibility-sensitive egalitarianism is undoubtedly incomplete in so far as it has not addressed these issues, but is there any reason to think that it cannot do so adequately? In its defence, it should be noted that it possesses some of the resources that are needed to justify claims about the injustice suffered by those that are the victims of processes that extend beyond borders. It offers principles that are designed to counteract the effects of differences in people's circumstances, and it is often these differences that make people vulnerable to exploitation in less developed states. It might plausibly be argued that the principles I defended in Chapter 6, such as the basic skills principle, which is grounded in a version of the sufficiency view, and the accumulation of wealth principle, which is a quasi-egalitarian principle, possess global scope, at least in a context where individuals are connected by a global economic structure.[15] If they do have global scope, when we fail to live up to these principles, whether domestically or globally, we are violating our obligation to treat people as equals. (Note, however, that in order to establish that these principles do have global scope, we would need to rebut the argument that what it is to treat people as equals depends, at least in part, on whether or not they are fellow citizens. Thomas Nagel, for

[14] These issues are related of course: for example, it may be that a group's failure to organize to address a structural injustice when they should do so means that it is fair to require its members to share some of the costs of that injustice.

[15] See Ch. 5, Ss II and IV.

example, maintains that the fact that citizens are both joint authors of a coercively imposed system and subject to its norms means that treating fellow citizens as equals imposes stronger requirements of distributive justice, requirements that would not follow from mere participation in the same global economic institutions.[16] It may also be the case that members of a state are bound by special obligations which sometimes take priority over global principles such as these and reduce their impact beyond the borders of the state.[17])

In response, it might be argued that even if responsibility-sensitive egalitarianism can show that the principles of justice it defends have global scope, it must still fall short on the grounds that it is unable to conceptualize the relevant issues properly because it is committed to a form of methodological individualism that cannot provide us with an adequate understanding of structural injustice. I address this issue in the next section.

III. *Methodological Individualism*

The highly implausible thesis of ontological individualism needs to be distinguished from the less implausible thesis of methodological individualism. Methodological individualism is formulated by different theorists in different ways but for my purposes it can be thought of as the view that 'all institutions, behavioural patterns, and social processes can in principle be explained in terms of individuals only: their actions, properties, and relations'.[18] One can be a methodological individualist in this sense without being an ontological individualist. For there is no inconsistency in believing that explanations of group behaviour must, in principle, be reducible to explanations which mention only the actions, properties, and relations of individuals whilst insisting that groups are part of the fabric of the world.

Is responsibility-sensitive egalitarianism committed to methodological individualism? Given that this form of egalitarianism is essentially concerned with what constitutes a just allocation of

[16] See Nagel, 'The Problem of Global Justice', 113–47.

[17] See A. Mason, *Community, Solidarity and Belonging: Levels of Community and Their Normative Significance* (Cambridge: Cambridge University Press, 2000; ch. 4 and 199–200).

[18] J. Elster, *An Introduction to Karl Marx* (Cambridge: Cambridge University Press, 1986; 22).

benefits and burdens, it is hard to see how it could be logically committed to methodological individualism, since the latter is a doctrine about the *explanation* of social phenomena. Anne Phillips thinks that luck egalitarianism (which is perhaps the dominant form of responsibility-sensitive egalitarianism and embraces the neutralization approach) nevertheless practices methodological individualism even if it could in principle reject that thesis, on the grounds that it 'treats structures of inequality as arising from the activities and choices of autonomous individuals'.[19] I do not wish to take sides on the issue of whether or not methodological individualism is defensible. Note, however, that methodological individualists can acknowledge the reality of these structures of inequality and recognize the way in which they are created and sustained not only intentionally but also unintentionally as a by-product of people's habitual (and not so habitual) behaviour. If, by doing so, they are treating 'structures of inequality as arising from the activities and choices of autonomous individuals', it needs to be shown what is wrong with such an approach.

It might nevertheless be argued that the dominant forms of responsibility-sensitive egalitarianism have not given an adequate role to groups and the structures that oppress some of them, and that any plausible version of this form of egalitarianism will need to do better.[20] Iris Young argues that because contemporary egalitarians often attribute outcomes to either 'choice' or 'chance', structures tend to be ignored because it is hard to know on which side of this dichotomy they fall.[21] The structures an individual confronts do not seem to be due to their choices but nor do they seem to be a product of mere chance. This does not seem to reflect a deep problem with responsibility-sensitive egalitarianism, however. We can see this more easily if we think in terms of the choice/circumstance distinction I have drawn. A person's circumstances are constituted by what lies outside of the space of his rational agency, including, in general,

[19] A. Phillips, 'Equality, Pluralism, Universality: Current Concerns in Normative Theory', *British Journal of Politics and International Relations* 2 (2000), 243.

[20] See I. M. Young, 'Equality of Whom? Social Groups and Judgements of Injustice', *Journal of Political Philosophy* 9 (2001), 1–19; Phillips, 'Equality, Pluralism, Universality', 244; A. Phillips, 'Defending Equality of Outcome', *Journal of Political Philosophy* 12 (2004), 15.

[21] See Young, 'Equality of Whom?', 8.

the opportunities he enjoys and the constraints he encounters, and these are, in part, a product of his group memberships and the social position he occupies. To maintain that something is part of a person's circumstances is not to deny that it may be the product of social structures. (A methodological individualist would want to explain social structures as the product of the relations between individuals, and patterns of individual behaviour, but, as I have suggested, even if this approach is misconceived, it is not clear that responsibility-sensitive egalitarianism is committed to it.)

In her earlier work, Young also argues that justice is not primarily a distributive notion, and that if we are to understand injustice properly, we must regard the notion of oppression as fundamental. (In arguing against luck egalitarianism, Elizabeth Anderson has also proposed that we need to understand equality as primarily a social relation rather than a mode of distribution.) From this standpoint it might be said that responsibility-sensitive egalitarianism has tended to focus on the issue of how costs and benefits should be distributed amongst individuals, whereas justice requires a wider perspective that is shaped by an understanding of the main forms of oppression. In this light consider how defenders of the neutralization approach have addressed the issue of what justice requires in relation to disability. Most have maintained that individuals with disabilities (at least in so far as they cannot legitimately be held responsible for those disabilities) should receive compensation when their disabilities cannot be remedied. Yet as critics have pointed out, this ignores the role of social structures and practices in the oppression of the disabled. For at least some of the disadvantages experienced by the disabled might be removed by changing these structures and practices. To give a mundane example that I also mentioned in Chapter 6, buildings might be made accessible to those in wheelchairs so that a wider range of services, facilities, and occupations become available to those whose mobility would otherwise be restricted.

There is much to be said in favour of a form of egalitarianism that regards equality as a multifaceted ideal, conceptually connected to the notion of oppression. It is hard to see why responsibility-sensitive egalitarianism in general (or indeed the particular mitigation approach I favour) should be disturbed by such a proposal, however. Even if there is much more to oppression than an unjust distribution of resources, the distribution of resources within a society cannot credibly be regarded as irrelevant to the issue of whether some are oppressed in it. Both Young and Phillips would agree with this, though perhaps neither would go so far as to claim (as I do in Chapters 5 and 6) that there may be reasons for regarding inequalities of a certain kind or degree as unjust independently of their causal effects—independently, for example, of their effects on the capacities necessary to be a full citizen. To the extent that the distribution of resources in a society is a question of justice, the role of structures in sustaining particular distributions will also come within the purview of justice. Indeed, responsibility-sensitive egalitarianism will evaluate these structures in terms of their ability to deliver outcomes which hold individuals appropriately responsible for their behaviour, in so far as that is possible in practice. (Even if luck egalitarianism has, in general, ignored the role played by social practices and institutions in disadvantaging disabled people, there is no reason in principle why versions of responsibility-sensitive egalitarianism cannot give due acknowledgement to these factors, and insist that justice requires these practices and institutions to be reformed in an appropriate way.)

Responsibility-sensitive egalitarianism does seem to be committed to the idea that the prosperity or flourishing of groups does not matter fundamentally. According to the different versions of this form of egalitarianism, what matters ultimately is that the relative levels of advantage enjoyed by individuals within and across these groups are appropriately sensitive to their choices but are not inappropriately affected by their circumstances. Structures and group membership matter only in so far as they are relevant to this issue. Again, however, it is not clear that there is anything objectionable in maintaining that it is the flourishing of individuals (in both absolute and relative terms) that matters fundamentally not the flourishing of groups, and that the flourishing of groups matters only in so far as it bears upon the flourishing of individuals.[22]

IV. *Atomistic Egoism*

Is responsibility-sensitive egalitarianism committed to atomistic egoism?[23] The notion of atomistic egoism is far from clear, and critics

[22] Young agrees, see 'Equality of Whom?', 6.

[23] See Anderson, 'What is the Point of Equality?', esp. 300, 311.

who level this charge against responsibility-sensitive egalitarianism have a variety of issues in mind, but one question that unavoidably arises is how it proposes to distribute the costs of caring for those who cannot meet their own needs. The answers that responsibility-sensitive egalitarianism gives to this question will depend in part on what approach it takes to the issue of when a person can legitimately be required to bear the costs of his behaviour. (In Chapter 7, I rejected what I called the control conception and the responsiveness to reason conception, arguing instead for a pluralist approach to this issue.)

The easiest cases for responsibility-sensitive egalitarianism to deal with are those where a person's needs are due entirely to his own genetic or biological constitution, and are not in any way the product of his own or other people's behaviour. In such cases responsibility-sensitive egalitarianism will regard these needs as part of a person's circumstances. As a result, it will hold that justice requires us to counteract the effects of these needs on people's relative access to advantage. When needs are partially or wholly the result of one's own actions, or partially or wholly the product of the actions of others, the issue is much tougher because they lie within the category of some agent's choice.

Consider cases where a person's needs are the result of his own actions. The control conception I identified in Chapter 7 will focus on whether the agent could have avoided creating those needs. If he could have done so, and there were no excusing conditions, then according to the control conception he can legitimately be required to bear the full costs of meeting those needs. Suppose, for example, that the agent engaged in a practice that he knew carried with it a serious risk of personal injury, without insuring himself against that prospect even though he had the resources to do so. If he suffers injury as a result, then the control approach would imply that it is legitimate to require him to bear its full costs, including the costs of medical treatment or the costs of nursing care. There would be no requirement of justice to help him if he is unable to bear those costs on his own. The responsiveness to reason conception is likely to reach the same conclusion.

Eric Rakowski, who defends a version of the neutralization approach, provides a good illustration of this way of thinking:

People who leap from airplanes, scale cliffs, or whirl around racetracks knowingly take their lives in their own hands and cannot expect others to foot their hospital bills or aid their dependents if fortune is uncharitable.[24]

Following Ronald Dworkin, Rakowski distinguishes between brute luck and option luck and argues that in so far as someone's needs are the consequence of his bad option luck (I refer to such needs as self-inflicted), he can legitimately be required to bear the costs of meeting those needs himself. If insurance against infirmity and other setbacks is available in a society, and its members are aware that such insurance is available, then those who fail to purchase this insurance can legitimately be required to bear the costs of these setbacks. Their needs are, in the relevant sense, self-inflicted, for the opportunity to purchase insurance means that these needs become a matter of bad option luck rather than bad brute luck. If someone is unable to meet the costs of self-inflicted needs, there is no requirement of justice that others contribute to the costs of doing so. Indeed, forcing others to provide the means to care for those who could have insured against infirmity arising from bad option luck but failed to do so might be seen as exploitation of the prudent who, in contrast, avail themselves of this insurance.[25] Rakowski is untroubled by these conclusions and indeed regards them as appealing implications of his account. But many egalitarians react against them. Can responsibility-sensitive egalitarianism, which holds people accountable for their choices in various contexts, be faulted for being too harsh in its treatment of those with self-inflicted needs?

In response it might be argued that responsibility-sensitive egalitarianism is consistent with a scheme of compulsory insurance, where premiums are set in the light of the risks to which individuals choose to expose themselves. A compulsory insurance scheme of this kind would not sanction the exploitation of the prudent by the imprudent, but it would run into the charge of paternalism, for it appears to involve restricting the freedom of both the imprudent and the prudent for their own good.[26] Since the freedom of both is restricted by a compulsory insurance scheme, it might be said that

[24] E. Rakowski, *Equal Justice* (Oxford: Oxford University Press, 1991; 79).
[25] Rakowski, *Equal Justice*, 82.
[26] See Anderson, 'What is the Point of Equality?', 301.

they nevertheless possess equal freedom.[27] But it remains the case that, as a result of the dispositions of the imprudent, the prudent lose what might be regarded as an important freedom, namely, the freedom not to insure, even if they would not take advantage of that freedom. The charge of paternalism is not insuperable, however. Indeed, we might respond to it by arguing that a compulsory insurance scheme can be justified by an independent reason or duty of justice to ensure that everyone is in a position to lead a decent life.[28] In other words, we might here appeal to some version of the sufficiency view, of the kind defended in Chapter 6, to justify a compulsory insurance scheme on non-paternalistic grounds.

In effect we would be appealing to the idea that there is a reason why it may be unfair to require a person to bear the full costs of his choices, even when he reflectively endorsed those choices at the time he made them, and no excusing conditions entered the picture, thereby providing further support for the pluralist view I defended in Chapter 7: if requiring a person to bear the full costs of his choices would mean that he would be destitute, then we have a reason of justice not to do so. Note, however, that the version of the sufficiency view we would require here would have to claim that we have a reason of justice to aid those who are unable to lead a decent life, regardless of how their needs came about. This version of the sufficiency view would not have to suppose, however, that those with self-inflicted needs are in precisely the same position, from the point of view of justice, as those with equivalent needs that are not self-inflicted, for it can be made sensitive to considerations of personal responsibility whilst acknowledging that there is a reason of justice to help the needy, irrespective of how their needs arose. There are two ways in which this might be done. First, it might be argued that individuals with self-inflicted needs nevertheless have a duty of justice to bear the costs of those needs. It is only when they are unable to do so that our duty of justice to aid those who are unable to lead a decent life kicks in. Second, it might be maintained that even though there is a reason of justice to benefit anyone below the threshold who is unable to benefit himself, there is also a reason of justice to give greater weight to benefiting those who are below

[27] See Carter, 'Equal Opportunity and Equal Freedom'.
[28] Cf. Carter, 'Equal Opportunity and Equal Freedom'.

the threshold through no fault of their own in cases of conflict. Suppose, for example, that there has been an unpredictable natural catastrophe which has resulted in many casualties, and collective provision funded by a scheme of compulsory insurance is insufficient to meet all of the needs that currently exist in the society. It might be argued that under these circumstances, other things being equal (that is, when benefits are of the same magnitude and there is the same number of potential beneficiaries), we have a reason of justice to give priority to those who are the victims of this natural catastrophe (and others who are needy through no fault of their own) over those with self-inflicted needs. In practice, of course, the costs of doing so, both moral and otherwise, may militate against prioritizing in this way.

V. *The Burdens of Childcare*

Responding to the charge of atomistic egoism also requires some account of how responsibility-sensitive egalitarianism would distribute the burdens of caring for children. Defenders of this form of egalitarianism have gravitated towards the conclusion that parents have responsibility for their children (in so far as they genuinely chose to have them), and hence should bear the costs of raising them, as well as enjoying the pleasures of doing so.[29] Rakowski describes what he sees as the implications of the neutralization approach for the issue of who can legitimately be required to bear the costs of raising children:

> Babies are not brought by storks whose whims are beyond our control. Specific individuals are responsible for their existence. It is therefore unjust to declare ... that because two people decide to have a child, or through carelessness find themselves with one, everyone is required to share their resources with the new arrival, and to the same extent as its parents.[30]

Rakowski would say the same of babies who are born with special needs, or who develop disabilities in childhood as a result of congenital defects, at least when it is possible to insure against that

[29] See, for example, P. Casal and A. Williams, 'Rights, Equality and Procreation', *Analyse und Kritik* 17 (1995), 103–14; E. Rakowski, *Equal Justice*, 150–5; Steiner, *An Essay on Rights*, 277–9.

[30] Rakowski, *Equal Justice*, 153.

possibility. When insurance is available, he would argue that giving birth to a disabled baby represents bad option luck, for in making decisions about whether to have children parents are, or should be, aware of this risk. (From this standpoint, it might even be argued that prospective parents should be required to insure against the risk of having a child with special needs, on the grounds described in the previous section, that we have a reason or duty of justice to ensure that everyone is in a position to lead a decent life which might otherwise not be fulfilled.)

Even if we accept the idea that parents by and large should bear the costs of looking after their children, this still leaves open the question of how those costs should be distributed within couples. To simplify matters, let us assume that each parent had a veto over the decision to have children and that each reflectively endorsed the decision, with no manipulation or indoctrinated involved.[31] From the perspective of both the control conception and the responsiveness to reason conception, there are two obvious ways in which responsibility-sensitive egalitarianism might require the costs of raising children to be distributed between the parents. First, they might require these costs to be distributed equally. Secondly, they might require these costs to be distributed in whatever way the parents agree.

The first proposal seems vulnerable to an overwhelming objection, namely, that it is insensitive to any discussions which might have informed a couple's decision to have children, for example, an agreement that the man or woman should bear the lion's share of those burdens. Prospective parents may want to have children to differing degrees, and as a result may come to different arrangements concerning how the various benefits and burdens of raising them should be distributed between them. (Indeed, a man may agree to inseminate a woman on the understanding that he bears none of the costs of any child that may result.) Against the second proposal, however, it might be argued that allowing the man and the woman to decide how the burdens of childcare should be distributed will make women vulnerable to exploitation in a society such as ours

[31] Of course, social reality is much more complex than this: children may be conceived through rape, or inadvertently as a result of contraceptive failure, or as a result of one party misleading the other about whether he or she is fertile. Responsibility-sensitive egalitarianism will also have implications for cases of these kinds.

in which gender roles are partially constituted by the norm that mothers should look after their children personally, even if men and women enjoy the same set of employment opportunities outside the home.

Indeed this difficulty arises more generally: for it is also partially constitutive of those roles, though perhaps to a lesser degree, that women should look after their elderly or sick relatives personally. Suppose gender socialization tends to mean that women feel special responsibility for those relatives who cannot meet their own needs, regardless of the cause. So they, more than men, feel special responsibility to look after their elderly or imprudent relatives personally, as well as their own children. Under these conditions responsibility-sensitive egalitarianism might appear to treat women who decide to care for dependants as if they simply have an expensive taste, even when they do so from the deep moral conviction that they, as women, owe special duties of care to family members.[32]

Advocates of responsibility-sensitive egalitarianism such as Rakowski may find this conclusion unobjectionable and deny that it makes women vulnerable to exploitation, and they might make various observations designed to provide support for it. First, they can insist that if social institutions and practices in effect assign women the primary obligation to care for these dependant relatives, because it is impossible for the women concerned to refuse to do so without their relatives being neglected, then justice requires that it be reformed. Suppose that many of those in need of care would be neglected unless their female relatives cared for them because their male relatives have not, as part of their upbringing or experience, acquired the skills to do so. Under these circumstances it seems that women cannot legitimately be required to bear the full costs of any decision they make to look after their relatives since they had no reasonable alternative but to do so. Both the control conception and the responsiveness to reason conception can support this conclusion.

Second, they can argue that each member of society has an equal share of the responsibility to provide the means to care for those in need when no one in particular (even the person in need) can legitimately be required to bear those costs. In cases such as these, men or women who decide to look after their infirm relatives are

[32] See Anderson, 'What Is the Point of Equality?', 297, 300, 311, 313, 324–5.

entitled to resources to do so. But if someone decides to look after them *personally* for whatever reason, then, provided that his choice is fully and properly under his control and reflectively endorsed, he should bear the extra costs of his decision.

Third, they can point out that responsibility-sensitive egalitarianism is not conservative in its implications for women's roles and may require wide-ranging reforms of social practices and institutions. In relation to childcare commitments in particular, responsibility-sensitive egalitarianism may require institutions and practices to be designed in such a way that they at least *permit*, and sometimes force, men and women to share the costs of their decision to have children.[33] (It can accept that forcing parents to share these costs would sometimes be unjust, for example, when they agreed in the first place to split these costs unequally.) This has potentially far-reaching implications for the organization of the workplace and domestic life. In some circumstances the best way of allowing men and women to share the relevant costs might involve providing more flexible work structures. When the parents live apart, responsibility-sensitive egalitarianism can insist that they should sometimes be required to share the costs of raising their children. If one of them plays no part in childcare, this may require him to pay the other parent, unless they agreed to some different arrangement when they decided to have children.

But these observations do not wholly answer the charge that responsibility-sensitive egalitarianism makes women systematically vulnerable to exploitation. We know that in practice it is likely to be women who are burdened with the care of their needy relatives and that they will often do so from a sense of special moral responsibility. This may be so even when they could have behaved otherwise, they

[33] I say 'may require' since according to some versions of responsibility-sensitive egalitarianism what matters is that men and women should have equivalent sets of options available to them. For example, according to Richard Arneson's initial formulation of equality of opportunity for welfare, it obtains between a group of people only if each faces 'an array of options that is equivalent to every other person's in terms of the prospects for preference satisfaction it offers' (R. Arneson, 'Equality and Equal Opportunity for Welfare', in L. Pojman and R. Westmoreland (eds), *Equality: Selected Readings* (New York: Oxford University Press, 1997; 233). In principle this approach would allow men and women to be assigned to separate spheres if (and this 'if' would be a big one) they had equivalent sets of options in the relevant sense.

reflectively endorse their decision to look after their relatives, and they are faced with other reasonable alternatives. In order to answer the charge, we need to return to the argument developed in the previous chapter. There I maintained that the extensive socialization which is shaped by (and fosters behaviour and expectations that accord with) the sexist norm that women should look after their children and needy relatives personally makes it unfair to require them to bear the full costs of the consequences of acting in a way that accords with that norm, even when they reject the norm. We should allow that there may be a variety of different reasons for not requiring a person to bear the costs of his choices, even when the agent had a wide range of options available and reflectively endorsed his choice. A pluralist approach of this kind can maintain that the operation of the norm that women should look after their children and other needy relatives personally provides reason not to require women who behave in accordance with it to bear the full costs of their behaviour.

VI. *Conclusion*

One of the most attractive features of responsibility-sensitive egalitarianism is the way in which it gives weight to the choices of individuals in determining what is to count as a just distribution. But it is precisely this feature, or at least the specific form it has taken, that has made some suspicious of responsibility-sensitive egalitarianism. In this chapter I have argued that it can give appropriate weight to personal responsibility without being committed to the problematic idea that an individual's just share of economic benefits and burdens can be decided independently of a scheme for determining what constitutes a just overall allocation of those benefits and burdens. I have also insisted that it need not deny the possibility of genuine collective responsibility, and that it need not neglect the role of others in sustaining the networks of support on which we all rely at some points in our lives, and that it is not committed to being excessively harsh towards those with self-inflicted needs.

CHAPTER 9

Conclusion

This book can be read as a partial critique of luck egalitarianism, the dominant form of responsibility-sensitive egalitarianism. Luck egalitarianism provides us with a particular account of what it is to level the playing field in the way that justice requires. It holds that inequalities are unjust if they derive from differences in people's circumstances, but are just if they are the product of their voluntary choices. It is, in effect, a combination of two different claims: first, that justice requires us to neutralize the effects of differences in people's circumstances; second, that it is just to require people to bear the costs, or allow them to enjoy the benefits, of their voluntary choices. In making these claims, luck egalitarianism invokes a distinction between choice and circumstance to which it assigns direct normative significance. Such an approach might be thought to offer the best way of understanding the ideal of equality of opportunity. Indeed, luck egalitarianism is attractive because it gives an account of what it means to level the playing field that goes further than traditional theories of equality of opportunity, but which at the same time aims to hold people accountable for their behaviour. I have nevertheless taken issue with luck egalitarianism in a number of different ways.

Against the idea that justice requires us to neutralize the effects of differences in people's circumstances, I have argued that it requires us merely to mitigate these effects, to prevent them from having an undue impact upon people's relative access to advantage. Competing versions of this mitigation approach are constituted by different sets of principles which give different determinations of what is to count as an 'undue effect'. I do not pretend to have offered a complete version of the mitigation approach, but it is clear, I hope, that the principles I have defended provide a vision of what it is to level the playing field that is rather different, at least at the level of fundamental principle, from the neutralization approach. I have defended a basic skills principle—that everyone should receive an education that enables them to acquire a set of skills which will mean that they have an adequate range of options—which I claimed is best grounded in a sufficiency view. I have also argued for two quasi-egalitarian principles that are designed to place limits on the degree of inequality that can permissibly emerge from differences in people's circumstances. The first of these is an educational access principle, which is grounded in the idea that the effects of differences in people's social circumstances should not be such that some but not others possess (or can reasonably be expected to acquire) the resources necessary to obtain a good that is important in general for a person's access to overall advantage. The second is an accumulation of wealth principle, which holds that the effects of differences in people's circumstances should not be such that some but not others can acquire the resources that are necessary in order to be able to lead a decent life whilst choosing not to work to earn an income.

The set of principles I have defended also involves a commitment to selecting the best-qualified candidates for jobs and places in higher education, grounded in the requirement that we respect each person's agency. This allows the distribution of advantaged social positions to be affected by differences in natural talent and ability in so far as they have been developed and exercised. Rather than treating my favoured version of the mitigation approach as if it were itself an account of equality of opportunity, my proposal is that we should see it as incorporating a meritocratic account of this ideal, made up of the principle that the best-qualified candidates should be appointed to advantaged social positions and by the principles that govern access to qualifications, that is, the basic skills principle and the educational access principle. This meritocratic account is then supplemented by further principles, such as the accumulation of wealth principle, which taken together provide us with an interpretation of what it means to level the playing field in the way that justice requires.

The mitigation approach also involves principles which determine when it is just to require a person to bear the costs of his behaviour. Here again I have rejected the luck egalitarian position on this issue, in particular the claim that it is always fair to require a person to bear the costs of his voluntary choices, favouring instead a more nuanced account which maintains that it is sometimes unfair to do so. The conditions under which people make choices may crucially affect whether it is fair to require them to bear the costs of these choices. Here I am not just thinking of cases where individuals are coerced, or are deprived of the information necessary to choose well. Luck egalitarians would not regard these as counter-examples to their thesis because under these conditions choice is not fully voluntary. But there are other cases that do constitute a threat to it, when people make choices that conform to the social ethos in their society, but in doing so face significant disadvantages. The particular case I discussed was that of the career-sacrificing mother, who acts in a way that accords with the norm that mothers should take primary responsibility for childcare. I argued that it would be unfair simply to require her to bear the costs of voluntarily acting in a way that complies with this sexist norm, given the way in which it informs the behaviour and expectations of others. Discussion of this kind of case and others led me to claim that there are a number of different considerations which may affect whether it would be just to require a person to bear the full costs of his choices. In this context I also appealed to a version of the sufficiency view, arguing that even when we give appropriate weight to personal responsibility, we have a reason of justice not to require people to bear the costs of their choices when that would leave them destitute.

Although I am a critic of luck egalitarianism, my opposition to it is not as radical as some theorists, such as Elizabeth Anderson. Anderson rejects luck egalitarianism in favour of what she calls democratic equality. Democratic equality, as she conceives it, has a positive and negative dimension. Its negative dimension consists in a rejection of oppression, that is, 'forms of relationship by which some people dominate, exploit, marginalize, demean, and inflict violence upon others'; its positive dimension consists in a commitment to a social order in which persons stand in relations of equality, which requires democracy understood as 'collective self-determination by means of open discussion among equals, in accordance with rules acceptable to all'.[1] Anderson regards democratic equality as a relational theory,

[1] Anderson, 'What is the Point of Equality?', 313.

whereas she claims that luck egalitarianism is a distributive theory because it conceives equality as a pattern of distribution.

This contrast is somewhat overdrawn: luck egalitarianism may be part of an account of what it is to treat people as equals, with equal concern and respect, whilst democratic equality (as indeed Anderson argues) has distributive implications even if it is not itself a theory of distribution. But the two accounts of equality do have a different character: luck egalitarianism is troubled by inequalities of access to advantage as such, whereas democratic equality is moved by them only in so far as they play a role in oppression or exploitation, or undermine democratic self-government. The theory I have defended shares with Anderson's account of democratic equality, a rejection of the idea that justice requires us to neutralize the effects of differences in people's circumstances, but it does not suppose that we need only object to inequality when it plays a part in oppression or undermines the conditions necessary for democratic self-government. Indeed, it allows that certain kinds of inequalities of access to advantage may be unjust *simply* because they are too great, or because they have a kind of character that is objectionable, irrespective of whether they are bound up in some way with oppression or exploitation and whether they undermine the conditions necessary for genuine democratic self-government. So understood, my theory can be seen as expressing what it is for individuals to be treated as equals and as maintaining that certain inequalities in the distribution of goods signal a failure to do so. It can hold that these inequalities are unjust in themselves not because of their effects on, say, democratic self-government, and without supposing that they are unjust because they are oppressive or exploitative.

In terms of my approach to these issues, the choice is not between regarding equality as a 'social ideal' which expresses what it is for people to be treated as equals, and regarding it instead as a distributive ideal concerned with giving equal amounts of something, whether it be resources, welfare, or capabilities.[2] Rather, the choice is between seeing equality as a social ideal which objects to certain kinds of distributive inequalities as such, and seeing it as a social ideal

[2] See Scheffler, 'What is Egalitarianism?'; S. Scheffler, 'Choice, Circumstance and the Value of Equality', *Politics, Philosophy and Economics* 4 (2005), esp. 17–23; T. Hinton, 'Must Egalitarians Choose Between Fairness and Respect?', *Philosophy and Public Affairs* 30 (2001), esp. 80–1.

which objects to these distributive inequalities only because they are the product of exploitation (or because they make some individuals vulnerable to exploitation), or oppressive (or make some vulnerable to oppression), or because they make it impossible or harder for some to enjoy or exercise their rights as citizens.

In the way that I have unpacked it, equality of opportunity, and the wider goal of levelling the playing field, is a complex ideal. The version of the mitigation approach I have defended gives no simple answer to the question: when are the effects of differences in natural endowments and social circumstances on access to advantage just and when are they unjust? The neutralization approach I have rejected, which is part and parcel of luck egalitarianism, does give a straightforward answer to this question at one level: it maintains that any inequalities of access to advantage that stem from differences in natural endowments and social circumstances are unjust. In contrast, according to the mitigation approach I favour, justice requires that these differences should not unduly affect access to advantage, then there are various principles governing access to different goods or different aspects of people's circumstances which, combined, spell out what it is for that to be the case. The particular version of the mitigation approach I have defended also gives a complex answer to the question: when is it just and when is it unjust to require a person to bear the costs of his behaviour? It maintains that a variety of different factors may affect the justice of requiring people to bear the costs of their choices, for example, the norms that are partially constitutive of the social ethos that governs the society in question.

It might be thought that the complexity of the mitigation approach—its reliance on a plurality of principles that work together but which may nevertheless come into conflict with one another—counts against that approach and provides at least one reason in favour of the neutralization approach, and indeed in favour of a version of it which holds that justice requires people to bear the full costs of their choices. But I do not think that considerations of complexity or simplicity have any bearing on the assessment of the mitigation approach, nor indeed the assessment of the neutralization approach, at the level of fundamental principle. At this level, simplicity is a virtue of a theory only if that theory is true, and the reasons I have given against the neutralization approach suggest that it is flawed. Simplicity at the most abstract theoretical level is also bound to give way to considerable complexity of principles at other levels when the issue of what principles are required for the regulation of policy and institutions is addressed.

In response, it might be argued that it is not complexity as such that counts against the mitigation approach, but rather the particular character of this complexity, especially the large role that it gives for judgement, and for the balancing of principles governing different aspects of people's circumstances and the access to different goods. Rawls aims to minimize the scope for intuitive judgement by providing priority rules for when principles conflict. This is at least partly because he wants to reduce the scope for non-rational factors to influence the trade-offs between these principles, and perhaps partly because of the need for publicity, that is, the need for principles which are such that others can check the extent to which a person's behaviour conforms to them. But intuitive judgement may be unavoidable if we are to remain faithful to our moral sensibilities. Rather than being suspicious of intuitive judgements, and seeking to minimize our reliance upon them, we would do better to distance ourselves from a conception of normative theory that strives to bring these judgements under fewer and fewer fundamental principles, with priority rules to settle conflicts between these principles, and where necessary abandoning those judgements that do not fit, without taking proper account of the burdens that this exercise may impose upon our normative sensibility. A conception of normative theory that gives a large role to judgement will allow non-rational influences greater play, but provided that law and policy which is given the job of balancing different principles is subject to democratic control, this should not trouble us too much.

I do not claim to have offered a definitive account of equality of opportunity and its proper place in egalitarian thought. There is no reason to expect convergence upon it, even if my arguments are any good. The fact that disagreement over what counts as equality of opportunity, and its proper role in egalitarian thought, is likely to persist does not show that whether it is accepted or rejected is ultimately a matter of personal preference. Disagreement does not preclude the possibility of rational argument concerning which is the best; we are not forced, for example, to adopt an emotivist understanding of the role and significance of moral and political judgements that sees these judgements as mere expressions of desire.

There is no incoherence in holding, on the one hand, that reasonable people may disagree over the nature of equality of opportunity (or egalitarian justice more generally) and that there is no reason to expect convergence on a single conception, whilst on the other hand maintaining that one conception is the best and the others mistaken.[3]

But the persistence of disagreement over which conception of equality of opportunity or egalitarian justice is best means that the political process has an important role to play in legitimating the adoption of one conception rather than others to shape institutions and policy. As Jeremy Waldron has argued, political philosophers need to address two different kinds of questions: first, the question of which conception of justice is best; second, the question of how we should proceed in the face of disagreement over which conception of justice is the best.[4] (Although these are different questions, they may not be entirely independent of each other. For it may be that justice itself places constraints on how we should proceed in the face of divergent conceptions of justice.) This book has addressed the first of these questions but both are of fundamental importance. It would be a mistake to conclude from the existence of disagreement about which conception of equality of opportunity (or egalitarian justice more generally) is the best, that the only questions of importance to political theorists concern the design of political processes to determine which conception should prevail in the development and reform of social and economic institutions. Likewise, however, those engaged in debates about which conception of equality of opportunity is the best, and about its proper role in egalitarian thought, of the kind found in this book should not suppose that these are the only important debates, or that procedures should be evaluated solely in terms of whether they are likely to promote justice properly conceived.

In the face of disagreement over which conception of equality of opportunity or justice is the best, the political process is of vital importance, for it can provide the authority to implement one of these conceptions rather than another. Of course, there will be disagreement over which set of political procedures is fairest, and

[3] See my *Explaining Political Disagreement* (Cambridge: Cambridge University Press, 1993;, ch. 2).

[4] See J. Waldron, *Law and Disagreement* (Oxford: Oxford University Press, 1999; 3).

this will be so even when there is broad agreement amongst people that democracy is the best form of government. In practice, existing political procedures will provide a 'pragmatic solution' to the existence of disagreement in so far as citizens believe that these procedures are acceptable, even if they do not believe that they are the best, or the fairest, or the most democratic. Provided citizens regard their procedures as authoritative, that is, believe they are sufficiently fair and well designed for there to be good reason to abide by them, then the existence of a range of disagreements about which electoral system is the best, whether there should be proportional representation, and whether there should be group rights, will not compromise the ability of these procedures to offer a pragmatic solution to the existence of disagreement over equality of opportunity and justice more generally. Indeed, questions about which political procedures are the best or the fairest can themselves be a matter for debate and decision within existing procedures.

This pragmatic solution to the problem of disagreement over which conception of justice is the best does not mean that democracy or order is being given priority over justice.[5] It would be a mistake to suppose that the argument I have rehearsed has as its conclusion that when their favoured conception of justice lacks widespread appeal, citizens should give democracy priority over justice. The question of which value should take priority, justice or democracy, is as much a matter of political contest as the proper way of understanding each of these values. The political process does not provide a principled solution to the problem of disagreement over which conception of justice is the best by ordering values in a way that everyone can find acceptable but rather provides a practical way of proceeding (and overcoming disagreement in this sense) for all those who, for different reasons no doubt, regard that process as acceptable.[6]

[5] See Waldron, *Law and Disagreement*, 160–1.

[6] On these grounds the normative theorizing in this book does not 'aim at the supersession of ... politics' (G. Newey, *After Politics: The Rejection of Politics in Contemporary Liberal Philosophy* (Basingstoke, UK: Palgrave, 2001; 2; see also 7–8).

BIBLIOGRAPHY

Anderson, E., 'What is the Point of Equality?', *Ethics* 109 (1999), 287–337.

Arneson, R., 'Equality', in R. Goodin and P. Pettit (eds), *A Companion to Contemporary Political Philosophy* (Oxford: Blackwell, 1991).

——'Equality and Equal Opportunity for Welfare', in L. Pojman and R. Westmoreland (eds), *Equality: Selected Readings* (New York: Oxford University Press, 1997).

——'Against Rawlsian Equality of Opportunity', *Philosophical Studies* 93 (1999), 77–112.

——'Luck Egalitarianism and Prioritarianism', *Ethics* 110 (2000), 339–49.

——'Why Justice Requires Transfers to Offset Income and Wealth Inequalities', *Social Philosophy and Policy* 19 (2002), 172–200.

Barry, B., 'Equal Opportunity and Moral Arbitrariness', in N. Bowie (ed.), *Equal Opportunity* (Boulder, CO: Westview, 1988).

——*Theories of Justice: A Treatise on Social Justice, Vol. I* (Hemel Hempstead, UK: Harvester-Wheatsheaf, 1989).

——*Culture and Equality: An Egalitarian Critique of Multiculturalism* (Oxford: Polity, 2001).

——*Why Social Justice Matters* (Cambridge: Polity, 2005).

Brighouse, H. and Swift, A., 'Parental Partiality: Legitimate and Excessive', a paper presented to the workshop on Equality of Opportunity at the ECPR Joint Sessions, Granada, 14–19 April 2005.

Brink, D., *Moral Realism and the Foundations of Ethics* (Cambridge: Cambridge University Press, 1989).

Broome, J., 'Equality Versus Priority: A Useful Distinction', in D. Wickler and C. J. L. Murray (eds), *'Goodness' and 'Fairness': Ethical Issues in Health Resource Allocation* (World Health Organization, forthcoming).

Brudney, D., 'Community and Completion', in A. Reath, B. Herman and C. Korsgaard (eds), *Reclaiming the History of Ethics: Essays for John Rawls* (Cambridge: Cambridge University Press, 1997).

Buchanan, A., 'Equal Opportunity and Genetic Intervention', in E. F. Paul, F. D. Miller and J. Paul (eds), *The Just Society* (Cambridge: Cambridge University Press, 1995).

Campbell, T. D., 'Equality of Opportunity', *Proceedings of the Aristotelian Society* 106 (1974–5), 51–68.

Caney, S., 'Individuals, Nations and Obligations', in S. Caney, D. George, and P. Jones (eds), *National Rights, International Obligations* (Oxford: Westview, 1996).

——*Justice Beyond Borders: A Global Political Theory* (Oxford: Oxford University Press, 2005).

Carter, I., 'Equal Opportunity and Equal Freedom', a paper presented to the workshop on Equality of Opportunity at the ECPR Joint Sessions, Granada, 14–19 April 2005.

Casal P. and Williams, A., 'Rights, Equality and Procreation', *Analyse und Kritik* 17 (1995), 93–116.

Cavanagh, M., *Against Equality of Opportunity* (Oxford: Oxford University Press, 2002).

Cohen, G. A., 'David Miller on Market Socialism and Distributive Justice', unpublished paper.

——'On the Currency of Egalitarian Justice', *Ethics* 99 (1989), 906–44.

——'Expensive Tastes and Multiculturalism', in R. Bhargava, A. Bagchi, and R. Sudarshan (eds), *Multiculturalism, Liberalism and Democracy* (New Delhi: Oxford University Press, 1999).

——*If You're an Egalitarian, How Come You're so Rich?* (Cambridge, MA: Harvard University Press, 2000).

——'Facts and Principles', *Philosophy and Public Affairs* 31 (2003), 211–45.

——'Expensive Taste Rides Again', in J. Burley (ed.), *Dworkin and His Critics* (Oxford: Blackwell, 2004).

——'Rescuing Justice from Constructivism', unpublished manuscript.

Crisp, R., 'Equality, Priority, and Compassion', *Ethics* 113 (2003), 745–63.

Daniels, N., 'Democratic Equality: Rawls's Complex Egalitarianism', in S. Freeman (ed.), *The Cambridge Companion to Rawls* (Cambridge: Cambridge University Press, 2003).

Darwall, S. L., 'Two Kinds of Respect', *Ethics* 88 (1977), 36–49.

Dworkin, R., 'What is Equality? Part 2: Equality of Resources', *Philosophy and Public Affairs* 10 (1981), 283–345.

——*Sovereign Virtue: The Theory and Practice of Equality* (Cambridge, MA: Harvard University Press, 2000).

——'Sovereign Virtue Revisited', *Ethics* 113 (2002), 106–43.

——'Replies to Critics', in J. Burley (ed.), *Dworkin and His Critics* (Oxford: Blackwell, 2004).

Elster, J., *An Introduction to Karl Marx* (Cambridge: Cambridge University Press, 1986).

Estlund, D., 'Liberty, Equality, and Fraternity in Cohen's Critique of Rawls', *Journal of Political Philosophy* 6 (1988), 99–112.

Fischer, J. M. *The Metaphysics of Freewill: An Essay on Control* (Oxford: Blackwell, 1994).

—— 'Recent Work on Moral Responsibility', *Ethics* 110 (1999), 93–139.

—— and Ravizza, M., *Responsibility and Control: A Theory of Moral Responsibility* (Cambridge: Cambridge University Press, 1998).

Fishkin, J., *Justice, Equal Opportunity, and the Family* (New Haven, CT: Yale University Press, 1983).

Flew, A., *The Politics of Procrustes* (London: Temple Smith, 1981).

Frankfurt, H., 'Equality as a Moral Idea', *Ethics* 98 (1987), 21–43.

Gaus, G., *Justificatory Liberalism: An Essay on Epistemology and Political Theory* (Oxford: Oxford University Press, 1996).

Goldman, A., 'The Justification of Equal Opportunity', *Social Philosophy and Policy* 5 (1987), 88–103.

Graham, K., *The Battle of Democracy* (Brighton, UK: Wheatsheaf, 1986).

Gutmann, A. and Thompson, D., *Democracy and Disagreement* (Cambridge, MA: Harvard University Press, 1996).

Harris, J. R., *The Nurture Assumption: Why Children Turn Out the Way They Do* (New York: Free Press, 1998).

Hart, B., and Risley, T., *Meaningful Differences in the Everyday Experience of Young American Children* (Baltimore, MD: Brookes Publishing, 1995).

Hart, H. L. A., 'Rawls on Liberty and Its Priority', in N. Daniels (ed.), *Reading Rawls* (Oxford: Blackwell, 1975).

Hill, T. E., *Autonomy and Self-Respect* (Cambridge: Cambridge University Press, 1991).

Hinton, T., 'Must Egalitarians Choose Between Fairness and Respect?', *Philosophy and Public Affairs* 30 (2001), 72–87.

Hirose, I., 'Equality, Priority, and Numbers', Ph.D. thesis, University of St Andrews 2003.

Holtug, N., 'Prioritarianism', in N. Holtug and K. Lippert-Rasmussen (eds), *Egalitarianism: New Essays on the Nature and Value of Equality*. Oxford: Oxford University Press (forthcoming in 2007).

Hsieh, N.-H., 'Moral Desert, Fairness and Legitimate Expectations in the Market', *Journal of Political Philosophy* 8 (2000), 91–114.

Hurley, S., *Justice, Luck, and Knowledge* (Cambridge, MA: Harvard University Press, 2003).

Jacobs, L., *Pursuing Equal Opportunities: The Theory and Practice of Egalitarianism* (Cambridge: Cambridge University Press, 2004).

Kershnar, S., 'Why Equal Opportunity Is Not a Valuable Goal', *Journal of Applied Philosophy* 21 (2004), 159–72.

Kymlicka, W., *Liberalism, Community, and Culture* (Oxford: Oxford University Press, 1991).

Kymlicka, W., *Multicultural Citizenship: A Liberal Theory of Minority Rights* (Oxford: Oxford University Press, 1995).

—— *Contemporary Political Philosophy: An Introduction* 2nd edn (Oxford: Oxford University Press, 2002).

Lareau, A., *Unequal Childhoods: Class, Race, and Family Life* (Berkeley and Los Angeles, CA: University of California Press, 2003).

Levin, M., 'Equality of Opportunity', *Philosophical Quarterly* 31 (1981), 110–25.

Lippert-Rasmussen, K., 'The Insignificance of the Distinction Between Telic and Deontic Egalitarianism', in N. Holtug and K. Lippert-Rasmussen (eds), *Egalitarianism: New Essays on the Nature and Value of Equality*. Oxford: Oxford University Press (forthcoming in 2007).

Lloyd Thomas, D. A., 'Competitive Equality of Opportunity', *Mind* 86 (1977), 388–404.

Macleod, C., *Liberalism, Justice, and Markets: A Critique of Liberal Equality* (Oxford: Oxford University Press, 1998).

Mason, A., *Explaining Political Disagreement* (Cambridge: Cambridge University Press, 1993).

—— *Community, Solidarity and Belonging: Levels of Community and Their Normative Significance* (Cambridge: Cambridge University Press, 2000).

—— 'Equality, Personal Responsibility, and Gender Socialisation', *Proceedings of the Aristotelian Society* 100 (2000), 227–46.

—— 'Equality of Opportunity, Old and New', *Ethics* 111 (2001), 760–81.

—— 'Egalitarianism and the Levelling Down Objection', *Analysis* 61 (2001), 246–54.

—— 'Social Justice: The Place of Equal Opportunity', in R. Bellamy and A. Mason (eds), *Political Concepts* (Manchester, UK: Manchester University Press, 2003).

—— 'Meritocracy, Desert and the Moral Force of Intuitions', in D. Bell and A. de-Shalit (eds), *Forms of Justice: Critical Perspectives on David Miller's Political Philosophy* (Lanham, MD: Rowman and Littlefield, 2003).

—— 'Equality of Opportunity and Differences in Social Circumstances', *The Philosophical Quarterly* 54 (2004), 368–88.

—— 'Just Constraints', *British Journal of Political Science* 34 (2004), 251–68.

Matravers, M., 'Responsibility, Luck, and the "Equality of What?" Debate', *Political Studies* 50 (2002), 558–72.

—— 'Luck, Responsibility, and "The Jumble of Lotteries that Constitutes Human Life"', *Imprints* 6 (2002), 28–43.

——'Responsibility and Choice', in M. Matravers (ed.), *Scanlon and Contractualism* (London: Frank Cass, 2003).

May, L., *Sharing Responsibility* (Chicago, IL: University of Chicago Press, 1992).

McDowell, J., *Mind and World* (Cambridge, MA: Harvard University Press, 1994).

McKerlie, D., 'Equality and Priority', *Utilitas* 6 (1994), 25–42.

——'Equality', *Ethics* 106 (1996).

Mendus, S., 'Choice, Chance and Multiculturalism', in P. Kelly (ed.), *Multiculturalism Reconsidered* (Cambridge: Polity, 2002).

Miller, D., *Market, State and Community: Theoretical Foundations of Market Socialism* (Oxford: Oxford University Press, 1989).

——'Recent Theories of Social Justice', *British Journal of Political Science* 21 (1991), 371–91.

——'Deserving Jobs', *Philosophical Quarterly* 42 (1992), 161–81.

——'In Defence of Nationality', *Journal of Applied Philosophy* 10 (1993), 3–16.

——*Principles of Social Justice* (Cambridge, MA: Harvard University Press, 1999).

——'Holding Nations Responsible', *Ethics* 114 (2004), 240–68.

——'Equality of Opportunity and the Family', a paper presented to the workshop on Equality of Opportunity at the ECPR Joint Sessions, Granada, 14–19 April 2005.

Munoz-Dardé, V., 'Is the Family to be Abolished Then?', *Proceedings of the Aristotelian Society* 99 (1999), 37–56.

Nagel, T., *Equality and Partiality* (New York: Oxford University Press, 1991).

——'The Problem of Global Justice', *Philosophy and Public Affairs* 33 (2005), 113–47.

Narveson, J., *The Libertarian Idea* (Philadelphia, PA: Temple University Press, 1988).

——'Egalitarianism: Partial, Counterproductive, and Baseless', in A. Mason (ed.), *Ideals of Equality* (Oxford: Blackwell, 1998).

Newey, G., *After Politics: The Rejection of Politics in Contemporary Liberal Philosophy* (Basingstoke, UK: Palgrave, 2001).

Nickel, J., 'Equal Opportunity in a Pluralistic Society', *Social Philosophy and Policy* 5 (1987), 104–19.

Nielsen, K., *Equality and Liberty: A Defense of Radical Egalitarianism* (Totowa, NJ: Rowman and Allanheld, 1985).

Nozick, R., *Anarchy, State and Utopia* (Oxford: Blackwell, 1974).

Nussbaum, M., 'Human Functioning and Social Justice: In Defence of Aristotelian Essentialism', *Political Theory* 20 (1992), 202–46.

Olsaretti, S., *Liberty, Desert and the Market: A Philosophical Study* (Cambridge: Cambridge University Press, 2004).

Otsuka, M.,'Luck, Insurance, and Equality', *Ethics* 113 (2002), 40–54.

Parekh, B., *Rethinking Multiculturalism: Cultural Diversity and Political Theory* (Basingstoke, UK: Macmillan, 2000).

Parfit, D., 'Equality and Priority', in A. Mason (ed.), *Ideals of Equality* (Oxford: Blackwell, 1998).

—— 'Equality or Priority?', in M. Clayton and A. Williams (eds), *The Ideal of Equality* (Basingstoke, UK: Macmillan, 2000).

Patten, A., 'Liberal Egalitarianism and National Cultures', *The Monist* 82 (1999), 387–410.

Phillips, A., 'Equality, Pluralism, Universality: Current Concerns in Normative Theory', *British Journal of Politics and International Relations* 2 (2000), 237–55.

—— 'Defending Equality of Outcome', *Journal of Political Philosophy* 12 (2004), 1–19.

Pogge, T., *Realizing Rawls* (Ithaca, NY: Cornell University Press, 1989).

—— *World Poverty and Human Rights* (Cambridge: Polity, 2002).

Price, T., 'Egalitarian Justice, Luck, and the Costs of Chosen Ends', *American Philosophical Quarterly* 36 (1999), 267–78.

Rakowski, E., *Equal Justice* (Oxford: Oxford University Press, 1993).

Rawls, J., *A Theory of Justice* (Cambridge, MA: Harvard University Press, 1971).

—— *Political Liberalism* (New York: Columbia University Press, 1993).

Raz, J., *The Morality of Freedom* (Oxford: Oxford University Press, 1986).

Richards, J. R., 'Equality of Opportunity', in A. Mason (ed.), *Ideals of Equality* (Oxford: Blackwell, 1998).

Ripstein, A., 'Equality, Luck, and Responsibility', *Philosophy and Public Affairs* 23 (1994), 3–23.

—— *Equality, Responsibility, and the Law* (Cambridge: Cambridge University Press, 1999).

Risse, M., 'How Does the Global Order Harm the Poor?', *Philosophy and Public Affairs* 33 (2005), 349–76.

Roemer, J., *Equality of Opportunity* (Cambridge, MA: Harvard University Press, 1998).

Rowe, D. C., *The Limits of Family Influence: Genes, Experience and Behaviour* (New York: Guilford, 1994).

Rowlinson, K., Whyley, C. and Warren, T., *Wealth in Britain: A Lifecycle Perspective* (London: Policy Studies Institute, 1999).

Sadurski, W., *Giving Desert Its Due* (Dordrecht, The Netherlands: Reidel, 1985).

Scanlon, T. M., 'The Significance of Choice', in S. Darwall (ed.), *Equal Freedom: Selected Tanner Lectures on Human Values* (Ann Arbor, MI: University of Michigan Press, 1995).

—— *What We Owe to Each Other* (Cambridge, MA: Harvard University Press, 1998).

Scheffler, S., *Boundaries and Allegiances: Problems of Justice and Responsibility in Liberal Thought* (Oxford: Oxford University Press, 2001).

—— 'What Is Egalitarianism?', *Philosophy and Public Affairs* 31 (2003), 5–39.

—— 'Distributive Justice and Economic Desert', in S. Olsaretti (ed.), *Desert and Justice* (Oxford: Oxford University Press, 2003).

—— 'Choice, Circumstance and the Value of Equality', *Politics, Philosophy and Economics* 4 (2005), 5–28.

Sher, G., 'Effort, Ability and Desert', *Philosophy and Public Affairs* 8 (1979), 361–76.

—— 'Qualifications, Fairness, and Desert', in N. Bowie (ed.), *Equal Opportunity* (Boulder, CO: Westview Press, 1988).

—— *Approximate Justice: Studies in Non-Ideal Theory* (Lanham, MD: Rowman and Littlefield, 1997).

Shiffrin, S., 'Egalitarianism, Choice-Sensitivity, and Accommodation', in R. J. Wallace, P. Pettit, S. Scheffler, and M. Smith (eds), *Reason and Value: Themes from the Moral Philosophy of Joseph Raz* (Oxford: Oxford University Press, 2004).

Singer, P., *Practical Ethics*, 2nd edn (Cambridge: Cambridge University Press, 1993).

Steiner, H., *An Essay on Rights* (Oxford: Blackwell, 1994).

Strawson, G., 'The Impossibility of Moral Responsibility', *Philosophical Studies* 75 (1994), 5–24.

Sumner, L. W., 'Positive Sexism', *Social Philosophy and Policy* 5 (1987), 204–22.

Swift, A., *How Not To Be a Hypocrite: Social Choice for the Perplexed Parent* (London: Routledge, 2003).

—— 'Social Justice: Does It Matter What the People Think?', in D. Bell and A. de Shalit (eds), *Forms of Justice* (Lanham, MA: Rowman and Littlefield, 2003).

—— 'Justice, Luck and the Family: Normative Aspects of the Intergenerational Transmission of Economic Status', in S. Bowles, H. Gintis, and M. A. Osborne (eds), *Unequal Chances: Family Background and Economic Success* (Princeton, NJ: Princeton University Press, 2005).

Temkin, L., *Inequality* (New York: Oxford University Press, 1993).

—— 'Egalitarianism Defended', *Ethics* 113 (2003), 764–82.

Temkin, L., 'Equality, Priority or What?', *Economics and Philosophy* 19 (2003), 61–87.

Vallentyne, P., 'Self-Ownership and Equality: Brute Luck, Gifts, Universal Dominance and Leximin', *Ethics* 107 (1997), 321–43.

—— 'Brute Luck, Option Luck, and Equality of Initial Opportunities', *Ethics* 112 (2002), 529–57.

Waldron, J., *Law and Disagreement* (Oxford: Oxford University Press, 1999).

Wallace, J. R., *Responsibility and the Moral Sentiments* (Cambridge, MA: Harvard University Press, 1994).

Weinstock, D., 'National Partiality: Confronting the Intuitions', *The Monist* 82 (1999), 516–41.

Wertheimer, A., 'Jobs, Qualifications, and Preferences', *Ethics* 94 (1983), 99–112.

Westen, P., 'The Concept of Equal Opportunity', *Ethics* 95 (1985), 837–50.

White, S., *The Civic Minimum: On the Rights and Obligations of Economic Citizenship* (Oxford: Oxford University Press, 2003).

Williams, A., 'Incentives, Inequality, and Publicity', *Philosophy and Public Affairs* 27 (1998), 225–47.

Williams, B., 'The Idea of Equality', in his *Problems of the Self* (Cambridge: Cambridge University Press, 1973).

Wittgenstein, L., *Philosophical Investigations*, trans. by G. E. M. Anscombe (Oxford: Blackwell, 1953).

Wolff, J., 'Fairness, Respect, and the Egalitarian Ethos', *Philosophy and Public Affairs* 27 (1998), 97–122.

—— 'The Dilemma of Desert', in S. Olsaretti (ed.), *Desert and Justice* (Oxford: Oxford University Press, 2003).

Young, I. M., *Justice and the Politics of Difference* (Princeton, NJ: Princeton University Press, 1990).

—— 'Equality of Whom? Social Groups and Judgements of Injustice', *Journal of Political Philosophy* 9 (2001), 1–19.

—— 'Responsibility and Global Labor Justice', *Journal of Political Philosophy* 12 (2004), 365–88.

—— 'Responsibility and Global Justice', *Social Philosophy and Policy*, 23 (2006), 102–3.

Zaitchick, A., 'One Deserving to Deserve', *Philosophy and Public Affairs* 6 (1977), 370–88.

INDEX

accumulation of wealth principle, *see* mitigation approach
advantage:
  comparative 99–109, 126, 126–9
  as currency of justice 95 n., 102 n. 16
advantaged social positions 16–8, 70–3, 82–7, 141
affirmative action, *see* discrimination, positive
Anderson, E. 206, 218–20
Arneson, R. 63–4, 114 n. 4, 122–4, 214 n.
atomistic egoism, *see* individualism

Barry, B. 17 n., 22 n. 10, 26, 77–80, 108
basic skills principle, *see* mitigation approach
bequests 146–50
Brighouse, H. 108 n. 25
Brink, D. 54 n. 36
Buchanan, A. 57 n. 42

Campbell, T. 6 n. 5
Caney, S. 52 n. 27, 121 n. 21, 201 n. 10
career sacrificing mother 182–8, 213–5
careers open to talents, *see* Rawls, J.
Cavanagh, M. 14, 30 n., 56–7
children 80–1, 99–109, 135–41, 144–5, 183–8, 211–5
choice 90, 91–4, 179, 205, 208; *see also* responsibility
  bearing the costs of:
  control conception 161, 162–4, 167–4, 191, 208
  pluralist conception 188–92, 210, 215
  responsiveness to reason conception 161, 164–70, 170–4, 174–8, 184, 186, 189, 208
circumstances, 90, 91–4, 179, 205, 208
  counteracting differences in 71, 74–6, 79–80, 82, 87, 89–90, 91–4, 150–2; *see also* neutralisation approach; mitigation approach

Cohen, G. A. 97 n., 99, 100 n. 14, 102, 163 n., 173 n. 23, 178–82
control conception, *see* choice
Crisp, R. 123–4, 126
culture 23–4, 27, 181–2; *see also* identity

Darwall, S. 58 n. 45
decent life, *see* sufficiency view
desert:
  and achievement or contribution 41–4, 45–51, 55–6
  of the best-qualified 39–41, 44
  comparative 49
  economic, *see* desert, and jobs
  and effort 45–51, 55–6
  institutional vs preinstitutional 50–1, 65
  and jobs 39–51
  and luck 42, 49
  and the market 41–4
  prejusticial 65–7, 110, 196
  Rawls and, *see* Rawls, J.
  realised virtue theory of 47 n. 16
  voluntarist conception 49
difference principle, *see* Rawls, J.
disability 152, 206–7
discrimination 29–32
  fair equality of opportunity and 72–3
  institutional 30–1, 72–3
  and the neutralisation approach 154–5
  positive 19, 38 n., 59–60, 77–8, 86
  principle of non-discrimination 29–30
  and respect for persons 56–60
  secondary sexism 30, 77–8
  simple view and 30–2
  unintentional 30, 77
distributional individualism, *see* individualism
Dworkin, R. 150–2, 164, 178, 186–8

educational access principle, *see* mitigation approach
effort, *see* desert
egalitarianism, *see also* quasi-egalitarian principles
  conditional 118 n. 14, 130 n. 30
  deontic vs telic 118–21, 127–8
  and the levelling down objection 116–20, 129, 142–3, 148
  luck 91, 205–6, 216–9
  responsibility-sensitive 90, 91, 94, 113–4, 158–93, 194–215
  scope of 120, 203–4
  strict 22, 113, 116–7
equality of opportunity:
  and careers open to talents, *see* Rawls, J.
  competitive vs non-competitive 18
  fair, *see* Rawls, J.
  and levelling the playing field 4–5, 6, 145
  meritocratic 38, 39–67, 68–88, 152–5
  and open competition 15–22, 24, 25–6, 35–7, 39–41, 56–62, 152–3
  radical conception 88, 89
  simple view 15–38, 70–2
equals:
  treating people as 121, 127–8, 139, 147–8, 219; *see also* respect for persons
excusing conditions, *see* responsibility
expensive tastes, 93–4, 169–70, 176–82, 213

fair equality of opportunity, *see* Rawls, J.
family, *see* children
Fischer, J. 173
Fishkin, J. 77 n. 13
Flew, A. 7, 15–16
Frankfurt, H. 115 n. 6, 172–3
fundamental principles 95–6, 97–9, 110, 126, 132, 156, 180, 220

gender identity, *see* identity
gourmand, *see* expensive tastes
Graham, K. 198

head hunting 19–21
health care 18, 141
Hirose, I. 113 n. 3
Holtug, N. 125
Hsieh, N. 43 n. 10
Hurley, S. 130 n. 29, 167, 171–2

identity:
  cultural 23, 175–8
  gender 182–8, 214–5
  moral 23, 175–8
individualism 194–215
  atomistic egoism 195, 207–15
  distributional 194–5, 195–7
  methodological 195, 204–5, 206
  ontological 195, 197–8
intuitions 44, 51–6, 65, 132, 221

Jacobs, L. 121 n. 20

Kymlicka, W. 90 n. 1, 181–2, 192

levelling down objection, *see* egalitarianism
Levin, M. 6 n. 5
libertarianism 13–14, 17
Lippert-Rasmussen, K., 119
luck egalitarianism, *see* egalitarianism
luck 146
  brute vs option 91–3, 179
  integral vs circumstantial 42, 49

Matravers, M. 92 n. 4, 166 n. 13, 172 n. 20
McDowell, J. 93 n.
McKerlie, D. 119
meritocratic ideal, *see* equality of opportunity
methodological individualism, *see* individualism
methodology 6–7, 51–6, 132–3, 156–7
Miller, D. 35 n. 27, 39–56, 64, 75 n.
mitigation approach 79, 94–7, 97–9, 109–11, 112–3, 129–31, 134–57, 161, 216–7, 220
  accumulation of wealth principle 147–50, 203
  basic skills principle 135–7, 143, 203
  educational access principle 138–41, 143
Muñoz-Dardé, V. 81

Nagel, T. 121, 203–4
neutralization approach 79, 91, 94–111, 112–3, 129–31, 144–5, 147, 150–2, 153–5, 156
Newey, G. 223 n. 6
Nozick, R. 110 n. 27

Olsaretti, S. 47 n. 17
ontological individualism, *see* individualism
open competition, *see* equality of opportunity
opportunity:
  account of 22–5, 86
  and open competition 16–18, 24
  as a primary good 85–6
  and reasonable choice 23–5
  and the simple view 16–18, 22–5
  subject dependency of 23–4
Otsuka, M. 151

Parekh, B. 23
Parfit, D., 112–3, 114 n. 5, 117–20; *see also* prioritarianism; egalitarianism, deontic vs telic; egalitarianism, and the levelling down objection; egalitarianism, strict
Patten, A. 182 n. 33
Phillips, A. 205, 207
pluralist conception, *see* choice
Pogge, T. 71 n. 4, 121 n. 21
positive discrimination, *see* discrimination
Price, T. 179 n. 28
priority view, *see* prioritarianism
prioritarianism 113–15, 122–6, 129–32, 142, 148
  extreme vs moderate 114–5, 122, 132
publicity 103–4, 221

qualifications 25–30, 32–5, 62–63; *see also* desert, of the best-qualified; equality of opportunity, simple view; respect for persons
  access to 36–8, 134–45
  and attitudes or reactions of others 17 n. 4, 26 n. 16, 32–5
  and culture 23, 26
  moralized account of 35
  nature of 34–5, 62–3
quasi-egalitarian principles 125–6, 126–9, 130–1, 142, 147–8, 152

Rakowski, E. 140–1, 208–9, 211–3
Rawls, J.:
  basic liberties, and their priority 69, 80–1, 83–4, 85–6
  careers open to talents 70–1, 77–9
  and desert 48 n. 20, 67
  difference principle 82–7, 114 n. 5
  fair equality of opportunity 70–88, 89–90
  family 80–1
  moral arbitrariness 71, 73, 78–80, 82, 97
reciprocity principle 148–9
reductionism 54, 132–3, 142, 148, 156–7, 221
religion 17, 25, 26
respect for persons 56–64, 153
responsibility, *see also* choice, bearing the costs of
  actual sequence vs alternate sequence requirements 167–8
  as attributability 162 n. 4
  and causal thesis 171
  collective 197–204
  and determinism 168
  excusing conditions 163, 167, 169, 189
  and expensive tastes 169–70, 176–82
  moral 162–3, 164–6, 167–8, 171–4
  and regression requirement 171–2
  responsibility-sensitive egalitarianism, *see* egalitarianism
  and self-government 164–6, 175
  and socialisation 168–70, 182–8, 189–91
  substantive 162 n. 4
  Young on liability vs political model 202–3
responsibility-sensitive egalitarianism, *see* egalitarianism
responsiveness to reason conception, *see* choice

rewards:
intrinsic or internal vs extrinsic or external 16–7, 41, 22, 85, 141, 153–4
Ripstein, A. 164 n. 7
Roemer, J. 189–91

Sadurski, W. 46 n. 15
Scanlon, T. M. 66, 162 n. 4, 164–8, 171, 189
Scheffler, S. 65, 195–6
self-government, *see* responsibility
Sher, G. 35 n. 27, 39 n., 57–64,
Shiffrin, S. 188 n.
simple view, *see* equality of opportunity
Steiner, H. 120 n. 18
sufficiency view 115–6, 122–6, 129–32, 136–7, 142–3, 210–11
moderate vs extreme 115–6, 122–4, 132, 136–7, 143
Swift, A. 100 n. 13, 106, 108 n. 25

Temkin, L. 117–8

Vallentyne, P. 91–2

Waldron J. 222
Wertheimer, A. 33 n., 35 n.
Westen, P. 5–6
White, S. 140
Williams, A. 103–4
Williams, B. 36–7
Wittgenstein, L. 53–4, 192
Wolff, J. 47 n. 16

Young, I. 26–9, 202–3, 205, 206–7

Lightning Source UK Ltd.
Milton Keynes UK
UKOW050632210313

207978UK00005B/25/P